1831

1831

YEAR OF ECLIPSE

LOUIS P. MASUR

HILL AND WANG

A DIVISION OF FARRAR, STRAUS AND GIROUX

NEW YORK

Hill and Wang
A division of Farrar, Straus and Giroux
19 Union Square West, New York 10003

Distributed in Canada by Douglas & McIntyre Ltd.
Printed in the United States of America
Published in 2001 by Hill and Wang
First paperback edition, 2002

Library of Congress Cataloging-in-Publication Data
Masur, Louis P.
    1831, year of eclipse / Louis P. Masur.— 1st ed.
        p.   cm.
    Includes bibliographical references and index.
    ISBN 0-8090-4119-7 (pbk.)
    1. United States—History—1815–1861.   2. United States—Politics and
government—1829–1837.   3. Eighteen thirty-one, A.D.   I. Title.

E381 .M37 2001
973.5—dc21   00–031969

Designed by Jonathan D. Lippincott

www.fsgbooks.com

1   3   5   7   9   10   8   6   4   2

FOR
SOPHIE AND BEN

Never, perhaps, since the period when history first speaks to us of the doings of man, did a year open upon the world that promises to be more rife with improvements and mighty changes, than that which commences today. The WORLD is in a state of revolution.

—Robert Dale Owen, *The Free Enquirer*, January 1, 1831

In dim eclipse, disastrous twilight sheds
On half the nations, and with fear of change
Perplexes monarchs
—John Milton, *Paradise Lost*

CONTENTS

ILLUSTRATIONS

ACKNOWLEDGMENTS

This book about a year has been many years in the making. I am grateful to the Mellon Foundation for a Faculty Fellowship in the Humanities at Harvard University, where I first started thinking about 1831. Additional support has come from the Rifkind Center for the Humanities at City College as well as the PSC-CUNY Fund. Two short-term fellowships allowed me to complete the research for this work. I served as a Kate B. and Hall J. Peterson Fellow at the American Antiquarian Society, where the collections and staff are superb. I am indebted to Georgia Barnhill, Nancy Burkett, Joanne Chaison, Alan Degutis, Ellen Dunlap, John Hench, and Marie Lamoureux. I also profited from an Andrew Mellon Foundation Fellowship at the Library Company of Philadelphia. My thanks to Jenny Ambrose, Jim Green, Phil Lapsansky, Erika Piola, Jessy Randall, Nicole Scalessa, John Van Horne, and Sarah Weatherwax. At City College, Martin Tamny, Jim Watts, and Frank Grande helped make certain I would have time to write.

Over the years, a number of friends have contributed in different ways to this project. They include Bob Allison, John Brooke, Tom Brown, Peter Coclanis, David Gerber, Christine Herbes-Sommers,

David Jaffee, Keith Mayes, David Nasaw, Carol Quirke, Richard Skolnik, and Darren Staloff. I so wish John Phillips were here to share in this moment. I do not know where I would be without Dave at the Bagel Dish, Ed at Raritan Video, the BLRB, occasional Friday nights with the Whites, Allan Lockspeiser and all our teams, and Jesse Wolpert and the guys at the Center School. I appreciate the interest in my work shown by the entire Fox and Mallin families. A few years ago, my parents, Sarah and Seymour Masur, moved five blocks away. They always ask "How is the book going?"—and, if it is not too much trouble, could I run an errand? I am fortunate that they live nearby. Dave Masur, Bruce Rossky, and Mark Richman would not think to look for their names here, and that is only one of many reasons why I cherish them.

I am lucky that Arthur Wang first expressed interest in this project and even luckier that Lauren Osborne became my editor. I am grateful to Lauren for encouraging me to write the book that I envisioned and improving the one that I wrote. Her assistant, Catherine Newman, ushered me through the publication process with efficiency and wit.

Kathy Feeley, Jim Goodman, Doug Greenberg, Peter Mancall, Aaron Sachs, and Tom Slaughter read the manuscript and provided insight, encouragement, and bottomless cups of coffee. They also danced at my son's bar mitzvah. For my fortieth birthday, Tom gave me a rock with the word CREATE carved in it, and soon thereafter I started writing. What I owe him can not be repaid with the next present I buy, but I will certainly try.

I promised Sophie that her name would go first this time. I promised Ben that I would not list all his accomplishments. And I promised Jani that for our twentieth wedding anniversary, we would vacation in Hawaii. Well, two out of three is not bad. Every day they show me that love is wild, love is real, love will not let you down.

LPM
Highland Park, N.J.
May 2000

CHRONOLOGY

January 1: William Lloyd Garrison publishes the first issue of *The Liberator* and emerges as a leader of the abolitionist movement in the United States.

February 12: Eclipse of the sun.

February 14: Congressman Edward Everett of Massachusetts speaks against Indian removal.

February 17: Correspondence between President Andrew Jackson and Vice-President John C. Calhoun is published.

March 7: Supreme Court hears arguments in *Charles River Bridge* v. *Warren Bridge*.

March 14: William Wirt, former attorney-general and lead counsel for the Cherokee Indians, addresses Supreme Court in *Cherokee Nation* v. *Georgia*.

March 18: Supreme Court issues decision in *Cherokee Nation* v. *Georgia*.

March 24: Dinner for Daniel Webster, senator from Massachusetts, at City Hotel in New York.

April 7: Resignations of Cabinet members in Jackson's administration begin.

April 26: New York legislature abolishes imprisonment for debt.

May 10: Alexis de Tocqueville and Gustave Beaumont arrive in New York from France and begin their tour of American society.

June 4–7: Meeting between Black Hawk, a Sauk warrior, and Major General Gaines of the United States Army at Rock Island, Illinois.

June 29: Magdalen Society Report on prostitution in New York is issued.

July 4: James Monroe, former President of the United States, dies.

> Senator Robert Hayne of South Carolina addresses the States Rights and Free Trade Party.
>
> Representative William Drayton of South Carolina addresses the Union and States Rights Party.
>
> John Quincy Adams, former president, addresses the town of Quincy, Massachusetts.
>
> Hymn "America" performed for the first time.

July 25: Cyrus McCormick, a Virginia farmer and inventor, tests his mechanical reaper.

July 26: John C. Calhoun issues Fort Hill letter irrevocably linking him to nullification.

August 5: Frances Trollope arrives home in England with the manuscript of *Domestic Manners of the Americans* in hand.

August 22: Nat Turner's rebellion begins.

August 25: John Quincy Adams delivers eulogy for James Monroe.

September 3: John James Audubon, artist and naturalist, arrives in New York.

September 24: Supreme Court Justice Joseph Story delivers consecration address at Mount Auburn Cemetery.

September 28: Anti-Masonic Convention in Baltimore nominates William Wirt as candidate for president.

September 30–October 7: Free Trade Convention, opposed to tariffs, meets in Philadelphia.

October 23: Charles Grandison Finney, a leading evangelical minister, delivers sermon "Sinners Bound to Change Their Own Hearts."

October 26: Friends of Domestic Industry Convention in support of tariffs is held in New York.

November 11: Nat Turner executed.

November 12: The *John Bull*, a steam-powered railroad car, makes its first trip.

November 25: *Confessions of Nat Turner* published.

December 12–16: National Republican Convention in Baltimore nominates Henry Clay of Kentucky for president.

December 14: Virginia legislature begins debate over the abolition of slavery.

December 24: Nicholas Biddle, director of the Second Bank of the United States, decides to apply early for rechartering of the institution.

December 26: Newspapers report that the cholera epidemic has reached England and is headed for the United States.

1831

1. "A Map of the Eclipse of Feb.ʸ 12th in Its Passage Across the United States," *American Almanac and Repository of Useful Knowledge* (Courtesy of the American Antiquarian Society)

ECLIPSE

✳

Everyone knew it was coming. "THE GREAT ECLIPSE OF 1831 will be one of the most remarkable that will again be witnessed in the United States for a long course of years," alerted *Ash's Pocket Almanac*. One editor reported that the February 12 eclipse would even surpass historic occasions when "the darkness was such that domestic fowls retired to roost" and "it appeared as if the moon rode unsteadily in her orbit, and the earth seemed to tremble on its axis."[1]

On the day of the eclipse, from New England through the South, Americans looked to the heavens. One diarist saw "men, women and children . . . in all directions, with a piece of smoked glass, and eyes turn'd upward." The *Boston Evening Gazette* reported that "this part of the world has been all anxiety . . . to witness the solar eclipse. . . . Business was suspended and thousands of persons were looking at the phenomena with intense curiosity." "Every person in the city," noted the *Richmond Enquirer*, "was star gazing, from bleary-eyed old age to the most bright-eyed infancy."[2]

Unlike previous celestial events, thought some commentators, the eclipse of 1831 would not produce superstitious dread that the world

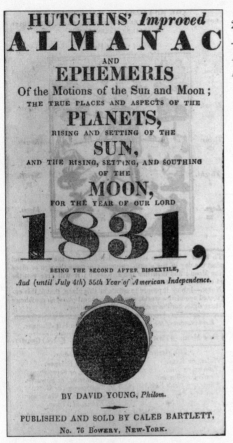

HUTCHINS' *Improved*
ALMANAC
AND
EPHEMERIS
Of the Motions of the Sun and Moon;
THE TRUE PLACES AND ASPECTS OF THE
PLANETS,
RISING AND SETTING OF THE
SUN,
AND THE RISING, SETTING, AND SOUTHING
OF THE
MOON,
FOR THE YEAR OF OUR LORD
1831,
BEING THE SECOND AFTER DISSEXTILE,
And (until July 4th) 55th Year of American Independence.

BY DAVID YOUNG, *Philom.*

PUBLISHED AND SOLD BY CALEB BARTLETT,
No. 76 BOWERY, NEW-YORK.

*2. Hutchins' Improved Almanac
. . . for the Year of Our Lord
1831* (Courtesy of the American
Antiquarian Society)

would end. "Idle fears and gloomy forebodings of evil formerly raised by the appearance of phenomena caused by the regular operation of natural laws," one writer claimed, "have yielded to pleasing admiration; a change which the march of science and general diffusion of knowledge have largely contributed to effect." Another writer mocked the notion that eclipses were "signs or forerunners of great calamities." Eclipses, he thought, "necessarily result from the established laws of the planetary revolution, and take place in exact conformity with those laws. . . . Those who entertain the opinion that eclipses of the sun are tokens of the Divine displeasure can produce no warrant from scripture for their irrational belief. If we would look for the signs of the displeasure of God towards a nation, we can see them, not in eclipses, but in national sins and depravity of morals."[3]

Rational explanations of atmospheric events, however, offered little solace to most Americans. In many, "a kind of vague fear, of impending danger—a prophetic presentiment of some approaching catastrophe"—was awakened, and "the reasonings of astronomy, or the veritable deductions of mathematical forecast," did little to diminish the anxiety. One correspondent reported that an "old shoe-black accosted a person in front of our office, the day previous to the eclipse, and asked him if he was not afraid. For, said he, with tears in his eyes, the world is to be destroyed to-morrow; the sun and moon are to meet . . . and a great earthquake was to swallow us all!—Others said the sun and the earth would come in contact, and the latter would be consumed. Others again, were seen wending their ways to their friends and relations, covered with gloom and sadness; saying that they intended to *die with them!*" The day after the eclipse, preachers employed Luke 21:25 as the text for their sermons: "there shall be signs in the sun." "In strict propriety of language," one minister observed, "it is not the sun that is eclipsed. Not the slightest shadow is cast upon the least portion of his broad disk. His beams are shot forth precisely the same. It is over us only that the momentary darkness is spread, and it is truly the earth that is eclipsed."[4]

The spectacle, however, proved anticlimactic. "The darkness being less visible than generally expected," the heaven-gazers felt "bamboozled." "At the moment of greatest obscuration," reported one paper, "a foolish feeling of disappointment was generally prevalent and this was expressed by many in such terms as they might have used after having been taken in by the quacking advertisement of an exhibitor of fireworks or phantasmagoria. It was not half as dark as they expected." "The darkness was that of a thunder gust," snorted one observer: "The light of the sun was sickly, but shadows were very perceptible." "The multitude have been sadly disappointed," reported one editor. "They looked for darkness and the shades of light; they expected to drink in

horrors, and feel the power of superstition without its terrors or appre-
hensions; they expected to work by candlelight, see cows come home,
and poultry go ultimately to roost—to count the stars and tell them by
their names; in short, to see something that they might talk about now
and hereafter—something to tell their children and grandchildren."[5]

With the anticipation more disturbing than the event, some sought
to cast blame. Almanac makers and newspaper editors were chastised
for their extravagant predictions of darkness and glowing descriptions
of the wonders that would be seen. Some thought the astronomers
deserved condemnation for offering elaborate calculations that fizzled.
Others blamed regional temperaments for the heightened expectations.
"Our Yankee proneness to exaggeration," thought the *Boston Patriot*,
"was manifested in a ludicrous manner on the occasion of the late
eclipse." Southerners agreed: "Our eastern brethren are, as usual, up
in arms about the matter—they talk of a convention. Truth to say,
expectations were scarcely realized. On such occasions, people now-a-
day show a shockingly morbid appetite—they look for portentous
signs, for ghastly gleanings of fiery comets, the rushing up, with dire
intimations of the 'northern lights,' and expect to see 'clouds of dark
blood to blot the sun's broad light, / And angry meteors shroud the
world in night.' "[6]

However much the eclipse disappointed, it served as metaphor and
omen. Edward Everett, politician from Massachusetts, reported that "a
motion was made in the House of Representatives to adjourn over till
Monday in consequence of the darkness which was to prevail." The
motion did not pass, and Everett quipped, "After sitting so frequently
when there is darkness inside the House, it would be idle I think to fly
before a little darkness on the face of the heavens." The *United States
Gazette*, which feverishly opposed the re-election of President Andrew
Jackson, joked that "the solar eclipse has not attracted as much attention here, as the late curious obscuration of one of the smaller stars in
the constellation, Jupiter Jackson." With greater sobriety, the editor of
the *Philadelphia Gazette* observed that "the affairs of the Eastern
hemisphere . . . have reached a thrilling and portentous crisis. An irre-

sistible spirit of reform seems burning with occult but mighty energy among the nations. . . . An eclipse in Europe at the present time might be considered as an omen. In this country, where it has lately occurred, the sunshine of regulated freedom appears alone to rest."[7]

Unmoved by editorial, ministerial, astronomical, or political pronouncements and predictions, on the day of the eclipse some Philadelphians went ice-skating. The coldest winter in decades had frozen the Delaware River, and thousands of citizens chose to pass the day in recreation. The *Saturday Bulletin* reported, "It is probable that fifteen thousand persons were amusing themselves by sliding and skating on the river, while the numerous booths, or travelling dram-shops which were located at short distances apart, throughout the whole city front, were observed to do a brisk business in hot punch, smoked sausages, crackers, and ten-for-a-cent cigars. Sober citizens, whom we have

SKATING.

SCENE on the RIVER DELAWARE at PHILADELPHIA. *Febr.y 12th 1831.*

3. Edward William Clay, "Skating: Scene on the River Delaware at Philadelphia, Feb.y 12th 1831" (Courtesy of The Historical Society of Pennsylvania)

observed never exceed a regular dog-trot, while walking our streets, were now capering around with the agility of a feather in a whirlwind."[8]

One artist drew the scene. On February 12, Edward William Clay set up his easel by the Delaware River and produced an image of citizens at play. Men of all classes slip and swirl, some into one another's arms, as they skate the day away. To the right, a rough-hewn citizen warms himself with a drink; a woman looks on contentedly. A black man, in stereotypical comic fashion, slides helplessly away, his hat lost. All is movement and motion, energy and action. But the sky is gray, the light is pale, and dusk is approaching.

SLAVERY AND ABOLITION

✳

NAT TURNER

The heavens darkened and Nat Turner prepared to strike. Rising from the gloom of Virginia's swamps, he resolved to slay his enemies. The February eclipse, a black spot on the sun, signaled that the time to act had arrived.

"I had a vision—and I saw white spirits and black spirits engaged in battle, and the sun was darkened—the thunder rolled in the Heavens, and blood flowed in streams."

The visions continued—blood drops on corn, pores oozing blood, markings on bloodstained leaves. He felt the Holy Spirit within, felt awakened and ordained for some special purpose. Following the eclipse, Turner told four other slaves of the work to be done, the "work of death" to begin on the Fourth of July.

The time for violent insurrection had arrived, but no one could decide how best to proceed. The conspirators squabbled over plans and Turner became ill. The Fourth passed without a strike for freedom. And then, on Saturday, August 13, "the sign appeared again." Across the East Coast, noted an observer in Philadelphia, the "western heavens seemed as one vast sea of crimson flame, lit up by some invisible agent. Thousands of our citizens gazed at the spectacle—some with wonder, others with admiration, and others fearful that it was a sad augury of coming evil."[1]

Newspaper editors tried at first to contain the fear that leaped like a brushfire from door to door. Word was spreading of a general insurrection in Southampton County, Virginia, where the enslaved outnumbered the enslavers by over a thousand. Across Virginia there were nearly five hundred thousand slaves, and the total throughout the South reached two million souls. It could not be, they told themselves. The slaves were content. Slavery was a righteous institution. They were good masters. Indeed, some of them were. Even Joseph Travis, Nat Turner attested, "was to me a kind master." But kindness did not save him at 2 A.M. on August 22 from the force of a blunt hatchet against his head, followed by the deathblow from an ax. Nor did it save Mrs. Travis. Nor four others, including an infant who was initially overlooked and then also killed. There were no innocents. In the stillness of a sultry night, the murders that fueled the rumors had begun.[2]

"On the road, we met a thousand different reports, no two agreeing, and leaving it impossible to make a plausible guess at truth." How many slaves were involved? Some accounts said only three, some said four hundred, and some claimed over a thousand rebels, banditti, brigands, villains, wretches, monsters—called every name but men. At first, the papers reported that the insurrection was led by about 250 runaways who emerged from the Great Dismal Swamp for the purpose of "plunder and rapine," "to rob and to do mischief." They had come from a "Camp Meeting," a religious revival, and were deceived by "artful knaves" into launching an attack. The plan, some said, extended deep into North Carolina, and was "started by a white man, for some design unknown." But then rumor had it that the rebels were slaves, "the property of kind and indulgent masters." It started not with hundreds, but with six, and "there appears to have been no concert with the blacks of any other part of the state." The plan came from a slave, Nat Turner, a literate preacher who acted "without any cause or provocation."[3]

Neither rumor offered much solace. "Runaways" meant the attack came from without; "slaves" meant it came from within. Although the one rumor frightened people by portraying the uprising as more widespread than it was, it also allowed citizens to explain the tragedy in terms of a need for food and clothing and as the work of outside agitators. The other rumor limited the scope of the event, but allowed it to be accounted for only in terms of retribution, a blow for freedom originating from inside the slave community. Had it been runaways, the residents of Southampton County might have gone on as before. But it turned out to be slaves, and Virginians knew they could "never again feel safe, never again be happy."

First reports minimized the bloodshed, stating only that several families had "fallen victim." Though editors cautioned readers not to believe "a fiftieth part" of what they read or heard, a letter written on August 24 and published two days later claimed that between "eighty and one hundred of the whites have already been butchered—their heads severed from their bodies." An editor for the *Constitutional Whig* in Richmond, John Hampden Pleasants, belonged to a mounted militia unit sent to suppress the rebellion. From Jerusalem, the main town in Southampton County, he forwarded the first accounts of the tragedy. Although rumors exaggerated the number of insurgents, "it was hardly in the power of rumor itself, to exaggerate the atrocities: . . . whole families, father, mother, daughters, sons, sucking babes, and school children, butchered, thrown into heaps, and left to be devoured by hogs and dogs, or to putrify on the spot." Among those murdered were Mrs. Levi Waller and the ten children in her school, the bodies "piled in one bleeding heap on the floor." A single child escaped by hiding in the fireplace. Pleasants misidentified Turner as "Preacher-Captain Moore" and placed the death toll at sixty-two. By August 29, when his letter appeared, the two-day insurrection was over, Turner was in hiding, and those captured rebels who survived faced trial and execution.[4]

For the next three months, newspapers in Virginia and throughout the nation tried to explain the tragedy. Many accounts kept returning to the innocence of children and the vulnerability of women. Near the end of the rampage, Turner's band approached Rebecca Vaughan's residence. It was noon. Mrs. Vaughan was laboring outside, preparing dinner, when she saw a puff of dust rising from the road. Suddenly, some forty mounted and armed black men came rushing toward the house. She raced inside, quivered at the window, and, through the snorting of horses and shouting of men, begged for her life. The shots that killed her brought her fifteen-year-old son, Arthur, from the fields. As he climbed a fence, he too was gunned down. A niece, Eliza Vaughan, "celebrated for her beauty," ran downstairs and out the door but made it only a few steps away. One editor could not conceive of a situation more "horribly awful" than that faced by these women: "alone, unprotected, and unconscious of danger, to find themselves without a moment's notice for escape or defence, in the power of a band of ruffians, from whom instant death was the least they could expect."

Lurking beneath these accounts was a dread that the rebels had raped the women, that the slaveholders had failed to protect not only the lives of their wives and daughters but their purity as well. Across the centuries, accusations of rape were never far from the surface when white men thought about black men with white women. Virginians worried feverishly about it here. Many rumors took wing in the late days of the summer, but writers sought quickly to assure readers, "It is not believed that any outrages were offered to the females."

Driven by hatred and fear, the forces that extinguished the rebellion displayed a ruthlessness that startled some observers. No one in the South, of course, defended the rebels, but the actions of the soldiers in putting down the rebellion generated controversy. Enacting scenes "hardly inferior in barbarity to the atrocities of the insurgents," the militia beheaded some of the rebels in the field. One of the mounted volunteers from Norfolk had in his possession "the head of the celebrated Nelson, called by the blacks, 'Gen. Nelson,' and the paymaster, Henry, whose head is expected momentarily." Soldiers stuck the severed heads of several dozen slaves on poles and planted them along the highway, a warning to all who passed by. Those who

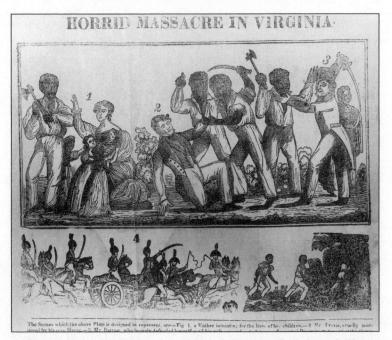

4. "Horrid Massacre in Virginia," fold-out frontispiece from Samuel Warner, *Authentic and Impartial Narrative of the Tragical Scene* (Courtesy of the American Antiquarian Society)

survived capture would be tried, and on September 4 the state started executing the convicted, but the summary justice in the field raised concerns. Pleasants was the first to express dismay over the decapitation of the rebels. "Precaution is even necessary to protect the lives of the captives," he concluded. He worried that revenge would "be productive of further outrage, and prove discreditable to the country." A week later, the paper altered its stance, stating that "the sanguinary temper of the population who evinced a strong disposition to inflict immediate death on every prisoner" was understandable and extenuated by their having witnessed unspeakable horrors to their wives and children. Readers, however, did not forget Pleasants's initial comments; perhaps here, in his call for restraint, he took the first step that would lead to his death when, fifteen years later, the editor of the *Rich-*

mond Enquirer accused him of abolitionist tendencies and shot him in a duel.

Some who warned against further revenge did so out of a desire to protect the owners of those slaves who did not participate in the insurrection and to re-establish the rule of law. "A public execution in the presence of thousands," advised the military commander, "will demonstrate the power of the law, and preserve the right of property. The opposite course, while it is inhuman and therefore not to be justified, tends to the sacrifice of the innocent. . . . This course of proceeding dignifies the rebel and the assassin with the sanctity of martyrdom."

Between private revenge and public justice resided conflicting messages. Barbaric revenge told the enslaved that, should they ever try to revolt again, genocide would be the result: "Another insurrection will be followed by putting the whole race to the sword." And yet such a threat carried with it a tacit acknowledgment that the enslaved were not loyal and contented, that slavery was not benign, and that the outnumbered white population could rule only through terror and fear. The enactment of legal, public justice demonstrated that whites could maintain civil society and that they viewed rebellion, however horrific, as an aberration. Yet it also suggested a concern with the property rights of slaveholders and a desire not to provoke the enslaved by creating martyrs to the cause of freedom. Either way, in the immediate aftermath of the rebellion, editors worried about accounts and actions that would "give the slaves false conceptions of their numbers and capacity, by exhibiting the terror and confusion of the whites, and to induce them to think that practicable, which they see is so much feared by their superiors."[5]

Stories of loyal slaves provided some solace. On the morning of August 23, before dawn, Turner and the rebels attacked the house of Dr. Simon Blunt, who by this time had heard of the insurrection. Crippled by gout, he chose to defend his ground. Alongside stood his fifteen-year-old son, an overseer, and three other white men. They had six guns and plenty of powder. Entering the yard, one rebel fired his weapon to test whether anyone was home. Twenty paces from the house, shots rang back, and the rebels scattered, one killed and one injured. Blunt's slaves, some attested, "nobly and gallantly" stood by their aged master and pursued the rebels with "shouts and execrations." One writer paid "tribute to our slaves . . . which they richly deserve. . . . There was not an instance of disaffection, in any section of our country; save on the plantations which Capt. Nat visited, and to their credit, the recruits were few." The remark said to have been uttered by the loyal slaves no doubt made the slave owners grin: "If they had to choose a master; it would never be a black one."[6]

In presenting Turner not as a liberator but as a false messiah, writers offered an answer to the question being asked across the country: "Who is this Nat Turner? Where is he from?" Accounts portrayed him as unremarkable-looking. A letter to the governor described Turner as "between 30 & 35 years old—5 feet six or eight inches high—weighs between 150 & 160 rather bright complexion but not a mulatto—broad-shouldered—large flat nose—large eyes—broad flat feet rather knock kneed—walk brisk and active—hair on the top of the head very thin—no beard except on the up-per lip and tip of the chin." However average he might be in appearance, his religious fanaticism distinguished him. In 1828, he had dipped into cool, dark water with a white man and emerged a baptized, self-anointed preacher. Writers called him "cunning" and "fanatical," a scoundrel who claimed to be a divinely inspired Baptist preacher. Turner's "preaching excursions" in Jerusalem and Petersburg allowed him, under the "cloak of religion," to concoct his insurrection scheme. He played off the "superstitious hopes and fear of others," using the eclipse to win adherents. "We are inclined to think," claimed one commentator, "that the solar phenomenon exercised considerable influence in promoting the insurrection."

His literacy also served as a means of persuasion, a way to "deceive, delude, and overawe" the minds of the enslaved. That Turner could preach and "read and write with ease" should serve as a warning: "no black man ought to be permitted to turn a Preacher through the country." The writer did not specify why, but he did not have to.

The religion of the slaveholders tried to contain the impact of biblical stories of salvation and liberation, but itinerant preachers along the frontier spread the word that man was a free moral agent and that redemption was available to those who sought it. Some writers said Turner was drunk and some said he sought only to plunder. But one Southerner understood that Turner acted on an "impulse of revenge against the whites, as the enslavers of himself and his race."[7]

The insurrection was over, and by the start of September the first of many executions had begun, but Turner remained at large and all were "at a loss to know where he has dropped to." Some said he had fled to another state; others declared that he remained hidden in the area. Most thought Turner vanished in the Great Dismal Swamp, an enormous bog, thirty by ten miles long, between Virginia and North Carolina, a place "beyond the power of human conception" where "runaway Slaves of the South have been known to secrete themselves for weeks, months and years, subsisting on frogs, terrapins, and even snakes." Time and again newspapers erroneously reported his capture. The *Norfolk Herald* told of a well-armed Turner being taken in a reed swamp. A writer to the *Richmond Enquirer* claimed that he spotted Turner some 180 miles away, on the road from Fincastle to Sweet Spring, headed for Ohio. One rumor had it that Turner drowned trying to cross New River. On another occasion, the body of a dead man thought to be Turner did not, on closer inspection, fit the description.[8]

It turned out that Turner had never left the vicinity of the insurrection, and on Sunday, October 30, around noon, he was captured. Turner had been hiding in the ground, in what some called a "cave" or a "den." He had covered himself with branches and pine brush from a fallen tree. Benjamin Phipps, a local farmer, was walking past when he saw the earth move and a figure emerge. He pointed his gun at the spot.

"Who are you?" he shouted.

"I am Nat Turner; don't shoot and I will give up."

The accounts all made Turner out to be a coward who surrendered and threw his sword to the ground. Phipps and others transported Turner to Jerusalem. As word spread, the citizens of Southampton

County gathered. The *Norfolk Herald* said that given the feelings of the people "on beholding the blood-stained monster . . . it was with difficulty that he could be conveyed alive." The *Petersburg Intelligencer*, by contrast, claimed "not the least personal violence was offered to Nat." All the reports sought to diminish the rebel's stature. Writers labeled him a "poor wretch," "dejected, emaciated, and ragged," a "wild fanatic or gross imposter" whose only honorable act was admitting the charges against him.[9]

On November 5, the state of Virginia tried, convicted, and sentenced Nat Turner. In the days prior to his trial, Thomas R. Gray, a lawyer and slave owner who had served as court-appointed counsel for several slaves tried in September, interviewed the prisoner in his cell. Gray spoke with Turner on November 1, 2, and 3; he also attended the examination of Turner by two justices on October 31. In an unsigned letter sent to the *Richmond Enquirer*, Gray called Turner a "gloomy fanatic" who gave "a history of the operations of his mind for many years past." Gray expressed dismay that "I could not get him to explain in a manner at all satisfactory" how the rebel conceived the idea of emancipating the slaves. The letter-writer teased that he intended to provide a "detailed statement of his confessions, but I understand a gentleman is engaged in taking them down verbatim from his lips."

Gray was himself that gentleman, and whatever other interests he had in Turner's story—civic duty, public curiosity, historical documentation—financial concerns topped the list. His holdings in land and slaves had been slashed over the preceding two years, and Gray seized the opportunity to produce a pamphlet guaranteed to sell. He obtained a copyright on November 10, and two weeks later he published *The Confessions of Nat Turner*. Gray had accurately gauged interest in Turner; the pamphlet sold tens of thousands of copies. It provided the fullest account of what had taken place and offered Turner's story through the prism of his interviewer's point of view.[10]

As a literary genre, last words and dying confessions dated back to the seventeenth century in America and served as part of the ritualistic requirements of execution day. In these texts, the condemned pro-

vided the details of the crime, pleaded for forgiveness, offered a warning to others, and displayed signs of true repentance. The actual
beliefs and feelings of the criminal played little part in the production,
which sought only to serve as a sign of the restoration of civil and religious order. *The Confessions of Nat Turner* stands apart from the dozens
of other works in this genre. The interviewer is a presence in the text;
both Gray and Turner have stories to tell; the prisoner does not warn others against following in his steps, nor does he seek forgiveness. Indeed,
he pled not guilty, "saying to his counsel that he did not feel so."

The *Confessions* begins and closes with Gray's effort to establish
authenticity. The opening page includes the clerk's seal of the full title
as submitted for copyright: "The Confessions of Nat Turner, the leader
of the late insurrection in Southampton, Virginia, as fully and voluntarily made to Thomas R. Gray, in the prison where he was confined,
and acknowledged by him to be such when read before the Court of
Southampton." The closing page includes a court document claiming
that the justices used the confessions at trial to convict Turner and that
when asked if he had anything to say Turner responded, "I have made
a full confession to Mr. Gray, and I have nothing more to say." The trial
record suggests otherwise. Neither Gray nor any confessions were
mentioned, and Turner said only that he had nothing more to say than
what "he had before said," more likely a reference to his interview with
the justices than with Gray. But Gray wanted to identify himself as a
central figure in the proceedings and to persuade the public not only
to trust the stories told in the *Confessions*, but also to buy the pamphlet.

Gray offered Southerners what they needed to hear and wanted to
believe. He opened the work with a signed address to the public, stating that the *Confessions* would at last provide an antidote to a "thousand idle, exaggerated and mischievous reports." Here at last, in the
words of Turner himself, the motives of the rebels would be revealed.
The insurrection, Gray declared, was "entirely local," the "offspring of
gloomy fanaticism." Its origins lurked in Nat Turner's history, in "the
operations of a mind like his, endeavoring to grapple with things
beyond its reach." Turner's revolt, Gray suggested, was a terrible aber-

ration, "the first instance in our history of an open rebellion of the slaves," and it should not alter the public's view of the enslaved as submissive and docile. When confronted, the rebels "resisted so feebly, when met by the whites in arms," and Turner himself, the "great Bandit," was captured by "a single individual . . . without attempting to make the slightest resistance." The lesson for the community was to "strictly and rigidly" enforce the laws that governed the enslaved. Gray did not have to specify that he meant especially those laws against teaching slaves how to read and permitting them to preach.

A perceptive reader might have found the brief opening more unsettling than comforting, for Gray hit upon an unresolvable tension at the core of American culture: whatever appearance might suggest, reality would prove otherwise. "It will thus appear," Gray lamented, "that whilst every thing upon the surface of society wore a calm and peaceful aspect; whilst not one note of preparation was heard to warn the devoted inhabitants of woe and death, a gloomy fanatic was resolving in the recesses of his own dark, bewildered, and overwrought mind, schemes of indiscriminate massacre to the whites." Who was to say that some other Nat Turner was not at this moment planning to strike? What made it worse was that Turner's actions were "not instigated by motives of revenge or sudden anger, but the results of long deliberation, and a settled purpose of mind." Unlike any other event, Turner's revolt punctured the fragile worldview of the slaveholding class. As long as slavery remained, Southerners would wonder and worry about the behavior of their chattels, and they would always have to watch their backs.

Turner also spoke of appearances—the appearance necessary to sustain the belief that he was destined for some special purpose: "Having soon discovered to be great, I must appear so, and therefore studiously avoided mixing in society, and wrapped myself in mystery, devoting my time to fasting and prayer." Turner's story is a narrative of religious awakening. To explain the insurrection, "I must go back to the days of my infancy, and even before I was born." As a child, Turner identified events that happened before 1800, the year of his birth. The slave community proclaimed that he would be a prophet; his parents interpreted marks on his body as indicating that he was meant "for some great purpose." Turner, deeply attached to his grandmother, "who was very religious," felt emboldened by his spiritual and intellectual gifts. He had a "restless, inquisitive and observant" mind and was self-taught in reading and writing. (Even Gray spoke of Turner's "natural intelligence and quickness of apprehension.") Turner heard the Spirit speak to him, and he believed that he was ordained for some special purpose. Twice Turner stated that he overheard others remark that "I had too much sense to be raised, and if I was, I would never be of any use to any one as a slave."

But in his first attempt at prophecy, he seemed to defend rather than attack slavery. In his early twenties, Turner ran away from an overseer and remained in the woods for thirty days, but he returned upon hearing the Spirit command him to follow "the service of my earthly master." The message of obedience that he brought back did not sit well with the other slaves. "The negroes found fault, and murmured against me, saying that if they had my sense they would not serve any master in the world." The story should have deepened the despair of Gray and his readers. Turner's decision to rebel against slavery came less from God than from fellow slaves. Immediately after being spurned, Turner had his first vision of darkened sun, rolling heavens, and red-flowing streams.

In every way, Turner's narrative resisted the interpretation Gray strove to provide. When Turner had told his interviewer of a revelation in 1828 that "the time was fast approaching when the first should be last and the last should be first," Gray asked, "Do you not find yourself mistaken now?" Turner responded with his own question: "Was not Christ crucified?" Asked whether the conspiracy spread beyond Southampton County, Turner inquired, "Can you not think the same ideas, and strange appearances about this time in the heavens might prompt others, as well as myself, to this undertaking." Neither the kindness of the individual master nor the impracticability of the scheme mattered. Turner chose to "carry terror and devastation" wherever he went, and he narrated the massacre of entire families with a dispassionate, almost scientific tone. Gray ended the *Confessions* by recounting the stories of individuals who by luck and grace survived, but Turner's "calm, deliberate composure" unsettled the interviewer: "I looked on him and my blood curdled in my veins."[11]

By the time the *Confessions* appeared, Turner had been hanged and dissected. Some said he sold his body for ginger cakes, but his body was not his to sell. Folk legends had it that he was skinned, his flesh fried into grease, and his bones ground into souvenirs. Whatever happened to his body, his voice remained, captured in the text published by Gray. One reader, at least, declined to believe that Turner spoke the words attributed to him. "The language," he claimed, "is far superior to what Nat Turner could have employed—Portions of it are even eloquently and classically expressed." The reader refused to accept the authenticity of Turner's words because to do so would violate his assumptions about the intellectual capacities of slaves. But such reservations helped make the case that the words transcribed from speech to print were indeed uttered by Nat Turner. Gray did not put the *Confessions* into a dialect meant to imitate the supposed everyday speech of slaves; the very literacy that would seem to belie the authenticity of the text helps confirm it. Furthermore, Gray repeatedly praised Turner for his qualities of mind. Preacher and prophet, Turner early in life discovered the power of language, and he used it to win adherents: "On the sign appearing in the heavens, the seal was removed from my lips, and I communicated the great work laid out for me to do."[12]

THE LIBERATOR

The work of liberation and retribution begun by Turner in Virginia opened a national debate that fueled sectional rivalries between North and South and triggered a wide-ranging discussion over what to do about slavery in Virginia. In assessing the multiple causes of the rebellion, Southern writers placed Northern interference high on their list.

Even in praising Northerners for their sympathy, Southern editors displayed acute sensitivity to sectional tensions. One writer expressed relief that in most Northern newspapers "we have seen no taunts, no cant, no complacent dwelling upon the superior advantages of the non–slave holding states. . . . We have no doubt, that should it ever be necessary, the citizens of the Northern states would promptly fly to the assistance of their Southern brethren." The *Alexandria Gazette* quoted New York papers that expressed support and offered "arms, money, men . . . for the defense of our Southern brethren." "The spirit of the times," opined the *New York Telegraph*, "rebukes discord, disorder, and disunion."[13]

The problem, thought most Southerners and Northerners, was a small but influential group of reformist demagogues and religious fanatics who nurtured disaffection and fomented servile insurrection. "Ranting cant about equality," a Southerner argued, heated the imagination of the enslaved and could create the only force that might lead to a general insurrection across the South—"the march of intellect." One writer cautioned "all missionaries, who are bettering the condition of the world, and all philanthropists, who have our interest so much at stake, not to plague themselves about our slaves but leave them exclusively to our management." Particularly obnoxious—and dangerous, from the Southern perspective—was the circulation of Northern abolitionist newspapers which "have tended, in some degree, to promote that rebellious spirit which of late has manifested itself in different parts" of the South. Refusing to believe slaves capable of plotting an insurrection on their own, and disavowing any precedents or provocations for rebellion among the enslaved, Southerners blamed the timing and ferocity of Turner's revolt not on the darkening of the heavens but on the actions of outside agitators. And of all the missionaries, philanthropists, politicians, and abolitionists who challenged slavery, one alone seemed culpable for the events at Southampton: William Lloyd Garrison and his newspaper *The Liberator*.[14]

In an address to the public on January 1, in the first issue of *The Liberator*, Garrison explained his position on slavery. Invoking the principles of the Declaration of Independence, Garrison demanded the immediate, unconditional abolition of slavery and vowed to use extreme measures to effect a "revolution in public sentiment." He proclaimed he would abjure politics and refuse to ally himself with any denomination. Instead, he desired a brotherhood of reformers willing to raise their voices to defend "the great cause of human rights." He warned that he would not compromise, nor would he rein in his words: "I *will be* as harsh as truth, and as uncompromising as justice. On this subject, I do not wish to think, or speak, or write with moderation. No! No! Tell a man whose house is on fire, to give a moderate alarm; tell him to moderately rescue his wife from the hands of a ravisher; tell the mother to gradually extricate her babe from the fire into which it has fallen;— but urge me not to use moderation in a cause like the present. I am in earnest—I will not equivocate—I will not excuse—I will not retreat a single inch—AND I WILL BE HEARD."

Garrison, who grew up in Newburyport, Massachusetts, began his working life as a writer and editor for assorted newspapers in New England. In 1829, at age twenty-four, he joined Benjamin Lundy in Baltimore as co-editor of the *Genius of Universal Emancipation*, an antislavery newspaper started by Lundy in 1821. The two men differed temperamentally. Lundy, a Quaker, had none of his associate's zeal. He favored gradual, moderate approaches toward the abolition of slavery and wrote in careful, measured phrases. But he knew that his paper needed revitalizing, and he chose the right person for the job. Though Garrison was not yet the radical abolitionist he would soon become, in 1829 he was already pushing the boundaries of the antislavery argument. In a Fourth of July address at the Park Street Church in Boston, he proclaimed that slaves possessed inherent and unalienable rights, that the churches did nothing for the enslaved, that the nonslaveholding states were complicit in the guilt of slaveholding, and that with freedom and education blacks would be equal to whites in every way. The time to act, he declared, was now: "If we cannot conquer the monster in his infancy, while his cartilages are tender and his limbs powerless, how shall we escape his wrath when he goes forth a gigantic cannibal, seeking whom he may devour. If we cannot safely unloose two millions of slaves now, how shall we unbind upwards of TWENTY MILLIONS at the close of the present century?"[15]

It did not take Garrison long to find an object for scorn and derision, a target for the words that fired forth with such intensity. When he discovered that a fellow townsman from Newburyport, Francis Todd, owned the brig *Francis*, which transported seventy slaves from Baltimore to New Orleans, it was too much for him to take. "I am resolved to cover in thick infamy all who are concerned in this nefarious business," he proclaimed. In a November 1829 issue of the *Genius*, he excoriated Todd and the boat's captain for their participation in the domestic slave trade. Exposing the source of their wealth, he labeled them "enemies of their own species—highway robbers and murderers." "Unless they speedily repent," Garrison warned, they would one day *"occupy the lowest depths of perdition."* For his vituperative comments, Garrison faced criminal and civil charges of libel. Following a brief trial, the editor was found guilty and fined fifty dollars and costs. He refused to pay, and authorities imprisoned him in the Baltimore jail for seven weeks in 1830 until a wealthy New York abolitionist, Lewis Tappan, paid the fine.[16]

Those weeks in jail transformed Garrison. From his cell, he wrote Todd: "I am in prison for denouncing slavery in a free country! You, who have assisted in oppressing your fellow-creatures, are permitted to go at large, and to enjoy the fruits of your crime." Garrison's rage deepened as he contemplated the injustice of his treatment. An editorial in his former paper, the *Newburyport Herald*, called him vain and vehement. Garrison responded: "If I am prompted by 'vanity' in pleading for the poor, degraded, miserable Africans, it is at least a harmless, and, I hope, will prove a useful vanity . . . a vanity calculated to draw down the curses of the guilty . . . a vanity that promises to its possessor nothing but neglect, poverty, sorrow, reproach, persecution, and imprisonment." As for vehemence, "the times and the cause" demanded it, because "truth can never be sacrificed, and justice is eternal. Because great crimes and destructive evils ought not to be palliated, or great sinners applauded." From his cell, Garrison witnessed firsthand the effects of slavery as he heard slave auctions conducted and observed as masters came to reclaim their fugitive slaves. He made eye contact with the enslaved and came to compare his own situation, his own "captivity," to their fate.[17]

In prison, Garrison experienced a final awakening. His confinement led him to identify so strongly with the sufferings of the enslaved that he felt he would burst if forced to endure one more day. To be sure, one can find in pre-Baltimore Garrison the views of post-Baltimore Garrison. But his prison experience liberated him: "The court may shackle the body, but it cannot pinion the mind." Garrison imagined what it meant to die unfree, to be made "an abject slave, simply because God has given a skin not colored like his master's; and Death, the great liberator, alone can break his fetters!"

Garrison fled Baltimore and found his way back to Boston, where in the fall he announced plans to start a newspaper that would insist upon the immediate abolition of slavery. He called it *The Liberator* and proclaimed that the slaves must be freed not in death but in life. Garrison sought public absolution from what he now saw as his earlier sinful belief that "the emancipation of all the slaves of this generation is most assuredly out of the question." On January 1, 1831, Garrison offered "a full and unequivocal recantation" of the gradualist position that left millions to die in slavery. He begged "pardon of my God, of my country, and of my brethren the poor slaves, for having uttered a sentiment so full of timidity, injustice, and absurdity."[18]

No one would ever again accuse Garrison of timidity. He not only agitated for the immediate abolition of slavery in the South, he also struggled for the equal rights of free blacks in the North. In June, he attended a convention of free people of color in Philadelphia. "I never rise to address a colored audience," he confessed, "without being ashamed of my own color." With Independence Day celebrations a few weeks away, Garrison admitted, "If any colored man can feel happy on the Fourth of July, it is more than I can do. . . . I cannot be happy when I look at the burdens under which the free people of color labor." "*You are not free*," he lamented, "you are not sufficiently protected in your persons and rights." Garrison saw hope in the Constitution of the United States, which "knows nothing of white or black men; it makes no invidious distinctions with regard to color or condition of free inhabitants; it is broad enough to cover your persons; it has power enough to vindicate your rights. Thanks be to God that we have such a Constitution." But just as Garrison came to see through gradual schemes of emancipation, so too did he lose faith in the Constitution when he recognized that, through such provisions as the three-fifths and fugitive-slave clauses, it defended slavery. Setting the document on fire, the flames lapping at his fingertips, he condemned the Constitution as a proslavery compact, "a covenant with death, an agreement with hell."

Garrison urged free blacks to embrace temperance, industry, and piety as the means to rise. He recommended trades and education, seeing "no reason why your sons should fail to make as ingenious and industrious mechanics, as any white apprentices," and calling "knowledge of the alphabet . . . the greatest gift which a parent can bestow upon his child." He had special hopes for the creation of a black college in New Haven that would combine manual arts with higher education. "What Yale College . . . has done for the whites," he wished, "may in time be done by the new college for the colored people." The delegates in Philadelphia agreed to raise ten thousand dollars in support of the school.[19]

The citizens of New Haven had other ideas. At a meeting on September 10, the mayor and aldermen resolved that a black college would be "destructive of the best interests of the City," and that, since slavery did not exist in Connecticut, and the college tacitly supported the immediate emancipation of slaves, a black college represented "an unwarrantable and dangerous interference with the internal concerns of other States." Abolitionists had miscalculated. They had selected New Haven because of the "friendly, pious, generous, and humane" residents of the town and were mortified by the way in which "a sober and christian community . . . rush[ed] together to blot out the first ray of hope for the blacks." The hypocrisy about not interfering with internal concerns was galling. After all, these same citizens sent flour and supplies to support revolutionaries in Poland, and evinced outrage over Georgia's treatment of the Cherokee Indians, yet themselves treated free blacks with the same disdain. A "Dialogue in Two Acts," printed in the *New-Haven Register*, exposed the contradictions:

FRIEND: Have you heard the Georgians are driving off the Indians?

PUBLIC SPIRIT: Yes! And my blood boils with indignation at the deed. . . . It is astonishing that in this christian country, the precepts of religion and humanity are so grossly violated. . . . Let us declare in the face of the world that we wage eternal war against ignorance and oppression. . . .

FRIEND: Have you heard of the proposition to establish a College in this place for the improvement of the colored youth? . . .

PUBLIC SPIRIT: *Colored youth*! What do you mean, Nigger College in this *place*! . . . Have you lost your senses! . . . Give a liberal education to a black man! Look at the consequences! Why the first thing he will do when educated will be to run right off and cut the throats of our Southern brethren; or if he should stay among us he will soon get to feel himself almost equal to the whites. . . . Send them off to Africa, their native country, where they belong.[20]

Samuel J. May, Unitarian minister in Brooklyn, Connecticut, and contributor to *The Liberator*, warned of the consequences of such prejudice. He despaired that whites were "shamefully *indifferent* to the injuries inflicted upon our colored brethren" and declared that "we are implicated in the guilt" of the slaves' oppression. Arguing that "men are apt to dislike most those whom they have injured most," he concluded that the intensity of racial prejudice was deepened "by the secret consciousness of the wrong we are doing them." "The slaves are men," alerted May. "They are already writhing in their shackles," he observed on July 3, and will "one day throw them off with vindictive violence."[21]

Among the many subjects broached in the pages of *The Liberator* in its first months of publication, slave insurrections received special attention. The focus of discussion was a brief work published by David Walker in the fall of 1829 and now in its third printing: *Appeal to the Colored Citizens of the World*. Walker had been born free in North Carolina, part of a growing, mainly urban, community of artisans, day laborers, and farmhands whose freedom dated from a spate of manumissions that followed the American Revolution. He traveled throughout the South and North before settling in Boston in the 1820s. He lectured against slavery, joined the Massachusetts General Colored Association, and served as local agent for *Freedom's Journal* and *Rights of All*, black papers published in New York. The *Appeal* took the form of a preamble and four articles.

Walker began by declaring, "We (colored people of these United States) are the most degraded, wretched, and abject set of beings that ever lived since the world began." Rejecting all gradual, ameliorative approaches to slavery, he appealed directly to his race: "Brethren, arise, arise! Strike for your lives and liberties. Now is the day and the hour." "When shall we arise from this death-like apathy?," he asked, "And be men!!"

Walker refuted Thomas Jefferson's racial beliefs as expressed in *Notes on the State of Virginia*. According to Walker, Jefferson believed "it is unfortunate for us that our creator has been pleased to make us black," but "we will not take his say so, for the fact." He implored all people of color to challenge Jefferson's judgment by showing they were men, not brutes, and by demonstrating that "man, in all ages and all nations of the earth, is the same." The way to accomplish this was by escaping the state of ignorance in which they were kept, by overturning the tenets of slaveholding religion for a gospel of equality, and by adhering to the words of the Declaration of Independence even if white Americans would not. Sounding both millennial and revolutionary chords, Walker alerted Americans, "Your DESTRUCTION is at hand."

Southerners sought immediately to suppress the publication and

circulation of the *Appeal*, which nonetheless made its way into Southern ports, carried by black sailors and ship's stewards who had been
approached by antislavery agents in Boston Harbor. One bemused
writer in North Carolina found it odd that, "when an old negro from
Boston writes a book and sends it amongst us, the whole country is
thrown into commotion." State legislatures met in closed session
and passed laws against seditious writings and slave literacy. Across
the South, prohibitions on slaves' reading, writing and preaching
were enacted. The mayor of Savannah asked the mayor of Boston
to arrest Walker, and newspapers reported prices as high as ten
thousand dollars on the author's head. Walker perished in 1830
under mysterious circumstances. One writer, "a colored Bostonian,"
had no doubt that Walker was murdered, a casualty of "Prejudice—
Pride—Avarice—Bigotry," a "victim to the vengeance of the public."[22]

In the second issue of *The Liberator*, Garrison condemned Walker's
call for violence. Garrison believed in the Christian doctrine of nonre-
sistance, that evil should not be resisted by force; moral, not violent,
means would transform public opinion and bring an end to slavery.
"We deprecate the spirit and tendency of this *Appeal*," he wrote. "We
do not preach rebellion—no but submission and peace." And yet,
while proclaiming that "the possibility of a bloody insurrection in the
South fills us with dismay," he averred that, "if any people were ever
justified in throwing off the yoke of their tyrants, the slaves are that
people." Garrison also observed, "Our enemies may accuse us of striv-
ing to stir up the slaves to revenge," but their false accusations are
intended only "to destroy our influence."

In the spring, Garrison published an extensive three-part review of
the *Appeal* by an unidentified correspondent. The writer acknowledged
that Walker was an extremist, but denied reports that the pamphlet was
"the incoherent rhapsody of a blood-thirsty, but vulgar and ignorant
fanatic." Quoting at length from the text and approving Walker's analysis, the correspondent proclaimed that insurrection was inevitable,
justifiable, even commendable. He recalled:

A slave owner once said to me, "Grant your opinions to be just, if you talk so to the slaves they will fall to cutting their master's throats."

"And in God's name," I replied, "why should they not cut their master's throats? . . . If the blacks can come to a sense of their wrongs, and a resolution to redress them, through their own instrumentality or that of others, I shall rejoice."[23]

When word of Turner's revolt came, Garrison did not rejoice, but neither did he denounce. "I do not justify the slaves in their rebellion: yet I do not condemn *them.* . . . Our slaves have the best reason to assert their rights by violent measures, inasmuch as they are more oppressed than others." Noting that the "crime of oppression is national," he directed his comments to New Englanders as well as Virginians. Indeed, it astonished him that Northern editors opposed to slavery would express support for the South. According to Garrison, *Badger's Weekly Messenger* offered the "tenderest sympathy for the distresses" of the slaveholders and the *New York Journal of Commerce* thought it understandable that "under the circumstances the whites should be wrought up to a high pitch of excitement, and shoot down without mercy, not only the perpetrators, but all who are *suspected* of participation in the diabolical transaction."[24]

Among those "suspected" of inciting the slaves to revolt was Garrison himself. Within several weeks of the insurrection, Southern editors were seeking information about the dissemination of abolitionist literature. The *Richmond Enquirer* asked its readers to "inform us whether Garrison's Boston *Liberator* (or Walker's appeal) is circulated in any part of this State." The Vigilance Association of Columbia, South Carolina, offered a fifteen-hundred-dollar reward for the arrest and conviction of any white person circulating "publications of a seditious tendency." In Georgia, the Senate passed a resolution offering a reward of five thousand dollars for Garrison's arrest and conviction. The *National Intelligencer* reprinted a letter claiming that *The Liberator* was published "by a white man with the avowed purpose of inciting rebellion in the South" and was carried by "secret agents" who if caught should be barbecued. Northern editors also evinced hostility and pledged "to suppress the misguided efforts of . . . short-sighted and fanatical persons." Garrison began receiving "anonymous letters, filled with abominable and bloody sentiments." He published some of the letters in *The Liberator* on September 10. One slaveholder, writing from the nation's capital, warned Garrison "to desist your infamous endeavors to instill into the minds of the negroes the idea that 'men must be free.' " The prospect of martyrdom only deepened the activist's resolve: "If the sacrifice of my life be required in this great cause, I shall be willing to make it." [25]

The attention turned out to be a boon for the fledging *Liberator*, and Garrison used it to promote the paper and the cause. Those who had never heard of him now wondered about this Boston abolitionist. "A price set upon the head of a citizen of Massachusetts," he cried. "Where is the liberty of the press and of speech? Where the spirit of our fathers? . . . Are we the slaves of Southern taskmasters? Is it treason to maintain the principles of the Declaration of Independence?" Subscriptions to *The Liberator*, limited largely in its first months to free blacks in Boston, now extended to New York and Philadelphia. Garrison used the momentum created by his success at the business of reform to call a meeting in November that consolidated the abolitionist movement in Massachusetts under his leadership. The constitution of the New-England Anti-Slavery Society (1832), a predecessor to the American Anti-Slavery Society (1833), declared its objective "to effect the abolition of slavery in the United States, to improve the character and conditions of the free people of color . . . and obtain for them equal civil and political rights and privileges with the whites." Had Southerners ignored the Boston weekly, it might have folded or limped along. But the attention it garnered in the form of accusation boosted circulation, brought in revenue, and provided Garrison with the platform he desperately sought. "The tread of the youthful *Liberator*," he thundered in October, "already shakes the nation." [26]

As to the charge of inciting the slaves to murder, Garrison proclaimed that *The Liberator* "courts the light, and not darkness." He reminded readers that he was a pacifist whose creed held that violence of any kind for whatever reason was contrary to Christian precepts. With typical sarcasm, he retorted that if Southerners wanted to prohibit incendiary publications they should ban their own statute books and issue a warrant for Thomas Gray, whose pamphlet on Nat Turner "will only serve to rouse up other leaders and cause other insurrections." The blow for freedom, he explained, originated in experiences, not words on the page: "The slaves need no incentives at our hands. They will find them in their stripes—in their emaciated bodies—in their ceaseless toil—in their ignorant minds—in every field, in every valley, on every hill-top and mountain, wherever you and your father have fought for liberty." Garrison likened Turner to other revolutionary leaders: "Although he deserves a portion of the applause which has been so prodigally heaped upon Washington, Bolivar, and other *heroes*, for the same rebellious though more successful conduct, yet he will be torn to pieces and his memory cursed."[27]

Garrison was not alone in viewing Turner's revolt as part of a transatlantic revolutionary movement. "The whole firmament," he believed, "is tremulous with an excess of light." In 1830 and 1831, across the Western world, blows for freedom were being struck. The Belgians obtained independence. In France, the king fled. The British Parliament debated the Reform Bill. In Poland, the Diet declared independence. David Child, the editor of the *Massachusetts Journal*, proclaimed "that the oppressed and enslaved of every country, Hayti and Virginia as well as France and Poland, have a right to assert their 'natural and unalienable rights' whenever and wherever they can." "These are the days of revolutions, insurrections, and rebellions, throughout the world," declared a New York editor. And yet "do we hear any portion of the American press rejoice at the success of the efforts of the *enslaved* AMERICAN to obtain *their* liberty—mourn over *their* defeats—or shed a solitary tear of sympathy and pity for *their* misery, unhappiness, and misfortune?" The writer denounced the hypocrisy of those who "rejoice at the success of liberty, equality, justice, and freedom, or mourn and sympathize at its defeat abroad," yet say nothing of its course at "home." By their actions, "some of the enslaved population of free America . . . have declared their independence." Had the writer known that Turner originally planned to strike on the Fourth of July, he would have had even more evidence for his analysis.[28]

The *Free Enquirer*, published in New York by Robert Dale Owen, the son of the famous utopian planner Robert Owen, also warned the slaveholders of the fate that awaited them in trying to resist the spirit of the times. Southerners might "suppress partial insurrections; by shooting and hanging, they may for a time intimidate and check that reforming and revolutionizing spirit which has always been extolled when successful; but a knowledge of the world's history, and man's nature should teach them that there is a point beyond which oppression cannot be endured, and they ought to anticipate the horrors of the oppressor when that day shall come."[29]

Southerners could not tolerate such talk. "Has it come at last to this," lamented Thomas Dew of the College of William and Mary, "that the hellish plots and massacres of Dessalines, Gabriel, and Nat Turner, are to be compared to the noble deeds and devoted patriotism of Lafayette, Kosciusko, and Schrynecki?" Dew and others placed the blame for the Southampton County tragedy on the mischievous effects of Garrison's *Liberator* and Walker's *Appeal*, not on a transatlantic revolutionary ideology of rights and liberties. Southerners sought a simple explanation for a tragedy they could not comprehend in any other way, because to do so would challenge the basis of Southern society. If slavery was wrong, if slaves were human, if liberty belonged to all and at some level every enslaved person knew it, then widespread rebellion and death would mark the future of the slaveholding states.[30]

The publication of incendiary publications raised another issue as well: the relationship of North and South under the federal government. Garrison often noted that "the bond of our Union is becoming more and more brittle" and thought "a separation between the free and slaves States" to be "unavoidable" unless slavery was speedily abolished. Governor John Floyd of Virginia reached similar conclusions for different reasons. In his diary on September 27, he wondered how it was possible that no law could punish the editor of *The Liberator* and other "Northern conspirators" who displayed "the express intention of inciting the slaves and free negroes in this and the other States to rebellion and to murder the men, women and children of those states." "A man in our States," he concluded, "may plot treason in one state against another without fear of punishment, whilst the suffering state has no right to resist by the provisions of the Federal Constitution. If this is not checked it must lead to the separation of these states."[31]

TRAVELERS IN AMERICA

Travelers to America in 1831 offered their own thoughts on the future of the United States and the dilemma of slavery in a republic that espoused freedom. James Boardman, an Englishman who left Liverpool in 1829 and returned in the summer of 1831, called America "the El Dorado of the age," a country "in which the great problem, can man be free, has been triumphantly solved." Boardman, for one, was reticent on the subject of slavery. While noting that he never hesitated to denounce the institution whenever "opportunities presented themselves," he expressed satisfaction that slave owners seemed reluctant to use the word "slave," substituting instead the word "servant" so as to avoid opprobrium. Another Englishman, the barrister Godfrey Vigne, sailed from Liverpool for New York on March 24, "alone, unbewifed, and unbevehicled . . . with the determination . . . of seeing all I could of the United States in the space of about six months." His brief comments on slavery are contradictory, a mirror of the tensions in the air. The slaves, he states, "are a very happy race," yet "they do as little as they can for their masters" and, if educated, would not "remain long in a state of bondage." Commenting on the aftermath of Turner's insurrection, Vigne noted that the Southern threat to secede would be checked by "the danger they would incur from their inability to defend themselves against their black population." "There can be no doubt," he predicted, "that the slaves, with an offer of liberty, would prove a most formidable weapon in the hands of an enemy."[32]

Other travelers offered more pointed denunciations of American slavery. In a letter written the day before Christmas, Henry Tudor, also an English barrister, described the horrors of the New Orleans slave market, where he witnessed "about *thirty of my fellow-creatures*—men, women, children, and *even infants at the breast*—put up indiscriminately to auction, and knocked down to the highest bidder, just like pigs or oxen in a market." "It was perfectly disgusting," he decried, "to observe the different purchasers . . . *feeling their joints* and *examining their bodies*, to ascertain if they were *sound and in good wind.* Several of them, in no delicate manner, as you may suppose, actually opened the *mouths* of some of these wretched victims of the white man's inhumanity, to satisfy themselves as to the *soundness of their teeth*, and possibly as to their *age*, as if they had been so many horses in a fair."

Sold for fourteen hundred dollars were a young man, wife, and infant, "a picture that would have softened a heart of stone"; sold for seven hundred was an attractive eighteen-year-old girl; sold for a thousand was a handsome man of twenty, "almost as white as myself." "Such a display as this, in a country declaring itself the *freest* in the world," Tudor asserted, "presents an anomaly of the most startling character; and as long as so foul a stain shall tarnish the brightness of American freedom, this otherwise prosperous, powerful, and highly civilised country, must be content to forego its proud claims to superior advantages over the rest of mankind."

For all his indignation, Tudor could not bring himself to advocate immediate abolition. Calling slavery "a subject surrounded by great and numerous difficulties," he concluded that "an indiscriminate course of emancipation would become a curse to the slaves themselves." He thought that slaves had to be prepared for freedom, educated in duties and obligations, and that only an act of gradual emancipation, completed with "the present generation of parents passing away," would protect the republic from convulsion.[33]

Of all the English travelers, Thomas Hamilton, who sailed from

England in the fall of 1830 and returned the following summer, offered the most biting condemnation of American slavery. Hamilton also witnessed a slave auction in New Orleans, and he recounted the sale of an emaciated woman evidently dying of consumption:

> "Now, gentlemen, here is Mary!", said the auctioneer, "a clever house servant and an excellent cook. Bid me something for this valuable lot. She has only one fault, gentlemen, and that is shamming sick. She pretends to be ill, but there is nothing more the matter with her than there is with me. . . ."
>
> Men began feeling the woman's ribs and asking her questions.
> "Are you well?" asked one man.
> "Oh, no I am very ill."
> "What is the matter with you?"
> "I have a bad cough and pain in my side."
> "How long have you had it?"
> "Three months and more."

The auctioneer interrupted: "Damn her humbug. Give her a touch or two of the cow-hide, and I'll warrant she'll do your work."

Mary sold for seventy dollars. Buyers joked that the woman would soon be food for land crabs, and "amid such atrocious merriment the poor dying creature was led off."

Scenes such as this one passed daily throughout the nation. Slavery, Hamilton noted, extended across "the larger portion of the territory of the Union." Especially galling was its perpetuation in Washington, where slaves served as waiters, coachmen, servants, and artisans. "While the orators in Congress are rounding periods about liberty in one part of the city, proclaiming, *alto voce*, that all men are equal, and that 'resistance to tyrants is obedience to God,' the auctioneer is exposing human flesh to sale in another." "That slavery should exist in the District of Columbia," thundered Hamilton, "that even the foot-print of a slave should be suffered to contaminate the soil peculiarly consecrated to Freedom, that the very shrine of the Goddess should be polluted by the presence of chains and fetters, is perhaps the most extraordinary and monstrous anomaly to which human inconsistency—a prolific mother—has given birth."

For those who excused the evil by stating that Americans had inherited the institution from the British, Hamilton had a piercing response: "Now when the United States have enjoyed upwards of half a century of almost unbroken prosperity, when their people, as they themselves declare, are the most moral, the most benevolent, the most enlightened in the world, we are surely entitled to demand, what have this people done for the mitigation of slavery? What have they done to elevate the slave in the scale of moral and intellectual being, and to prepare him for the enjoyment of those privileges to which, sooner or later, the coloured population *must* be admitted? The answer to these questions unfortunately may be comprised in one word—NOTHING."

As for the abolition of slavery in the Northern states, Hamilton expressed disdain. "Slavery has only ceased in those portions of the Union, in which it was practically found to be a burden on the industry and resources of the country," he argued. "*Wherever it was found profitable, there it has remained*, there it is to be found at the present day, in all its pristine and unmitigated ferocity." Because Northern abolition came gradually, slave owners had time to sell their most valuable property to the South. As a result, when the "day of liberation came, those who actually profited by it, were something like the patients who visited the pool of Bethesda,—the blind, the halt, the maimed, the decrepit, whom it really required no great exercise of generosity to turn about their own business, with an injunction to provide thereafter for their own maintenance."

Freedom, proclaimed Hamilton, entailed more than liberation from the power of compulsory labor: "If the word means anything, it must mean the enjoyment of equal rights, and the unfettered exercise in each individual of such powers and faculties as God has given him." Free people of color, he observed, "are subjected to the most grinding and humiliating of all slaveries, that of universal and unconquerable prejudice. The whip, indeed, has been removed from the back of the

Negro, but the chains are still on his limbs, and he bears the brand of degradation on his forehead. What is it but the mere abuse of language to call him *free*. . . . The law, in truth, has left him in that most pitiable of all conditions, *a masterless slave*."

The condition of free blacks served to highlight further the disingenuousness of slaveholders who pretended to acknowledge the evils of slavery but did not care at all about the fate of the black race. Southerners tried to disarm critics by inviting them to suggest a plan of abolition, to offer a "glimmering of light through the darkness by which this awful subject is surrounded." But if the slaveholders favored abolition, observed Hamilton, it was "abolition of a peculiar kind, which must be at once cheap and profitable; which shall peril no interest, and offend no prejudice; and which, in liberating the slave shall enrich his master." Hamilton concluded by wondering how long the slave owners "can hold out against nature, religion, and the common sympathies of mankind. . . . My own conviction is, that slavery in this country can only be eradicated by some great and terrible convulsion. The sword is evidently suspended; it will fall at last."[34]

Some travelers who admired the South (one writer called New Orleans "one of the most wonderful places in the world") decried state laws that prohibited anyone from teaching slaves to read. In his *Guide for Emigrants*, J. M. Peck declared that "to keep slaves entirely ignorant of the rights of man, in this spirit-stirring age, is utterly impossible. Seek out the remotest and darkest corner of Louisiana, and plant every guard that is possible around the negro quarters and the light of truth will penetrate. Slaves will find out, for they already know, that they possess rights as men." The slaves, Peck predicted, were "prepared to enter into the first insurrectionary movement proposed by some artful and talented leader."[35]

Rumors of widespread insurrections flowing from Turner's revolt seemed to substantiate these travelers' observations. Reports of a rebellion in Raleigh, North Carolina, led authorities to arrest every free black in the city. In Fayetteville, Tennessee, citizens believed they discovered a plot by a group of slaves to set fire to several buildings and, during the confusion, "seize as many guns and implements of destruction as they could rescue and commence a general massacre." James Alexander, another of the British travelers who toured America in 1831, noted in his *Transatlantic Sketches* that in New Orleans "there was an alarm of a slave insurrection. . . . Hand-bills of an inflammatory nature were found, telling the slaves to rise and massacre the whites; that Hannibal was a Negro, and why should not they also get great leaders among their number to lead them on to revenge? That in the eye of God all men were equal; that they ought instantly to rouse themselves, break their chains, and not leave one white slave proprieter alive; and, in short, that they ought to retaliate by murder for the bondage in which they were held."[36]

A German immigrant, twenty-five-year-old Johann Roebling (who would go on to build the Brooklyn Bridge), also heard rumors that in New Orleans "the blacks . . . had made a plan to massacre the whites, and thus attain their freedom by force." Roebling restated in his own words what seemed to him the common wisdom of the day: "All reasonable Americans agree . . . that slavery is the greatest cancerous affliction from which the United States are suffering." He arrived in Philadelphia on August 6 and immediately began contemplating where to settle. Of one thing he became certain: "We have made our decision to settle in a free state." "We have been frightened away from the South," he confided, "by the universally prevailing system of slavery, which has too great an influence on all human relationships and militates against civilization and industry." Fearing that in time "we should see ourselves compelled to hold slaves," Roebling headed west from Philadelphia and settled outside of Pittsburgh, where, from a distance, he could "wish the blacks all good fortune in their endeavors to be free."[37]

Two other travelers considered the problems of slavery and race in America; unlike others, they continued to contemplate the issues once they returned home. Alexis de Tocqueville and Gustave Beaumont, twenty-five and twenty-nine years of age, were court magistrates under Charles X and opponents of Louis-Philippe's rise to the throne in the revolution of July 1830. Although hostile to the new king, the young magistrates took an oath of allegiance and then sought an honorable way to wriggle out of their low position in the regime. They asked for leave to visit America to examine the prison system and report back. They hoped not only to fulfill a desire to visit North America, but also to restart their careers by becoming experts on penal discipline and by playing a role in the reform of the justice system in France. The compatriots left Le Havre on April 2 and, after a voyage that early on left Tocqueville "sick and depressed" but Beaumont "well and cheerful," they arrived in New York thirty-eight days later. In letters written shipboard, they disclosed their intentions to extend their investigation into nothing less than the nature of America and republican government itself and revealed the analytical mind-set for which they would long be remembered. Tocqueville, for example, contemplated life on a ship, where "the necessity of living on top of each other and of looking each other in the eye all the time establishes an informality and a freedom" unknown elsewhere. "This is the true land of liberty," he proclaimed, "but it can only be practiced between four wooden planks, there's the difficulty." Unlike other travelers, who came simply to praise or damn, Tocqueville and Beaumont came to understand. They wrote letters, kept diaries and journals, conducted interviews, and, in an attempt to explain America, published works that combined philosophy, history, sociology, and fiction.[38]

A consensus emerged from the many conversations Tocqueville recorded in his notebook: Americans increasingly viewed slavery as an evil, but almost no one thought blacks and whites could live together peaceably. Calling slavery "the one great plague of America," a Georgia planter told Tocqueville, "I do not think that the blacks will ever mingle sufficiently completely with the white to form a single people with them." In Maryland, John Latrobe, son of the famed architect, proclaimed, "The white population and the black population are in a state of war. They will never mix. It must be that one of the two will surrender the ground to the other." Joel Poinsett, a South Carolinian and former minister to Mexico, thought it "an extraordinary thing how far public opinion is becoming enlightened about slavery." While acknowledging that the idea of slavery as "a great evil" had been "gaining ground," Poinsett also asserted that plans to buy the slaves and transport them elsewhere were impracticable and extravagant. "I hope the natural course of things will rid us of the slaves," he confessed, but what that course was he could not say. On October 1, Tocqueville interviewed John Quincy Adams. He asked the former president, newly elected to Congress, whether he viewed slavery "as a great plague for the United States." "Yes, certainly," answered Adams. "That is the root of almost all the troubles of the present and fear for the future." The lawyer Peter Duponceau, who had settled in America during the Revolutionary War, painted the darkest picture: "The great plague of the United States is slavery. It does nothing but get worse. The spirit of the times works towards granting liberty to the slaves. I do not doubt that the blacks will all end by being free. But I think that one day their race will disappear from our land. . . . We will not get out of the position in which our fathers put us by introducing slavery, except by massacres."[39]

Added to what Tocqueville and Beaumont heard was what they saw. Prejudice and segregation permeated the states, free as well as slave. In Massachusetts, free blacks had the rights of citizenship, "but the prejudice is so strong against them that their children cannot be received in the schools." At the Walnut Street prison in Philadelphia, Tocqueville noticed "that the blacks were separated from the whites even for their meals." Beaumont attended the theater and was "surprised at the careful distinction made between the white spectators and the audience whose faces were black." "The colour white is here a nobility, and the colour black a mark of slavery," he wrote his brother. On October 29, they attended the horse races in Baltimore. A black man, "having ventured to come on to the ground with some whites," received "a shower of blows with his cane without that causing any surprise to the crowd or to the Negro himself." Of all the scenes touching on race that they witnessed, the most horrible occurred on November 4 at the Baltimore Almshouse. There they encountered "a Negro whose madness is extraordinary." A Baltimore slave trader, notorious for his cruelty, brutalized not only the body of the enslaved, but in this case the mind as well. "The Negro," Tocqueville recorded, "imagines that this man sticks close to him day and night and snatches away bits of his flesh. When we came into his cell, he was lying on the floor, rolled up in the blanket which was his only clothing. His eyes rolled in their orbits and his face expressed both terror and fury. . . . This man is one of the most beautiful Negroes I have ever seen, and he is in the prime of his life."[40]

Neither Tocqueville nor Beaumont had come to America to study race, but race forced itself on the sympathies of the travelers and figured prominently in their writings once they returned to France. Tocqueville concluded the first volume of *Democracy in America* (1835) with an essay on "The Present and Probable Future Condition of the Three Races That Inhabit the Territory of the United States." Reflecting upon his journey and synthesizing his experiences, Tocqueville offered a somber assessment of race in the United States. "The most formidable of all the ills that threaten the future of the Union," he began, "arises from the presence of a black population upon its territory." Slavery, he reported, seemed to be receding, but "the prejudice to which it has given birth is immovable . . . [and] appears to be stronger in the states that have abolished slavery than in those where it still exists; and nowhere is it so intolerant as in those states where servitude has never been known." Blacks and whites were separated in theaters, hospitals, churches, even cemeteries, where the "distinction of condition prevails even in the equality of death." A free person of color "can share neither the rights, nor the pleasures, nor the labor, nor the afflictions, nor the tomb of him whose equal he has been declared to be; and he cannot meet him upon fair terms in life or in death."[41]

Tocqueville gave little credence to the argument that enlightened attitudes had precipitated the abolition of slavery in the North. Rather, the small number of slaves and their nonessential role in the Northern economy facilitated emancipation. Moreover, the gradual abolition of slavery in the North led to a double migration as slaves were shipped south and immigrants flooded Northern cities. In places such as New York, concluded Tocqueville, abolition "does not set the slave free, but merely transfers him to another master, and from the North to the South." Of the remaining free blacks, segregation and diminishing numbers as a percentage of the population meant that emancipation posed little danger and the freedmen who remained in the North had time to learn "the art of being free."

"The art of being free." The phrase encapsulated Tocqueville's understanding, and he applied it not only to blacks but to whites as well. Struck by the differences between Kentucky and Ohio—the one a slave state, the other free—with the two separated only by a river, Tocqueville observed, "Slavery, which is so cruel to the slave, is prejudicial to the master." He offered a reading of American character based on the "different effects of slavery and freedom." In Kentucky, the presence of slavery degraded work and made free men idle and enervated, "ignorant and apathetic"; in Ohio, where slavery did not exist, "active and enlightened" laborers worked for prosperity and improvement. Kentuckians contented themselves with what they had; Ohioans struggled to get more, "to enter upon every path that fortune opens to [them]." Slavery undermined the work ethic and led inhabitants to live in the world of today; freedom exalted it and spawned the energy and enterprise that led to tomorrow. No wonder, he noted, that "it is the Northern states that are in possession of shipping, manufactures, railroads, and canals." In December 1831, while in Cincinnati, Tocqueville observed, "Slavery threatens the future of those who maintain it, and it ruins the State; but it has become part of the habits and prejudices of the colonist, and his immediate interest is at war with the interest of his own future and the even stronger interest of the country. . . . *Man is not made for slavery; that truth is perhaps even better proved by the master than by the slave.*"[42]

Slavery would be abolished; about that much Tocqueville was fairly certain. But he was at a loss to understand how blacks and whites could ever live together in the South. "We do not know what to do with

the slaves," a Louisville merchant told him, and that problem perplexed Tocqueville, who, early in his visit to America, confessed to
"wearing myself out looking for some perfectly clear and conclusive
points, and not finding any." Along with most Americans, Tocqueville
assumed that the races could not coexist. Gradual emancipation
schemes that liberated future generations could not succeed, he
argued, because such laws would "introduce the principle and the
notion of liberty into the heart of slavery. . . . If this faint dawn of freedom were to show two millions of men their true position, the oppressors would have reason to tremble." Furthermore, emancipating the
slaves without providing for their survival, leaving them in "wretchedness and ignominy," would only worsen the condition of the freedmen.
"The very instruments of the present superiority of the white while
slavery exists"—control of land, wealth, and arms—exposes the former slave "to a thousand dangers if it were abolished." Following
emancipation, "the Negroes and the whites must either wholly part or
wholly mingle," but Tocqueville had already concluded that prejudice
and inequality made the latter impossible. If the races "do not intermingle in the North of the Union, how," he wondered, "should they mix
in the South?" Yet emancipating and removing the black race, as some
advocated, was impossible. The cost of purchasing and transporting
some two million slaves exceeded the revenues of the federal government. Such a scheme "can afford no remedy to the New World."[43]

Tocqueville despised slavery, but he did not believe slaves could
be emancipated without being prepared for freedom. A conversation
with Sam Houston on a steamboat headed for New Orleans compelled
Tocqueville to think about the differences between Indians and slaves.
Houston had been governor of Tennessee before temporarily abandoning his political life to live among the Cherokee Nation, where he
acquired an Indian wife and a Cherokee name meaning "the Raven."
He was traveling to Washington along with a delegation to appeal to
Andrew Jackson on behalf of the Southeastern tribes, who were being
compelled to abandon their ancestral lands. Houston himself was in
the midst of abandoning his life among the Cherokee for a career that

would lead him to fame in Texas. When Tocqueville asked Houston about the "natural intelligence" of Indians, the Southerner answered, "I do not think they yield to any other race of men on that account. Besides, I am equally of the opinion that it is the same in the case of the Negroes. The difference one notices between the Indian and the Negro seems to me to result solely from the different education they have received." Born free, the Indian could act as a free man, with intelligence and ingenuity. But "the ordinary Negro has been a slave before he was born," and had to be taught how to live as a free man. As a slave owner in Texas, Houston would acquire the reputation of educating his slaves, but he never emancipated them.[44]

Tocqueville concluded that Southerners had two choices. They could educate, emancipate, and intermingle with the black population or, "remaining isolated from them, keep them in slavery as long as possible." He had no doubt that the latter would be their course, but recognized that this might terminate shortly "in the most horrible of civil wars and perhaps in the extirpation of one or the other of the two races." Though Tocqueville tried to look ahead, he acknowledged that "in every picture of the future there is a dim spot which the eye of understanding cannot penetrate." This much he foresaw: "Slavery, now confined to a single tract of the civilized earth, attacked by Christianity as unjust and by political economy as prejudicial, and now contrasted with democratic liberty and the intelligence of our age, cannot survive. By the act of the master, or by the will of the slave, it will cease; and in either case great calamities may be expected to ensue."[45]

Tocqueville approached the question of race as a theorist. Beaumont took a different path. He too published a work about America that flowed from his visit in 1831. Only his work was a novel about slavery that included extended appendixes about the condition of the United States. *Marie, or Slavery in the United States*, appeared the same year as *Democracy in America*. Traveling across the country, Tocqueville had often taken gun in hand to stalk game while Beaumont sat on a hillside and sketched pictures. Something of that difference carried over into their writings. Whereas Tocqueville observed, Beaumont personalized. Tocqueville, the hunter, aimed for the intellect; Beaumont, the artist, probed the emotions.

Marie is the story of a Frenchman who travels to America in 1831 and encounters a hermit named Ludovic living outside of civilization in the wilderness near Saginaw. Like the traveler, Ludovic is something of a visionary and reformer. He comes to the United States to experience the new society and to visit his friend Daniel Nelson, who lives in Baltimore with his children, George and Marie. Ludovic falls in love with Marie, especially after a visit to the almshouse, where he sees her soothe a raging, terrified black man who believes that a slave trader seeks to cut his flesh into strips and eat them. Nelson tries to warn Ludovic away from his daughter and tells him his story. The son of a Boston merchant, Nelson as a young man went to New Orleans, where, he was told, "If you don't die of yellow fever you will make a fortune." He married Theresa Spencer, an orphan whose great-grandmother had been a mulatto. When Theresa's bloodlines were revealed, the family plunged from the heights of New Orleans society to its depths. "The whiteness of Theresa's complexion was dazzling," recounted Nelson, but "tradition condemned her."

Ludovic continues to pursue Marie, and the novel goes on to offer an extended meditation on prejudice, racism, and segregation in the United States, where even those "freed from bondage . . . are denied entrance into free society." Blacks, Ludovic observes, are excluded from public schools and hospitals and kept apart from whites in courts, churches, and cemeteries. "I was continually witnessing some sad happening which revealed to me the profound hatred of the Americans for the blacks," laments Ludovic. In the United States, "there is but one crime from which the guilty can nowhere escape punishment and infamy: it is that of belonging to a family reputed to be *colored*. The color may be blotted out; the stain remains." In New York, Ludovic and George are mobbed and removed from the theater when someone identifies George as a mulatto; in Baltimore, George votes but his ballot is invalidated when it is claimed he has tainted blood.

Reluctantly, Nelson allows Ludovic and Marie to marry, but at a chapel in New York they are swarmed by a mob that denounces all abolitionists as traitors and condemns any amalgamation of the races. From there, Nelson, George, Ludovic, and Marie seek refuge in different ways. Nelson travels to Georgia to help the Cherokee, who are being forced off their lands, but his efforts are in vain. George becomes a revolutionary and heads to North Carolina to lead a combined insurrection of slaves and Indians, but the militia murder him. And Ludovic and Marie look west, away from the scrutiny of civilization and toward the solitude of the forest. But their journey exhausts the lovers, and Marie succumbs to a fever just as they reach a resting place in the "wilderness full of hope."

Beaumont had gone further in his assessment than most. He saw that slavery could not stand: "When one considers the intellectual movements stirring in the world, the opprobrium which stigmatizes slavery in the opinion of all peoples; the rapid conquest which the ideas of liberty over the servitude of the blacks have already made in the United States; the progress which enfranchisement is continually making from North to South; the necessity in which, sooner or later, the Southern states will be substituting free for slave labor, under the threat of being inferior to the Northern states; in the presence of all these facts it is impossible not to foresee a more or less imminent epoch in which slavery will have completely disappeared from North America." Slavery would be abolished, but black men and women, Beaumont feared, would never be free from racial prejudice: "The freed black has almost no characteristic of the freeman; in vain will the blacks receive their liberty; they will still be regarded as slaves. Custom is more powerful than law; the Negro slave has been considered an inferior or degraded being; the degradation of the slave will cling to the freed man. His black color will perpetuate the memory of his servitude, and seems an eternal obstacle to the mingling of the two races."

"The storm is visibly gathering," warned Beaumont; "one can hear its distant rumblings; but none can say whom the lightning will strike."[46]

THE VIRGINIA DEBATE OVER SLAVERY

Southerners were not deaf to the coming storm. Ever since the Revolution, when Northern states enacted plans of gradual emancipation, some Southerners had struggled with the problem of how to eradicate a system that they viewed as a "necessary evil." Necessary because slavery provided the labor and wealth of the region. Evil because relations between white and black, and between slaveholders and non-slaveholders, created social tensions and personal excesses that were intolerable.

In some ways, the formation of the American Colonization Society in 1816 marked an attempt to do something about slavery. Supported by leading statesmen such as President James Monroe, Representative Henry Clay, and Chief Justice John Marshall, the society sought to settle emancipated slaves and free blacks in a West African territory that became Liberia. Believing that blacks could never rise above their condition, colonizationists concerned themselves more with ending the black presence in America than with attacking slavery. "Our society has nothing to do directly with the question of slavery," admitted the speaker at the annual meeting of the society in 1831. They hoped that gradually, through voluntary emancipation and expatriation, slavery would dwindle away and the race problem would be removed to a foreign shore. As of 1830, nearly two thousand blacks had been transported to Africa. The American Colonization Society stayed in business for decades, providing statesmen from Jefferson to Lincoln with a panacea for the problem of racial harmony in America.[47]

After 1831, few abolitionists supported colonization. Garrison, once a proponent of gradualism, developed a blistering critique of the concept. In his *Thoughts on African Colonization* (1832), he condemned the society for not opposing slavery, for not supporting immediate abolition, for being hostile to the black race, and for ignoring the desires of the supposed beneficiaries of colonization. "The moving and controlling incentives of the friends of African Colonization," he explained, "may be summed up in a single sentence: *they have an antipathy against blacks.* They do not wish to admit them to an equality. They can tolerate them only as servants and slaves, but never as brethren and friends. They can love and benefit them four thousand miles off, but not at home."

In cities from Boston to Washington, free black citizens gathered to condemn colonization: "We will resist all attempts made for our removal to the torrid shores of Africa, and will sooner suffer every drop of blood to be taken from our veins than to submit to such unrighteous treatment. . . . We know of no other place that we can call our true and appropriate home, excepting these United States, into which our fathers were brought, who enriched the country by their toils, and fought, bled and died in its defence, and left us in its possession—and here we will live and die."[48]

In fighting removal, these African Americans shared the ordeal of the Southeastern Indian tribes who at that moment also faced forced migration from their homes. For many white Southerners, Turner's rebels could only be compared to heathen Indians. The revolt and the savagery associated with the insurrection reminded them of earlier incursions by red men upon white settlements. Just as it did not matter that the Indians had accepted Christianity and abandoned traditional ways, so it seemed not to matter that black men had been in Virginia almost as long as whites. Garrison too saw a connection. The masthead of *The Liberator* showed a slave auction in the Capitol.

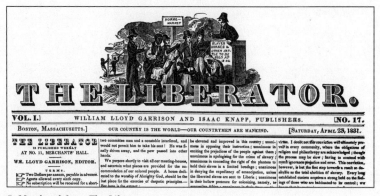

5. Masthead from *The Liberator* (Courtesy of the American Antiquarian Society)

Beside the whipping post, to which a slave is chained, "down in the dust, our Indian treaties are seen." At least one free black recognized the affinity between the two besieged groups. In a letter to Governor Floyd, he warned of his heavenly hopes to "enlist the Indians of Georgia in our common cause." That alliance, of course, was not to be. In the wake of Turner's revolt, some of the seventeen hundred free blacks in Southampton County prepared to leave. Blamed for circulating inflammatory publications and inciting the slaves, these artisans and farmers faced further restrictions on their freedom and threats to their lives. "Suffering severely in consequence of the late insurrection," several hundred free blacks boarded the *James Perkins* in Norfolk on December 9 and emigrated to Liberia.[49]

The new recruits thrilled colonizationists who sought to profit further from the upheaval. The "excitement produced by the late insurrection," reasoned Chief Justice John Marshall, provided an opportunity to raise money and win supporters. To the majority of white Virginians, voluntary removal might have offered a welcome means for eliminating the free black population, but few saw it as a practicable solution to the dilemmas posed by slavery. Indeed, one foreign commentator observed, "Its operations seemed rather calculated *to perpetuate than extinguish slavery*." Colonization was not emancipation, and the real issue was not the fate of those who were free but of those who were enslaved. As a result of Turner's rebellion, the unsettling question of how, if at all, to end slavery filled everyday discussion and led to an extraordinary moment: the Virginia legislature debated the future of slavery in the state.[50]

The question of abolition did not emerge formally until December 14, when William Henry Roane, Patrick Henry's grandson, introduced a Quaker antislavery petition calling for legislative action on emancipation. But in political circles, private talk of the need to do something dated from the moment Turner struck. Jane Randolph, the wife of Jefferson's grandson Thomas Jefferson Randolph, spoke for many of the women of the gentry class when she exclaimed that the horrors at Southampton County "aroused all my fears which had nearly become dormant, and indeed have increased them to the most agonizing degree." She even asked her husband to consider moving west to Ohio. Governor Floyd was also contemplating Virginia's future. On November 19, he wrote the governor of South Carolina and explained his belief that "the spirit of insubordination . . . had its origin . . . from the Yankee population." He confided that he planned in his annual message to the legislature to recommend laws "to confine the Slaves to the estates of their masters—prohibit negroes from preaching—absolutely to drive from the State all free negroes—and to substitute the surplus revenue in our Treasury annually for slaves, to work for a time upon our Rail Roads etc etc and these sent out of the country, preparatory, or rather as the first step toward emancipation." Two days later, in his diary, he confessed, "Before I leave this government, I will have contrived to have a law passed gradually abolishing slavery in this State." And on the day after Christmas: "I will not rest until slavery is abolished in Virginia."[51]

Floyd owned slaves, and his concern over the institution had more to do with the prosperity of the state than with the fate of the enslaved. Like most other Virginians, he believed that any plan of emancipation would have to provide for the eradication of the black presence. Some legislators thought it improper to discuss the issue at all. They believed it fell beyond the scope of the select committee created in response to the governor's annual message, which called for an examination of "the subject of slaves, free negroes and the melancholy occurrences growing out of the tragical massacre in Southampton." William Osborne Goode moved that the Quaker petition should not be referred to the committee. Agreeing with another member that the only appropriate question was "how we should get rid of our free black population," he warned that "agitation" on the question of abolition was "worse than useless."

The chair of the select committee, William Henry Brodnax, who led the militia during the insurrection, disagreed. The committee's mandate, he thought, was wide in scope, and a respect for the opinions of constituents necessitated their being heard. Shocked that the august body feared a petition, Brodnax wondered if the legislature wanted the world to believe that Virginia "was not even willing to think of an ultimate delivery from the greatest curse that God in his wrath ever inflicted upon a people." In asking that the petition be admitted, Brodnax confessed that he did not think the legislature "would take any direct steps toward the emancipation of the slaves." Another legislator agreed that the appearance of open discussion was necessary to put the public mind at rest. As for slavery, it was an evil, but one "so interwoven with our habits and interests . . . it was too late to correct it."[52]

By a vote of ninety-three to twenty-seven, the House accepted the Quaker petition, and for several weeks the select committee sifted through additional petitions, memorials, and resolutions. William Goode could not tolerate it any longer, and on January 11, 1832, he moved that the committee be discharged and that the body rule that "it is not expedient to legislate on the subject" of emancipation. He argued that "a misguided and pernicious course of legislation" had to be arrested, because the legislature was now treading dangerously close to considering whether "they would confiscate the property of the citizens" of Virginia. Talk of emancipation, moreover, only increased the likelihood of future rebellions: "The slaves themselves were not unconscious of what was going forward here. . . . They are an active and intelligent class, watching and weighing every movement of the Legislature. . . . By considering the subject [of emancipation], their expectations were raised; expectations that were doomed to disappointment, the effect of which might be the destruction of the country." Why, Goode wondered, continue the charade of consideration? After all, action was impossible, because the means of carrying any project into effect did not exist, and words caused anxiety, suffering, and, in the long run, even rebellion.

In offering his motion, Goode miscalculated. Others now rose to express their views on the abolition of slavery. Thomas Jefferson Randolph, newly elected as a delegate, presented a substitute motion that provided a specific plan of gradual emancipation: "The children of all female slaves, who may be born in this state, on or after the 4th day of

July, 1840 shall become the property of the Commonwealth, the males at the age of twenty-one years, and females at the age of eighteen, if detained by their owners within the limits of Virginia, until they shall respectively arrive at the ages aforesaid, to be hired out until the net sum arising therefrom, shall be sufficient to defray the expense of their removal, beyond the limits of the United States."

Under the terms of Randolph's emancipation plan, no slaves currently in bondage would be freed, freedom would come only to those slaves whose masters had not sold them farther south by a certain age, and those eligible for freedom would have to work off the costs of their transportation to Africa. Such was the "plan" that generated passionate discussion and induced the governor to describe the legislature as divided into slave and abolition parties. The slave-party delegates hailed from the Tidewater and Piedmont districts in the east. The abolition party drew its strength from the trans-Allegheny region in the west. Floyd himself had come from there, the first Virginia governor from west of the Alleghenies. House members in the Tidewater and Piedmont owned 1,080 slaves; those from the trans-Allegheny owned a total of ninety-five. Sectional tensions in Virginia had become acute just two years earlier in a battle of reapportionment. The western regions had lost their attempt to have representation based solely on the white population, and as a result the slaveholders of eastern Virginia received an extra seven seats. In some respects, then, the debate over slavery was between easterners opposed to interference with slavery and westerners who wanted to see the institution eradicated one day.

But the ideological differences between the slave and abolition parties were not nearly so severe as the names might signify. Merely being willing to consider some form of future gradual emancipation made one a member of Floyd's abolition party; it did not make one an abolitionist by any definition of the word a Northern activist might recognize. When the *Richmond Enquirer* proclaimed that "the seals are broken, which have been put for fifty years upon the most delicate and difficult subject," the editors were not commenting on Goode's or Randolph's motions, but on the astonishing and disturbing opinions being voiced, opinions that had always been whispered in private but almost never shouted in public. Almost no one in 1831–32 believed that the legislature would actually enact a plan that might lead one day to the disappearance of slavery from Virginia. Plans did not pose the danger; speech did. Every Virginian knew that David Walker and William Lloyd Garrison and Nat Turner breathed fire, and every resident of Southampton County knew someone enveloped by the flames. But now a white Virginian rose in the House of Delegates and declared through open doors, "Slavery as it exists among us may be regarded as the heaviest calamity which has ever befallen any portion of the human race. . . . The time will come, at no distant day, when we shall be involved in all the horrors of a servile war which will not end until . . . the slaves or the whites are totally exterminated." A Virginian rose and declared that, based on the principle that all men are by nature free and equal, "it is an act of injustice, tyranny, and oppression to hold any part of the human race in bondage against their consent."[53]

The comments shocked James Gholson, who owned twenty slaves. He spoke for the slave party of the Tidewater and the Piedmont. Deprecating a discussion that "from its very nature should never be openly" conducted, he denounced Randolph's proposal as "monstrous and unconstitutional." Slaves, he reminded his colleagues, were property and the source of wealth. "Private property is sacred" and could not be appropriated by the state for public use without just compensation. Only under extreme necessity might the legislature consider such an action, and such conditions did not currently apply. Gholson offered his own history of Turner's revolt: "An ignorant, religious fanatic, conceived the idea of insurrection. He succeeded in involving four or five others, of his *immediate neighborhood*, in his designs: they commence the massacre—they traverse a region of country containing hundreds of slaves; but neither threats, promises, nor intoxication, could secure more than forty to fifty adherents—they remain embodied something more than twenty-four hours—they disperse without being forced—are taken without resistance—and are at last hung on evidence of persons of their own class and color." With safety and order quickly restored, "the people of our country again sleep quietly on their pillows, and would, in all probability, have enjoyed uninterrupted repose, had it not been for this false legislative cry of 'Wolf!' 'Wolf!' "

The slaves of Virginia, Gholson asserted, "are as happy a laboring class as exists upon the habitable globe, . . . contented, peaceful, and harmless." But if the legislature adopted Randolph's plan, the slaves would become dangerous. A law that only freed a future generation would create untold resentments: "It argues but little knowledge of human nature to suppose that we reconcile one generation to servitude and bondage by telling it that [the one] to follow shall be free." Such a scheme not only failed to meet the demands of the putative emergency created by Turner, it threatened to offer the lesson that, "if *one insurrection* has been sufficient to secure the liberty of *succeeding* generations, might it not be inferred that *another* would achieve the freedom of the present?"

Gholson did not wish to argue "the abstract question of slavery, or its morality or immorality." "Will you believe it," he chided the legislators from the west, that the "great men of the revolution *owned slaves*? Yes, actually owned slaves, and worked them too—even died in possession of them, and bequeathed them to their children." There were no "lights of the age" dating from the Revolution, no beacons of freedom for all. "I have heard of these lights before," Gholson averred, "but I have looked for them in vain." Turner thought "*he* saw them . . . and now, all his lights and all his inspirations are shrouded in the darkness of the grave." Northern lights had indeed appeared in the form of incendiary publications, but "these are not lights of the age, or lights from heaven," but "a darkness visible." Rather than spreading illumination, this "unjust, partial, tyrannical, and monstrous measure," meant to commence no less on the Fourth of July, a day made sacred by Randolph's grandfather, would forever extinguish the "lights of liberty and justice."[54]

John Thompson Brown, from Petersburg, also denounced any scheme of abolition. He warned that, for the government to generate sufficient surplus revenue to purchase and remove the black population, it would have to impose "high duties on imports." "It is a well known fact," he added in the midst of South Carolina's threat to nullify the tariff, that "the burden would rest chiefly on the Southern states. It would be nothing more or less than drawing from the pockets of the slaveholders, by indirect taxation, the money with which their slaves were eventually to be purchased." "It would be better economy to abandon them at once," he snorted, "without compensation, than to go through the troublesome and expensive ceremony of furnishing the means to have them bought."

An even greater danger lurked beneath the reliance on government surplus revenue. By allowing the federal government a direct role in the disposition of slavery, Southern states would yield their autonomy. "When the general government shall have obtained the control of this subject," predicted Brown, "and the slave holding states lie defenceless at her feet, you will hear no more of the purchase and removal of slaves. You will be told that they are persons and not things. . . . The bill of rights will be quoted to prove that they are men and entitled to their freedom. They will be removed and slavery extinguished, but it will be without compensation, and at your expense." Brown dismissed those who averred that because of slavery "the body politic is languishing under disease." Slavery, he concluded, "is our lot, our destiny—and whether, in truth, it be right or wrong—whether it be a blessing or a curse, the moment has never yet been, when it was possible to free ourselves from it."[55]

William Brodnax, who owned twenty-six slaves and chaired the special committee, spoke next. He regretted that matters had come to this, because he believed that the committee's final report would have recommended against any action on the subject. Brodnax, a representative from Dinwiddie County in the eastern Piedmont district, disagreed with Gholson over whether the subject should be discussed: "The people all over the world are thinking about it, speaking about it, and writing about it. And can *we* arrest it, and place a seal on the subject? We might as well attempt to put out the light of the sun." He also disagreed with Gholson and Brown on the perniciousness of slavery:

"That slavery in Virginia is an evil, and a transcendent evil, it would be idle, and more than idle, for any human being to doubt or deny." Calling slavery an "incubus" that sapped the energies of the state and retarded its advancement, he argued that *something* should be done to alleviate it or exterminate it . . . *if any thing can be done*, by means less injurious or dangerous than the evil itself."

Randolph's proposal, however, was not the thing to be done. Calling it "nauseous to the palate," Brodnax denounced it for violating the three axioms that had to be met in considering any plan for abolition: "That no emancipation of slaves should ever be tolerated, unaccompanied by their immediate removal from among us; that no system should be introduced which is calculated to interfere with, or weaken the security of private property, or affect its value;—and, that not a single slave or any other property he possesses, should be taken from its owner, *without his own consent*, or an ample compensation for its value."

Brodnax, an ardent colonizationist, was willing to support emancipation provided that the state expelled all the slaves and that the slaveholders did not suffer financially. In reality, there was not much difference between Gholson, a slaveholder who defended the institution, and Brodnax, one who questioned it. It was easy to call slavery an evil and then refuse to pay a price to eliminate that evil. Brodnax suggested that legislators forget about the enslaved until they first demonstrated they could do something about the free black population. Before the state could deal with over 450,000 slaves, it must first show it could remove nearly fifty thousand free blacks. Brodnax argued that free blacks had an injurious influence on the slave population and played an indirect role in "fomenting conspiracies and insurrections." He recommended targeting six thousand per year for colonization in Liberia. Acquiring Texas and making it an independent black state ("a sable nation") had been discussed, but such a plan would prove unpalatable to the bordering slaveholding states to the east. Rather, Brodnax thought it imperative to restore "these people to the region in which nature had planted them, and to whose climates she had fitted their constitution." The colonization of all the free blacks would be accomplished in less than a decade, paid for by state taxation and by monies rightfully received from the federal government "without the slightest violation of those strict State Right principles which distinguish our Virginia political school."[56]

Thomas Jefferson Randolph knew all about that school. In 1798, his grandfather authored the resolutions adopted by the Kentucky legislature in protest against the Alien and Sedition Acts. Those resolutions declared, "The several States composing the United States of America are not united on the principle of unlimited submission to their General Government." Randolph was close to his grandfather. He lived nearby, managed Monticello for the last ten years of Jefferson's life, and served as executor of his estate. It was Randolph who sold Jefferson's slaves in order to pay off debts of forty thousand dollars.

Thomas Jefferson never figured out what to do about slavery. In 1787, he proposed a plan of gradual emancipation in which the children of slaves would be raised and educated at public expense until a certain age and then declared "a free and independent people." Throughout his life, he thought this a sound and practicable solution. Any abolition scheme, he believed, had to be accompanied by colonization. To the question "Why not retain and incorporate the blacks into the state?" he answered: "Deep rooted prejudices entertained by the whites; ten thousand recollections, by the blacks, of the injuries they have sustained; new provocations; the real differences which nature has made; and many other circumstances, will divide us into parties, and produce convulsions which will probably never end but in the extermination of the one or the other race."[57]

In retirement, Jefferson watched and at times worried as slavery became an increasingly divisive national issue. In 1814, he received a letter from Edward Coles, James Madison's private secretary. Coles implored Jefferson to use his influence to promote a plan of gradual emancipation. He told the statesman that, given his lifelong "professed and practiced" principles of liberty and independence, the "duty . . . devolves particularly on you." Coles confessed that slavery was so repugnant to him that he had decided to abandon his native soil and emancipate his slaves.

Jefferson wrote back that he believed that the "hour of emancipation is advancing" and that the most expedient plan would provide for the "education and expatriation" of blacks born after a certain date. The work of emancipation, however, was not for his generation: "This enterprise is for the young; for those who can follow it up and bear it through to its consummation." Thinking it preferable to be a benevolent slave owner, he advised Coles not to leave Virginia but to reconcile himself "to your country and its unfortunate condition" and through "the medium of writing and conversation" labor to change public opinion.

"I can not agree with you that [prayers] are the only weapons of one of your age," retorted Coles. "The difficult work of cleansing the escutcheon of Virginia of the foul stain of Slavery" required not only the energy of the young but the experience and influence of the "revered Fathers" of the nation. He reminded Jefferson that at the end of life another luminary, Ben Franklin, was "actively and usefully employed" in opposing slavery.[58]

Coles had the last word. In 1819, he left Virginia for Illinois and emancipated his slaves as he crossed the Ohio River. Elected governor of Illinois in 1822, he defeated proslavery forces within the state. As for Jefferson, he continued to worry, but felt unable to act. In the aftermath of the Missouri Crisis of 1819–20, when Missouri entered the Union as a slave state, Maine as a free state, and Congress prohibited slavery north of a geographic line located at 36°30', Jefferson confessed that the division of the union into slave and free states was an issue that, "like a fire bell in the night, awakened and filled me with terror." Yet he saw no "*practicable*" way out except for some plan of gradual emancipation and expatriation. Aged and tired, the statesman feared that the sacrifice of the Founding Fathers to "acquire self-government and happiness . . . is to be thrown away by the unwise and unworthy passions of their sons," the very generation Jefferson had told Coles would have to lead the way.[59]

Jefferson's relations tried to take action. In 1820, his son-in-law, Governor Thomas Mann Randolph of Virginia, suggested using tax monies to remove slaves to Santo Domingo. The legislature did not pursue the recommendation. And in 1831, thirty-nine-year-old Thomas Jefferson Randolph was elected for the first time to the House of Delegates. Without question, he burned with beliefs and ambitions fueled by bloodlines as well as book lines. He internalized his beloved grandfather's attitude toward the younger generation and felt the need to demonstrate his worthiness by proving himself in the public arena. As the House began to discuss the various petitions submitted in the aftermath of Turner's insurrection, Randolph received a message from a former neighbor who in August had been defeated in his bid for a seat in Congress.

Edward Coles was still writing letters. He informed Randolph, "Now is the time to bring forward & press on the consideration of the people & their representatives, not only the propriety but absolute necessity of commencing a course of measures for the riddance of . . . the colored population of Va." Appealing to the grandson's place in history, Coles told Randolph that he had "inherited the feelings & principles" of his "illustrious Grand Father" and that "no one of the young generation could be more suitable to lead or could bring more moral and political weight of character to aid the good work than his grandson."

Coles suggested a plan that would commence in 1840 and free children at the age of twenty-one. If they then had to work for two years to pay costs of transportation to Africa, "it would bring the year 1863 before the first Negro under this act would be sent out of the country." Coles lived through the Civil War, and if he stayed true to his conscience, on January 1, 1863, the day the Emancipation Proclamation took effect, he squirmed to remember what he had proposed three decades earlier.[60]

On that frigid day in January 1832 when Thomas Jefferson Randolph rose in the Virginia House of Delegates to move for a plan of gradual emancipation, he did so because Turner's insurrection horrified his wife, because he was a Jefferson and a Randolph, and because a letter had arrived that he, unlike his grandfather, took to heart. But as he rose to speak, his words evaporated. The thoughts that had flowed so easily when conceived in his closet vanished "as mist before the sun" when presented in public. His lineage summoned the oracle of Virginia's past, dead not even five years. The "weight" of his grandfather's name, Randolph complained, "was thrown into the scale to press me down farther." Randolph did not want to debate whether Thomas Jefferson would have supported this specific proposal, but he quoted from Jefferson's letter to Coles to show that throughout his life the sage of Monticello thought it "expedient" to do something about slavery.

Expedient. That was the word over which so many words issued forth in the Virginia debate on slavery. Randolph proclaimed that he had never intended his resolution to be debated so vociferously. It was not a bill, only a resolution of inquiry designed to probe the possibility of some future plan. Brodnax's committee reported that it "is inexpedient for the present legislature to make any legislative enactment for the abolition of slavery." A trans-Allegheny representative, William Preston, moved to strike the word "inexpedient" and substitute "expedient." Randolph was one of only six Piedmont representatives to vote for it; the motion lost seventy-three to fifty-eight. Ultimately, "inexpedience" won. A preamble to the report of the special committee, moved by Archibald Bryce, a slave owner from Piedmont, offered that "further action for the removal of the slaves should await a more definite development of public opinion." No one knew what that meant. Bryce said he only wanted to submit the question to the people. Preston said he would vote for it if it was intended as a declaration that the House would one day act. Another delegate offered that "slavery was not an evil in Virginia." One representative observed that if he voted for the preamble and afterward was asked what he had voted for he would be unable to answer.[61]

Bryce's preamble to the special committee's report passed by a vote of sixty-seven to sixty, and the Virginia debate came to an end. Unable to act against slavery, the legislature acted against what it believed to be the sources of insurrectionary spirit. Within weeks, a colonization bill to provide for the removal of free blacks moved swiftly through the legislature. A "police bill" further eroded the rights of free blacks,

denying them trial by jury and allowing for their sale and transportation if convicted of a crime. The legislature also revised the black
codes, barring slaves and free blacks from preaching or attending religious meetings unaccompanied by whites. In the aftermath of Nat
Turner, Virginians sought to reassure themselves that in the future
"successful insurrection would be impossible."

Thomas Jefferson Randolph was not so certain. Perhaps, in the
event of a full-scale revolt, if Virginia's resources proved inadequate,
the federal government would send troops and "reclaim a country
smoking with the blood of its population." Far more likely, he thought,
"there is one circumstance to which we are to look as inevitable in the
fullness of time; a dissolution of the Union. God grant it may not hap-
pen in our time, or that of our children; but . . . it must come, sooner or
later; and when it does come, border war follows it, as certain as the
night follows the day." Randolph imagined an invasion by Virginia's
enemy "in part with black troops, speaking the same language, of the
same nation, burning with enthusiasm for the liberation of their race;
if they are not crushed the moment they put foot upon your soil, they
roll forward, an hourly swelling mass; your energies are paralyzed,
your power is gone; the morass of the lowlands, the vastness of the
mountains, cannot save your wives and your children from destruction."[62]

With the eclipse of the sun, Nat Turner's prophecy came to pass. In
time, Randolph's would as well.

RELIGION AND POLITICS

✳

RELIGION AND REFORM

A man in a daydream drifts toward the precipice of Niagara Falls unaware of the danger. On the opposite side, someone watches. Just as the man is about to plunge, the observer cries out "STOP!" The shout awakens the man from his reverie, and at the critical moment he is saved. A crowd gathers.

"That man has saved my life."

"But how?"

"O, he called to me at the very moment I was stepping off, and that word, STOP, snatched me from destruction. O, if I had not turned that instant, I should have been dashed to pieces. O, it was the mercy of God that kept me from a horrible death."

Charles Grandison Finney introduced this Niagara Falls parable in a sermon delivered at Boston's Park Street Church in late October 1831, and he often repeated it to answer the question "What must I do to be saved?" The wandering sinner, Finney suggested, must act immediately in response to the voice of the preacher who shouts the word that originates with God. The sinner must choose salvation. A conversion experience occurs because the preacher is an effective

instrument, the word awakens, and the spirit is present. When all
works in unison, the unbeliever is "brought out of darkness into mar-
velous light."[1]

Finney arrived in Boston at the peak of a revivalist surge that he
helped to create and define. In 1831, he later recalled, began "the
greatest revival of religion throughout the land that this country had
then ever witnessed." Finney's rival, Lyman Beecher, who questioned
his colleague's methods and tried to dissuade him from coming to
Boston, went further when he declared, "This is the greatest revival of
religion that has been since the world began." The "extraordinary
excitement" of evangelical enthusiasm engulfed numerous cities and
towns across the United States. In August, the secretary of the American Education Society reported that as many as a "thousand congre-
gations in the United States have been visited within six months . . .
with revivals of religion; and the whole number of conversions is probably not less than fifty thousand." In New England and the Mid-

CAMP-MEETING

6. "Camp-Meeting," c. 1829 (Courtesy of the American Antiquarian Society)

Atlantic regions particularly, the fires of revivalism burned intensely. Evangelical Protestantism had swept through the southwestern frontier in the first decades of the century, leading to a proliferation of Baptist and Methodist churches. Now Presbyterians and Congregationalists, employing frontier techniques such as prolonged camp meetings and extemporaneous preaching, entered into the competition for souls. Whereas the newer denominations in the South appealed to the poor and dispossessed, those in the North attracted evangelical converts from the middle and upper classes. "The Lord," Finney proclaimed, "was aiming at the conversion of the highest classes of society."[2]

Finney himself was becoming a member of those classes when his conversion came. He was born in 1792 and reared in Oneida County in western New York, an area that would come to be known as the "burned-over district" because the flames of revivalism roared most intensely there. Finney taught for a while in New Jersey and then decided to study for the law. He later claimed that at the time he had had no interest in religion and that he had begun reading the Bible only because his law books contained so many references to the Mosaic Code. One day in the fall of 1821, he took a walk in the woods and suddenly began contemplating the issue of his own salvation. Then and there, in an open space surrounded by fallen trees, he decided to give his heart to God. The struggle with his excessive pride and sinfulness took all day, and he returned to his office to pray. Though the room was dark, it appeared to him as "perfectly light." At that moment, his religious conversion was completed, and he decided to preach the Gospel. Due in court at 10 A.M., he told his client that he could not handle his case because "I have a retainer from the Lord Jesus Christ to plead his cause."[3]

Finney studied theology, and the Oneida Presbytery ordained him in 1824. For the next few years, he led revivals across western New York and Pennsylvania and in New York City. In the fall of 1830, he accepted Rochester as his client. As recently as 1821, Rochester had been a small village of fifteen hundred settlers. The opening of the Erie Canal, which provided access to market for the goods of western New

York, transformed the town. Farmers bought land and devoted their energies to wheat production. Merchants and laborers flooded the city. By 1830, the boomtown had become a bustling entrepôt of ten thousand residents. The boundaries between civilization and the wilderness were so distinct that one visitor commented, "The transition from a crowded street to the ruins of the forest, or to the forest itself, is so sudden, that a stranger, by turning a wrong corner in the dark, might be in danger of breaking his neck over the enormous stumps of trees."[4]

But with growth came discord. The middle class divided on political and religious issues and united against the laboring classes on moral questions such as the consumption of alcohol. The story repeated itself in scores of other towns and cities. With expansion and wealth came dissension and strife. Only a revival of religion, many believed, could preserve the nation "from our vast extent of territory, our numerous and increasing population, from diversity of local interests, the power of selfishness, and the fury of sectional jealousy and hate."[5]

When the Third Church invited Finney to preach, they were without a minister and embroiled in a controversy with the First Church. "Religion was in a low state," Finney recalled. His friends advised against going to Rochester: too "uninviting a field," they warned. He agreed, and prepared to head east from Utica for New York City, a far richer field for someone trying not only to win souls but also to make a career. Upon further reflection, however, he concluded that the reasons "against my going to Rochester, were the most cogent reasons for my going." With his change of heart, he boarded the canal packet boat with his family and headed west to Rochester, where he filled the pulpit of the Third Church from September 10, 1830, through March 6, 1831.

Finney preached three evenings a week and three times on Sunday. His eyes were irresistible, deeply set and piercing blue; when they fixed on you, it was hard to look away. Hour after hour, day after day, his "clear, shrill" voice pierced the congregation. He spoke without notes, stared into the crowded aisles, and made his case. "It did not sound like preaching," recalled one congregant, "but like a lawyer arguing a case before court and jury. . . . The discourse was a chain of logic brightened by the felicity of illustrations and enforced by urgent appeals from a voice of great compass and melody." To sway sinners, whom he knew to be particularly anxious about their souls, he reserved an area in front of the pulpit and made certain that ushers led them to these seats. These "anxious inquirers" sat in what was known as the "anxious seat," and Finney expected them "then and there to give up their hearts." Considering the social and psychological pressures being applied, it is not surprising that more often than not those at the front publicly renounced their ungodly ways. By the time he left Rochester, some eight hundred residents had converted and joined the churches.[6]

Finney's work at Rochester culminated in a Protracted Meeting that lasted five days and blazed from morning to night, while all business in the city was brought to a stop. At the conclusion, Finney was exhausted. Physicians diagnosed him with consumption and advised him to rest. They told him he would not live long. Decades later, Finney chuckled at how the "doctors did not understand my case." He kept going, and after leaving Rochester, he led a revival in Auburn and then participated in a Protracted Meeting in Providence. The evangelist had his eyes set on Boston, a city crowded with Calvinists (orthodox Presbyterians and Congregationalists) and Arminians (liberal Unitarians and Universalists), the city where Lyman Beecher held sway. For years, Beecher had challenged Finney's beliefs and methods, claiming that they violated the strictures of Calvinist doctrine: innate depravity, predestination, limited atonement. Although the two had thrashed out their differences at meetings in New Lebanon, New York, in 1827 and Philadelphia in 1828, tensions and suspicions remained. Beecher tried to be diplomatic, telling Finney, "Boston was not the best place of entrance for you into New England," but Finney knew that Beecher had "solemnly pledged himself to use his influence to oppose me." The Union Church Committee of Boston decided to send a minister to Rhode Island to hear Finney preach, "to spy out the land

and bring back a report." But after hearing several sermons, Benjamin Wisner, from Boston's Old South Church, converted to Finney's side and embraced the minister. "I came here a heresy-hunter," he confessed, "but here is my hand, and my heart is with you."[7]

Finney arrived in Boston the first week of September and began preaching at the Park Street Church, where Beecher's son, Edward, was pastor. Toward the end of October, Finney delivered a new sermon, "Sinners Bound to Change Their Own Hearts." The year and the text were one: Ezekiel 18:31—"Make you a new heart and a new spirit: for why will ye die, O house of Israel?" The sermon encapsulated Finney's beliefs, displayed his oratorical gifts, and initiated a protracted debate over its meaning. Dispensing with the Calvinist idea of man's helplessness, Finney proclaimed, "All Holiness . . . must be voluntary." How could it be, he inquired, "that God requires us to make a new heart, on pain of eternal death, when at the same time he knows we have no power to obey; and that if ever the work is done, he must himself do the very thing he requires of us." It made no sense that the sinner was expected to be "entirely passive" in his own salvation, as if waiting for "a surgical operation or an electric shock." Changing one's heart was no different from changing one's mind. The heart was "something over which we have control; something voluntary; something for which we are to blame and which we are bound to alter." Conversion was the requirement to change our "*moral character*; our *moral disposition*; in other words, to change the abiding preference of our minds." The "actual turning, or change, is the sinner's own act," and not "the gift and work of God." God induces one to turn, but still it must be "your own voluntary act" and it must come now—"another moment's delay and it may be too late forever."

Finney offered the Niagara Falls parable and several other stories to illustrate his point. "Tell stories," Finney advised in his *Lectures on Revivals of Religion* (1835), "it is the only way to preach." Here was one key to Finney's success: his democratic style. He rejected the formality and obscurity of the educated ministry, and his preaching was theatrical, conversational, and practical. He defended his approach with an anecdote. The bishop of London once asked the actor David Garrick why actors, playing fictional roles, moved audiences to tears, whereas ministers, representing sober realities, were ignored. Garrick replied: "It is because we represent fiction as a reality and you represent reality as a fiction." Finney made reality palpable and forced congregants to participate in the drama of salvation. He talked in terms well understood by his audience, using analogies to professional ambitions, commercial arrangements, and domestic relations, going so far as to mention "improper intimacy with other women." The spirit of God was necessary to promote conversion, he reasoned, in the same way that the power of the state was necessary to compel debtors to pay their obligations. The sinner should see himself as a member of a jury who weighs the arguments of the lawyer "and makes up his mind as upon oath and for his life, and gives a verdict upon the spot."[8]

As Finney spoke, one man sat scribbling. Asa Rand, Congregationalist minister and editor of *The Volunteer*, a monthly publication devoted to traditional theology, copied down an abstract of the sermon. He published it, along with critical commentary, and issued his thoughts separately as a pamphlet titled *The New Divinity Tried*. Rand rejected the theological innovations of the previous decade (variously called New Divinity, New School, or New Haven theology) and remained true to eighteenth-century Calvinist strictures holding that salvation was a gift of divine agency and that regeneration was a physical, not moral, transformation. Rand's summary read like an indictment. Finney preached *"that a moral character is to be ascribed to voluntary exercises alone, and a nature cannot be either holy or unholy;—that the heart, when considered in relation to God, is nothing but the governing purpose of man;—that the depravity or moral ruin of man has not abridged his power of choosing right with the same ease that he chooses wrong;—and that conversion is effected only by moral suasion, or the influence of motives."*

Simply put, Finney ascribed too much power to the individual and not enough to God. Rand challenged Finney's parable, arguing, "If the Spirit *only* cries to the sinner stop, and does not *stop* him, he will go on to destruction. If the Spirit *only* warns, alarms and persuades, the awakened sinner is gone forever." Conversion and salvation, Rand restated, did not flow from the decision of the sinner and did not come instantaneously, "on the spot." Regeneration was not a career choice, not "like a man resolving to be a lawyer or a merchant, or changing his purpose about his worldly affairs as people do every day;—changes which might require no sacrifices, no regrets, no self-denial, no surmounting of inward obstacles." Change came not through choice but entirely through the inaudible, invisible, imperceptible "special agency of the Spirit of God."[9]

Rand objected not only to Finney's doctrines, but also to the measures he employed. Along with other orthodox ministers, he denounced the anxious seat as likely to produce "a selfish or spurious conversion." Ministers fretted deeply that, "at a time when *true* conversions are multiplied with such unprecedented rapidity, it is difficult for Christians to detect those which are false." How to tell the truly penitent from the false had always been a dilemma in Christian theology, but never more so than during a revival that invited sinners to reveal themselves and gave them a platform to enact their conversion. Rather than drawing out genuinely troubled sinners, the anxious seat would likely be filled by "the forward, the sanguine, the rash, the self-confident, and the self-righteous," not "the modest, the humble, the broken-hearted." In the hands of Finney, religion had been turned into a "business of self-examination," in which "conversion is simply an act of will," based almost exclusively upon a "self-determining power." Like "the morning cloud and the early dew," such a faith, Rand predicted, would soon dissipate.[10]

Rand misjudged. The essence of Finney's religious belief—individual action—flooded the American firmament. To be sure, he faced persistent opposition. The orthodox continued to hunt heretics, eventually trying even Lyman Beecher and his son for wandering away from strict religious tenets. In 1836, Finney withdrew from the Presbyterian Church altogether. Denunciation of revivals also rained down from the other side of the religious spectrum, not from Calvinists who denied free will but from the increasing power of Arminians who reveled in it. In Boston especially this meant the Unitarians, who controlled Harvard, as well as the Universalists. These liberal denominations differed from all Calvinists in their view of doctrinal matters. But, like the orthodox, they decried revivals for the measures employed to win converts: Protracted Meetings, emotional appeals, and uneducated ministers. Revivals, they argued, were being contrived by evangelicals. Women in particular, "young, simple, inexperienced, and uninformed are the very materials suited to the purpose of the actors." Once converted, they created a "petticoat government in religion." Speaking at the First Universalist Church in Boston, Walter Balfour snorted that "some *clergymen* now, can calculate when a revival of religion is to take place, yea, can produce one any time they please. Getting up revivals, is now a thing so well understood, and the means of producing them so well known, that some religious sects, draw their plans, and proceed with such certainty to produce them, as a mason, or a carpenter does to build a house. But an *astronomer*, though he can calculate to a moment the time of an eclipse, has as yet discovered no measure to produce one at his pleasure."[11]

The immediate concern of the Unitarians and Universalists was that, by emphasizing free will and free agency, Finney poached on liberal ground and threatened to increase the power and numbers of what, to them, remained the orthodox party. Revivals, protested one opponent, "are promoted as the last expedient for maintaining the sinking cause of orthodoxy." Had liberal ministers been able to look past doctrinal and denominational differences, they might have recognized what they shared with the New Divinity ministers: an abiding faith in the power of the individual.[12]

If Finney led a rebellion against orthodox Calvinism, there also loomed in Boston an incipient rebel against liberal Arminianism—Ralph Waldo Emerson. In February, the twenty-seven-year-old Unitarian minister faced a spiritual crisis when his wife died. "My angel is gone to heaven this morning & I am alone in the world and strangely happy," he confessed to his aunt. To read Emerson's journals for the year is to see how he and Finney, each moving away from starkly opposed religious tenets, galloped in stride: "self makes sin"; "we were made to become better"; "because you are a free agent, God can only remove sin by the concurrence of the sinner." Emerson shunned the denominations of the day. "In the Bible," he reasoned, "you are not directed to be a Unitarian or a Calvinist or an Episcopalian." Denouncing both religious and political strife, he proclaimed that "a Sect or Party is an elegant incognito devised to save a man from the vexation of thinking." Emerson would emerge out of the "dim confusion" of 1831, resign his pulpit, repudiate "corpse-cold" Unitarianism, and establish himself as the premier philosopher of American individualism in what he called, for better and worse, the "age of the first-person singular."[13]

Finney and Emerson, evangelicalism and transcendentalism, worlds apart yet part and parcel of an American spirit. Reform yourself, they proclaimed, and then reform society. No idea was more important to the day than the belief that man had the power to improve society, perhaps even to perfect it, and in so doing help usher in the millennium. Institutions and behaviors that only a few years earlier had received little notice now became the objects of organized moral-reform efforts: slavery, alcohol, criminality, deviance. Organizations such as the New England Anti-Slavery Society, the American Temperance Society, the Prison Discipline Society, and the Infant School Society competed for membership and funds. Leading ministers, politicians, and social activists frequently joined more than one society, but neither Finney nor Emerson ever embraced organized social activism to the extent of their friends and followers. When they did speak out, they did not go far enough (Finney banned slaveholders from his New York congregation in 1833, but he refused to abolish segregated seating and sought to avoid "angry controversy" on the subject of slavery). Or they regretted it (Emerson delivered a speech and public letter denouncing the removal of the Cherokee from their homeland, but the experience dragged him down "like dead cats around one's neck"). Compared with denominations, Emerson confessed that he preferred a "sect for the suppression of Intemperance or a sect for the suppression of loose behaviour to women," but he never warmed to the idea of organized reform.[14]

If revivals and reforms disturbed some Northerners, they disgusted at least one Southern visitor to New York. John Quitman, who as governor of Mississippi promoted secession, observed in July from Rhinebeck, New York: "Among the masses in the Northern States, every other feeling is now swallowed up by a religious enthusiasm which is pervading the country. Wherever I have traveled in the free states, I have found preachers holding three, four, six, and eight days' meeting, provoking revivals, and begging contributions for the Indians, the negroes, the Sunday-schools, foreign missions, home missions, the Colonization society, temperance societies, societies for the education of pious young men, distressed sisters, superannuated ministers, reclaimed penitents, church edifices, church debts, religious libraries, etc., etc.: clamorously exacting the last penny from the poor enthusiast, demanding the widow's mite, the orphan's pittance, and denouncing the vengeance of Heaven on those who feel unable to give. . . . They are not only extortionate, but absolutely insulting in their demands; and my observations lead me to believe there is vast deal of robbery and roguery under this stupendous organization of religious societies."[15]

Some men might have mocked and resisted (in Boston, one group posted a broadside for the formation of an "Intemperance Society"), but middle-class women in particular embraced religion and reform. Where women "were most active, revivals were most powerful," observed one western New Yorker. Women constituted a higher percentage of converts than did men, often joining the church first and then inducing their husbands, sons, and brothers to enlist. Finney's first convert in Rochester, he recalled, was "a lady of high standing, . . . a gay, worldly woman, very fond of society," who renounced "sin, and the world and self." "From that moment," he observed, "she was outspoken in her religious convictions, and zealous for the conversion of her friends." Unlike other ministers, Finney allowed women equality with men during services by permitting them to pray aloud in mixed gatherings, a practice that scandalized the orthodox. Opponents cried, "Set women to praying? Why, the next thing . . . will be to set them to preaching." Finney responded with sarcasm: "What dreadful things," he mocked. The wife of one pastor summarized one of the ways women believed evangelical religion empowered them: "To the Christian religion we owe the rank we hold in society, and we should feel our obligation. . . . It is that, which prevents our being treated like beasts of burden—which secures us the honorable privilege of human companionship in social life, and raises us in the domestic relations to the elevated stations of wives and mothers."[16]

Bolstered by Christian encomiums, the ideal of domesticity reigned over the middle-class household. One of the best-selling volumes of the year was *The Mother's Book*, by Lydia Maria Child. Capitalizing on the success of *The Frugal Housewife* (1829), Child's contributions to the advice literature genre added to her growing reputation as a writer of children's stories and sentimental fiction. "She is the first woman in the republic," hailed William Lloyd Garrison in 1829. Child despaired over the moral condition of the nation. "If the inordinate love of wealth and parade be not checked among us," she warned, "it will be the ruin of our country, as it has been, and will be, the ruin of thousands of individuals. What restlessness, what discontent, what bitterness, what knavery and crime, have been produced by this eager passion for money!"

The burden fell to mothers to check the appetites of husbands and children and to use their position to inculcate principles of domestic economy and moral restraint. "What a change would take place in the world if men were always governed by internal principle," she argued. For women as well as men, all change "must begin with her *heart*, and religiously drive from thence all unkind and discontented feelings." Child's belief that "the mind of a child . . . is a vessel empty and pure," to be formed and filled by environmental influences, contradicted Calvinist notions but fit comfortably with the emphasis on individual volition that reached from Finney to Emerson. Child herself moved from Congregationalism to Unitarianism. The "tone of *radicalism*" perceived by one reviewer—a tone evident in Child's contempt for the idleness of the upper classes—became a clarion call when she sacrificed her literary reputation, embraced immediate abolition, and published *An Appeal in Favor of That Class of Americans Called Africans* (1833), a work that asked readers to "try to judge the negro by the same rules you judge other men."[17]

The question that echoed, like the tolling of the steeple bell, was how to judge one's self. Henry Ware, Jr., thought he knew the answer, and he explained how in his essay *On the Formation of the Christian Character*. No other American work articulated the middle-class vision of self as clearly as Ware's; it passed through at least fifteen editions. Readers, Ware reported, "speak to me of it with tears in their eyes." The author was a Unitarian minister and professor of pastoral theology, the son of the man whose election as Hollis Professor of Divinity at Harvard in 1805 led orthodox members to resign and establish a more conservative seminary at Andover. Ware's work sounded again and again the themes of self-denial, self-discipline, and self-improvement. The state of society made individuals "*anxious* about themselves, about their characters, their condition, their prospects." Only by "vigilant self-examination," by replacing external, superficial, public standards for internal, spiritual, private ones, could one obtain a Christian character. This work must be "the business of . . . life," because God has opened "a free highway to the kingdom of life, through which all may walk and be saved." Religion, he claimed, "is a personal thing," and men "should first and most seriously study its relation to their own hearts." "Man's own labors are essential to his salvation," Ware insisted. Advising Christians to exert themselves immediately in prayer, meditation, and reading, he reminded them, "The work before you is wholly within your power."[18]

It is not surprising that orthodox reviewers condemned Ware's book as "defective" in its religious understanding. "The sinner is directed to be a philosopher," wrote a bemused Calvinist in *Spirit of the Pilgrims*, "and by retiring into himself and forming good resolutions" to achieve salvation. But what some found faulty, others found sound.

Ware preached a gospel of self-help that offered a solution to the problems that afflicted Americans: anxiety, ambition, competition, dislocation. Through solitude one achieved "quiet self-possession" and then was suited to enter the public world of business to partake in "secular affairs." The home, nurtured by women, became sacralized as a haven against the disordering effects of "the distractions of common life." An emphasis on self-help and individual responsibility also offered a ready explanation for why some succeeded and others failed. The urban laboring classes in particular suffered from long hours, low wages, mounting debts, and increasing poverty and unemployment. The solution to their problems, some argued, rested not with unions, or public relief, or reconfiguring relations between capital and labor, but with the workers themselves. Anyone could rise if he applied himself by gaining an education. At the inaugural Franklin Lectures in Boston, aimed "to promote useful knowledge . . . among that class from which [Franklin] himself sprung," the speaker told the assembled laborers and mechanics that "we are all equal" in the ability "to compare, contrive, invent, improve, and perfect." "It depends mainly on each individual" whether or not he or she advances.[19]

The laboring classes had their own perspective on the religious and moral enthusiasm that surrounded them. The *Working Man's Advocate* denounced the revivals as "a gigantic effort" on the part of "a certain class of theologians . . . to get power into their hands, to be used for the destruction of our republican institutions." Citing Jefferson, the paper reminded its readers that, "of all the forms which ambition assumes, the ecclesiastical is the most dangerous." Particularly upsetting was the movement on the part of evangelicals to prohibit Sunday public activities, such as mail delivery and stagecoach rides, and to introduce religious education into the public schools. If the evangelicals seemed suspicious, the myriad new religious societies germinating from the spiritual preoccupations of the day seemed insane. Most curious of all were the Mormons, led by Joseph Smith, who claimed that he could perform miracles and that angels revealed to him a lost portion of the Bible. Focusing on cooperative enterprise, theocratic rule, and male authority, the Mormon Church won converts by the thousands. Opponents denounced them as "a strange and ridiculous sect" led by "knaves pretending to have found some holy writings" and peopled by "blind and deluded" followers from "the lazy and worthless classes of society." One editor condemned the religion as "mental cholera morbus." In 1831, the Mormons, persecuted in western New York, settled in Kirtland, Ohio, the first stop on a trail west that would eventually lead them to Salt Lake City, Utah. Religious enthusiasms from evangelicalism to Mormonism, concluded the editor of the *Working Man's Advocate*, had created not only a class of "fanatics, but lunatics and maniacs" all bent on "enslaving the minds, preparatory to enslaving the bodies, of the *rising* generation."[20]

WOMEN AND WORKING CLASSES

Questions of religion, gender, and class became linked when the Magdalen Society in New York issued its first report in June. This society, established in 1830, sought to provide an "asylum for females who have deviated from the paths of virtue, and are desirous of being restored to a respectable station in society by religious instruction and the formation of moral and industrious habits." As its name suggested, the Magdalen Society focused on prostitution and set out to build a "place of refuge" where fallen women could be reformed through religious conversion and education. Arthur Tappan, a wealthy New York merchant who, along with his brother Lewis, supported various reform efforts including the abolition of slavery, presided over the society. The report claimed, "The number of females in this city, who abandon themselves to prostitution is not less than TEN THOUSAND!!" That figure comprised only "public" prostitutes; the figure doubled if one considered the "private harlots and kept misses, many of whom keep up a show of industry as domestics, seamstresses, and nurses in the most respectable families." These prostitutes, the report insisted, generate six million dollars a year, "a waste of wealth . . . when weighed beside the loss of hundreds of thousands of immortal souls." The author of the report claimed to have a list of names of "the men and boys who are the seducers of the innocent, or the companions of the polluted." Proclaiming that many of these prostitutes came from the working-class neighborhoods of the city and were "harlots by choice," the report made clear the society's objective of succeeding "not merely by *rescuing* and *reforming* them, not merely by affording a *refuge from misery*, but by providing a *school of virtue*; not simply to destroy the habits of idleness and vice, but to substitute those of honorable and profitable industry, thus *benefiting society*, while the *individual is reclaimed*."

It was the clearest statement of the objectives of evangelical middle-class reform yet written. Substitute for the prostitute the criminal, the drunkard, the pauper, even the slave, and the same formula applied. Not everyone in New York, however, shared the worldview of Tappan and his associates. The public received the report with "unbounded indignation," denounced it as "grossly revolting and disgraceful," and declared it a calumny upon the working classes of the city. In addition to newspapers, tracts, and handbills condemning the report, two anti-Magdalen meetings were held at Tammany Hall, and salacious drawings that portrayed Tappan's "real" interest in prostitution circulated widely. Opponents directed part of their attack against the facts presented in the report, facts that "are nearly impossible to be true." If the Magdalen Society numbers were accurate, then, based on a population of just over two hundred thousand, "one out of three of the marriageable females of New York at this moment received the wages of prostitution. One out of every six, is an abandoned, promiscuous prostitute . . . [and] more than half of the adult males, married and unmarried, visit prostitutes more than three times a week!" If, as the report claimed, thirteen million dollars were spent annually on prostitutes, then each male, assuming a fourth of the men between the ages of fifteen and sixty contributed, paid $1,177.68 per year for sexual gratification. Using the word as an adjective rather than a noun, one writer concluded that it was the statistics that were prostitute.[21]

The Magdalen Society needed such outrageous numbers, opponents claimed, to bolster their evangelical aims: "Motive is always to be suspected when *religion* seems to be the real or ostensible one." The society acted as an auxiliary to "the church and state party" that sought to fuse religion with politics. Those who blew orthodox bubbles did not realize that "fear of punishment in another world has never yet restrained people from the practice of vice in this," and that the failure of religion to prevent immorality "is the very proof of its inefficiency." Indeed, corruption progressed most easily under the cloak of religion. In *Confessions of a Magdalen*, one woman told of being seduced and forced into prostitution by her pastor. "The presence of darkness," she warned, "sometimes appears as the angel of light." If these ministers and seminary students who located prostitutes "were as pure and honest as they ought to have been, they could not know anything of this vice." Wondering about the private asylum planned by the Magdalen Society and echoing fears of conspiracy that ran deep in the American character, one writer inquired, "How is the public to know what is done within these secret walls? What is to prevent it from becoming an engine of religious torture to some?"

Readers found the profiles of the prostitutes as infuriating as the statistical impossibilities and religious homilies of the Magdalen Report. Though conceding that prostitutes came from all backgrounds, the report focused on the working classes as the source of the evil: "Hundreds, perhaps thousands of them, are the daughters of the ignorant, depraved, and vicious part of our population, trained up without culture of any kind, amidst the contagion of evil example, and enter upon a life of prostitution for the gratification of their unbridled passions." In October, months after the initial controversy, the board of directors of the Magdalen Society issued a second report, in which they acknowledged "inaccuracies" and "ambiguities" in the statistics but reaffirmed the view that the "lower classes crowded together in our cities who come under no favorable moral influence" turn to prostitution.[22]

If some working-class women turned to prostitution, it was because of economic hardship, not cultural inferiority, responded opponents. Men like Tappan, who shielded themselves behind religious intentions, actually did more to promote prostitution than abate it. After all, as a leading retailer in the city, he forgot "that his own traffic is the cause, indirectly, of making more prostitutes than all the distilleries in the country." Instead of "prayers, bibles, and tracts," why not "afford them the means of an honest living by an honest employment." At the time the report appeared, the tailoresses of New York went on strike to raise their wages and receive a fair price. The *Working Man's Advocate* struggled to awaken interest in the cause of the "oppressed and almost enslaved Tailoresses," whose condition, "as regards the necessities and comforts of life, is undoubtedly worse than that of the Southern slaves." Several writers made the connection between the Magdalen Society and the plight of the women workers: "Those who work as tailoresses, are at present standing out for higher wages, in order to prevent being crushed to the earth, sunk to utter degradation. Let this society assist them in their laudable endeavors to get an honest living." Though the critique of the Magdalen Society as an engine of religious oppression and an elitist assault upon the working classes and urban poor of New York did not win citywide support for the working women, it did have its effect: on December 7, the board of directors of the Magdalen Society voted to cease operations.[23]

Organized as never before, the working classes sought to advance their interests. Newly formed workingmen's societies served as self-improvement and self-empowerment associations. In an address at Dedham, Massachusetts, Samuel Whitcomb explained to the audience why farmers, mechanics, and laborers were more useful and important to society than lawyers, merchants, and capitalists. Arguing that the trading and commercial portion of the population constituted one million out of ten, he asked whether this fraction merited its disproportionate control over at least half the property in the nation. "Suppose some providential dispensation should at once remove the whole of this class of persons from our country—would the remaining nine million starve and perish? Would our Republic be brought to an end—our Union be dissolved—our civil institutions be abandoned—our churches and school-houses be shut up, think ye, for the loss of a mil-

lion of merchants, lawyers, and capitalists?" Whitcomb then reversed
the inquiry: "Suppose all our farmers, and mechanics, and manufacturers, and artisans and labourers, were to be suddenly removed from
the country—what would become of the rest? What would . . . this delicate and enterprising million of people do for food to eat, raiment to
put on, dwellings to shelter, fire to warm, and comforts of every sort to
cheer them on their journey to heaven?"[24]

Buoyed by a growing awareness of their power in society, mechanics and laborers formed political parties. In Philadelphia, the party
grew out of the Mechanics Union of Trade Associations in 1828. In
New York, the Working Men's Party showed considerable strength in
the city elections of 1829. The New England Association of Farmers,
Mechanics & Other Working Men was formed at a meeting in Providence in December. For the first time, newspapers devoted to worker's
interest appeared: the *Mechanics' Free Press*, the *Working Man's Advocate*, the *New England Artisan and Farmers, Mechanics, and Laboring
Man's Repository*. Every issue of the *Working Man's Advocate*—edited
by George Henry Evans, a recent British emigrant—carried a list of
Working Men's measures:

EQUAL UNIVERSAL EDUCATION
ABOLITION OF ALL LICENSED MONOPOLIES
ABOLITION OF CAPITAL PUNISHMENT
ABOLITION OF IMPRISONMENT FOR DEBT
AN ENTIRE REVISION OR ABOLITION OF THE PRESENT
    MILITIA SYSTEM
A LESS EXPENSIVE LAW SYSTEM
EQUAL TAXATION ON PROPERTY
AN EFFECTIVE LIEN LAW FOR LABORERS ON BUILDINGS
A DISTRICT SYSTEM OF ELECTIONS
NO LEGISLATION ON RELIGION

It seems like a motley list, but all lists have their logic, and this one
was guided by workers' fears of the encroachment of power upon lib-

erty. In its control of laws and elections and institutions, the state held excessive power. And with the power to coerce came the power to imprison, enslave, and execute. Religion, with its strictures and secrecies, posed the greatest threat against liberty. Only education—free, public, universal—offered hope that through knowledge and self-improvement workers could resist the forces of capital that pressed down upon them. In his *Working Man's Manual*, Stephen Simpson, a leader of Philadelphia's labor movement and the editor of the *Mechanics' Free Press*, declared that the workers had not yet commenced their own American revolution. "Let the producers of labor but once fully comprehend their injuries and fully appreciate their strength at the polls," he declared, "and the present oppressive system will vanish like the mists of morning, before the rising sun."[25]

Of the various issues identified by the Working Men's movement, the abolition of imprisonment for debt received the most action, in part because politicians and reformers other than workers found problems and injustices with the practice. "It seems to be now almost universally admitted that the present system imperiously demands a reform," reported one commentator in the *North American Review*. The board of managers of the Prison Discipline Society reported the numbers of those imprisoned for debt annually in various states: three thousand in Massachusetts, ten thousand in New York, seven thousand in Pennsylvania, three thousand in Maryland. The majority of these debtors, they found, were imprisoned for trifling sums, often less than five dollars. Of conditions in all the states surveyed, they found "nothing worse, in the whole length and breadth of the land, than in New Jersey," where a high proportion of debtors languished in filthy facilities and the state spent more than the original debt to recover the debt, while providing no support at all for those in prison—just "walls, bars, and bolts."

The arguments against imprisonment for debt came from all directions. Some focused on the injustice and inexpedience of the punishment, pointing to the wretched prison conditions and arguing that incarceration would not increase the creditor's chances of recovering the debt. Others focused on the paltry sums for which debtors could be confined. In the examinations of the causes of debt, a distinction emerged between fraud and honest debt, the one deserving the harshest penalties and the other deserving sympathy and understanding. "The inability to pay one's debts is itself no proof of crime," declared Edward Everett, senator from Massachusetts. "It may, and often does, arise from the act of God, and misfortune in all its forms. A man may become insolvent in consequence of sickness, shipwreck, a fire, a bad season, political changes." Bad luck, not bad intentions. Stephen Simpson shifted the focus from the honest worker to the despotic capitalist. Since a complaint from the creditor led to the imprisonment of the debtor, the law thereby "invests the creditor with the power over the PERSON, the BODY, and consequently the LIFE of the debtor, who in vain pleads the *will* to pay, but appeals to God to show that he has no *ability* to second his will. . . . Capital and law have usurped a power, contrary to the natural laws of labour, as well as repugnant to the principles of the American Declaration of Independence."[26]

A number of states had already instituted changes in the laws governing debtor's prison (eliminating the jailing of female debtors, raising the minimum amount of debt, compelling creditors to pay an allowance for bread money), but New York went a step further and, on April 26, passed a law abolishing imprisonment for debt. Responding to the governor's address to the Assembly, in which he proclaimed imprisonment for debt "repugnant to humanity," legislators prepared a report that recommended abolition. Intentions, they argued, mattered. Not paying a debt afforded "no evidence of moral turpitude or criminal intent, and without such evidence, we have no authority to invade the right of personal liberty." Imprisonment was an appropriate punishment for fraud, but not for debt. Further, under current laws, the presumption of innocence and the right to a speedy trial before an impartial jury were abandoned in favor of the "*presumption* of fraud arising in the mind of one individual," the creditor. The debtor "is put to the torture and starved into a compliance with the wishes or designs of his creditor." The effect of the punishment in this case was retribution against an individual, not reformation of a criminal, because "*indebtedness* is not a crime, . . . *misfortune* is not an offence." Jail serves only to "swell the amount of [the debtor's] afflictions, and press him more heavily to the earth than before."

In passing an act that abolished imprisonment for debt as a civil procedure and established guidelines for the criminal prosecution and punishment of fraudulent debtors, the legislature acted on a growing consensus within the community. To be sure, the language of working-class radicalism found its way into the discussion, particularly where the writers of the Assembly report presented themselves as counter-weights to the oppression of the poor and the weak by the wealthy and influential: "The cries of the slave will long be heard before the sympathies of the master will be awakened—the voice of the poor is feeble and petitioning, that of the rich, powerful and commanding." But the creditors also saw their own interests advanced by abolition and a different line of reasoning swayed them. Not only did it cost time and money to pursue debtors, but many of these creditors were themselves in debt to others. Misfortune could visit anyone. It was the responsibility of the creditor to demand some collateral for the debt, because accidents were "among the ordinary occurrences of life." The creditor "trusted to the good fortune of the debtor as the merchant to the prosperity of the voyage. If the one be unfortunate and the other unsuccessful, the loss must rest where the risk occurred. The debtor promises to pay if he has *ability* to do so; the creditor agrees to trust to his *ability*, consequently if the debtor has not the *ability* to pay, he has not forfeited his promise. . . . If a man agrees to go to London and dies before he can arrive there, it will scarcely be said he has violated his promise; and is it not equally impossible for a man to pay a debt, when he had nothing wherewith to pay it?"[27]

The harsh winter in New York made abstract questions of misfortune palpable. Within a week's span in February, more than three thousand people applied for poor relief. Philip Hone, the former mayor, noted, "The long continuance of extreme cold weather and the consequent difficulty of bringing wood to the city have occasioned great distress to the poor." George Evans reported, "Poor creatures are to be seen at every corner, in every alley, shivering with cold and hunger, unable to procure employment, and doomed to utter starvation." Frozen conditions clotted the commercial arteries of the city and the working classes suffered acutely. Whatever joy the Working Men's Party felt over the abolition of imprisonment for debt, they lamented the little progress in other areas. The militia system, which required citizens to stop working and turn out for a three-day period every fall or pay a fine, remained intact; a lien law, to protect workers from builders who did not fulfill contracts, was not passed, although procedures for recovery were put into place; an attempt to organize public meetings to call for a ten-hour workday failed. Some workers feared it would lower wages, and others mocked the very idea that the expectation of twelve hours' labor made the *"employer . . . oppressive and the employed* a slave."

The Working Men of New York, like similar groups in other cities, claimed not to be a political party ("they disclaim connexion and sympathy with all parties, except that great party which includes the nation"), but the factionalism of politics accelerated their demise. Two of the leaders of the movement that emerged in 1829, Thomas Skidmore and Robert Dale Owen, battled each other publicly in 1831 over the question of birth control. The men had already parted ways in their approach to Working Men's activism. Skidmore, the author of *The Rights of Man to Property* (1829), called for the abolition of all inheritance laws and the reallocation of wealth. He rejected the concept of private property, seeing it as a violation of natural rights: "Why not sell the winds of heaven, that man might not breathe without price? Why not sell the light of the sun, that man should not see without making another rich?" Whereas Skidmore advocated redistribution, Owen stressed reform. The son of the famous utopian Robert Owen, who created a communitarian society at New Harmony, Indiana, in 1825, Owen came to New York in 1829 from New Harmony and joined Frances Wright, the advocate of free thought and women's rights, whom he had met two years earlier. They published the *Free Enquirer*, a weekly paper devoted to rational inquiry and reform. Unlike Skidmore, who sought equal wealth, Owen and Wright stressed equal education. Sounding as much like middle-class reformers as like working-class radicals, they advocated the creation of nonsectarian state-run schools that would educate all children equally and inculcate the values of industry, temperance, and discipline. It was not that Skidmore did not believe in education, but, as one Owenite put it, "he thinks that if means were equal, education would be universal; I think if right education were universal, means would be equal."[28]

Birth control fit into Owen's education scheme, and he raised the delicate subject in a work that quickly went through several editions, *Moral Physiology; or, A Brief and Plain Treatise on the Population Question*. It was not a new issue. Political economists and philosophers such as Thomas Malthus and David Ricardo had shocked the post-Enlightenment world by arguing that population increased faster than society's ability to provide sustenance; as a consequence, poverty and misery, not progress and happiness, would mark the future. Despairing that nations relied upon war, famine, and disease as checks upon unrestrained population growth, Owen sought rational measures that returned autonomy and control to the individual. He spurned celibacy as unnatural and unhealthy. Owen sympathized with the Shakers, a religious sect who had taken vows of celibacy and whose name came from an elaborate dance that was part of their service; he urged, however, that the reproductive instinct need not contribute to misery and profligacy but, rather, that "its temperate enjoyment is a blessing." Though preferable to a life of dissipation, "a life of rigid celibacy," Owen proclaimed, "is yet fraught with many evils. Peevishness, restlessness, vague longings, and instability of character are among the least of these." The key was individual self-control, and Owen advocated "the *desirability* and *possibility*" of denial and restraint. Only by self-mastery over his instincts did man distinguish himself from "brute creation" and demonstrate the "power to improve, cultivate, and elevate his nature, from generation to generation." To restrain population growth further, Owen recommended various measures for preventing conception—withdrawal, the insertion of a sponge, and the use of a covering. After reading *Moral Physiology*, one writer exclaimed, "A new scene of existence seemed to open before me. I found myself, in this all important matter, a free agent, and, in a degree, the arbiter of my own destiny."[29]

In *Moral Physiology Exposed and Refuted*, Thomas Skidmore denounced Owen's proposals as an assault upon the working classes. Owen, in essence, argued that "the gratification of one of the most important appetites of our nature and the consequent production of beings like ourselves is a criminal act with all who have not a certain amount of property, [that] poor men may not have as large families as their wealthy neighbors." Labeling Owen's work "morose and chilling" and calling the author an "imposter-reformer," Skidmore argued that a "life of unremitting toil and poverty is *not* the consequence of having a large family. . . . It is the effect, directly, immediately, and wholly, of an unjust and vicious organization of government." With "meretricious sophistry," Owen was "guilty of throwing out false lights to decoy the wretched from the discovery of the true remedy of their distresses": the unequal division of property. "Better, far better, it appears to me," proclaimed Skidmore, "to set about discovering the means of preventing the existence of enormous incomes, derived from the labor of others. . . . Destroy this, and it will be a long time before Robert Dale Owen, or any other man, will have any cause to complain of the number of mouths."[30]

With the debate over birth control, the Working Men's movement in New York reached its denouement. At the end of the year, Owen left New York for a journey to Indiana and back. He married, traveled to Europe, and on his return settled at New Harmony. Skidmore, the oldest of ten children, died in 1832 in the cholera epidemic that ravaged the city. Evans maintained his ideals but, by 1833, folded the *Working Man's Advocate* "because of insufficient patronage." Elsewhere, the story was much the same. In Philadelphia, Stephen Simpson discontinued his *Mechanics' Free Press*, changed political allegiances, and started the *Pennsylvania Whig*. Workers in New England, late to organize, never had as much impact as their brethren did elsewhere. The demise of the Working Men's movement was symbolized by the closing of the Hall of Science in New York. Established by Wright and Owen when they came to the city, the Hall served as a lecture lyceum, printing office, and lending library for the advance of secular knowledge and free thought. For the price of three cents for men and no charge for women, visitors heard talks on astronomy, anatomy, and perspectival drawing as well as debates on such questions as whether "the light of reason is a trustworthy and sufficient guide to happiness." But economic reality impinged on the pursuit of knowledge and, in a move that represented the triumph of religious revivalism over radical reform, Owen announced in November that he had sold the Hall to a Methodist congregation.[31]

ANTI-MASONS AND NATIONAL REPUBLICANS

As a political party, the Working Men's movement could not sustain itself. But political frenzy pulsated through the nation like an electrical force. "Party politics and prices current," lamented Owen, "are the alpha and omega of men's thoughts." Most foreign travelers thought it remarkable that Americans agreed on the basic principles of government, but as a result "it was not easy to become master of the distinctions" on which parties rested. "America has had great parties," proclaimed Tocqueville, "but there are not any more now." He thought that the Federalists and the Republicans of the Revolutionary era held to high moral principles but he did not recognize in the National Republicans and Democrats, the immediate descendants of these parties, similar virtues. "In the whole world," declared Tocqueville, "I do not see a more wretched and shameful sight than that presented by the different coteries (they do not deserve the name of parties) which now divide the Union. In broad daylight one sees all the petty, shameful passions disturbing them which generally one is careful to keep hidden at the bottom of the human heart."[32]

Whatever one called them—coterie, faction, or party—one group that galvanized American politics was the Anti-Masons, who became the first third party in American history and invented the presidential nominating convention. As their name disclosed, the Anti-Masonic Party set itself against Masonry, a private, fraternal organization that originated in England early in the eighteenth century. At the time of the Revolution, there were some one hundred lodges and several thousand members in America, including Ben Franklin and George Washington. Freemasonry continued to expand as entrepreneurs, professionals, and artisans sought social camaraderie and business connections. In January, the *New York Register* posited the existence of two thousand fraternities with a hundred thousand members. Andrew Jackson and Henry Clay, among many other leading statesmen, belonged at one time or another to a Masonic lodge. Though its exclusive membership, private oaths, and hierarchical orders may have seemed anathema to republican America, Masonry stirred little controversy until 1826, when one mason, William Morgan, disappeared.

Morgan, a fifty-two-year-old artisan in western New York, had planned to publish a pamphlet, *Illustrations of Masonry*, that exposed the secret rituals of the Masonic order. Local officials, many of them Masons, used all means possible to prevent publication: they burned down the shop that intended to print it and arrested Morgan, first for theft and then for a small debt that he owed. Morgan was languishing in a chilly prison cell in Canandaigua, New York, when someone paid his debt of $2.69 and carried him off in a carriage. They carried him to Rochester and Lewiston and Fort Niagara and, ultimately, to someplace where secrets are never revealed and silence is permanent.

Investigators never found Morgan's body. Between 1826 and 1831, New York launched over twenty grand-jury investigations and at least eighteen trials but never secured a conviction. Each indictment and trial served only to inflame passions. It seemed that judges, lawyers, and jurors were all Masons; with each acquittal came a new chorus of denunciation for what could only be seen as a conspiracy against liberty. Masonry became a dividing line in American politics, and local candidates in New York, Pennsylvania, and Vermont, and eventually across New England and the Midwest, gained office by running against the seemingly antidemocratic fraternal organization.

Morgan's was not the only story that roused suspicions that Masonry was akin to tyranny. The case of Pastor George Witherell, a Mason who sought to leave his Masonic temple, was widely discussed throughout the spring of 1831. A Knight Templar in the Masons, Witherell decided he would no longer attend meetings or abide by the oaths and signs that bound members to each other. One evening while the pastor was away, Lucinda Witherell and her son heard footsteps in the darkened house. "Father, have you got home?" the son called. Suddenly, two men with black silk handkerchiefs covering their faces cried out: "Now you damned, perjured rascal, we will inflict upon you the penalty of your violated obligations." They seized Mrs. Witherell by the throat, but fled when the son came at them.

Investigations failed to identify the culprits, though most citizens suspected they were two Masons seeking to silence the apostate pastor. Shortly after the incident, newspapers throughout western New York printed a bogus trial transcript that purported to be the testimony of the Witherells before a magistrate. Lucinda comes across as little more than a prostitute, and the pastor incriminates himself in the planning and execution of the assault. The forged transcript outraged the community as much as the original assault. Here was deviousness at its worst, accusing Anti-Masons of feigning the assassination in order to win adherents to their cause. "To what acts of depravity," people wondered, "will not Masonry descend to be revenged on Seceders?"

Political Anti-Masonry flourished from the cultural anxieties that had been unleashed. In local elections in western New York, Massachusetts, and Vermont, more than 80 percent of the electorate turned out to vote. Anti-Masonic candidates won seats in state assemblies and helped send candidates to Congress. More than a hundred Anti-Masonic newspapers sprouted across the nation. With an eye toward nominating a candidate for president, Anti-Masons began soliciting the opinions of leading politicians. Deeming Freemasonry "dangerous

7. *Anti Masonic Almanac for the Year 1831* (Courtesy of the American Antiquarian Society)

to our political and moral welfare," the Anti-Masonic Committee of Correspondence for York County, Pennsylvania, asked Richard Rush if he was a member. On May 4, Rush, who at various times held the positions of attorney general, secretary of state, minister to England, and secretary of the Treasury, published a response. He offered a lengthy denunciation of the place of secret societies in America: "Of all governments existing, ours is the one, which would be most justified in watching, with constant and scrupulous care, the conduct of societies profoundly secret." He expressed shock that Morgan's murderers remained free and outrage "at seeing human life and liberty so sported with, by a power [that] rides in darkness." "A secret combination," capable of thwarting the law, contaminated "the heart of the republic." Rush condemned the editors of newspapers for failing to uphold the role of a free press "to raise and keep up the alarm." "Silence," he believed, "is participation," but "the press on this occasion has fallen into stupefaction, or turpitude." Had the press done its duty, "this conspiracy against Morgan would long since have been laid bare, and public justice been vindicated." Rush concluded by complimenting the Anti-Masonic movement for the efforts they were making against Masonry, "to root out its bad influence from the face of our land." [33]

Rush would have made an ideal Anti-Masonic candidate for president, but he privately declined any nomination. John Quincy Adams, the former president who at the end of the year took a seat in the House of Representatives, also entered into Anti-Masonic politics. On July 11, he attended an Anti-Masonic oration at Faneuil Hall in Boston. Lyman Beecher opened the meeting with a prayer, but Adams was struck by how few of his Boston friends were in attendance, evidence of how Anti-Masonry brought new faces into the political arena. Adams declared that he would not take part in the next presidential election but acknowledged that "the dissolution of the Masonic institution" was the most important issue facing "us and our posterity." In September he allowed a series of letters against Masonry to be published, and for several years he continued to decry the institution. He even ran as Anti-Masonic candidate for governor of Massachusetts in 1833. As a "zealous anti-mason," Adams made his position clear: because of the atrocious crimes committed in the Morgan affair, it was the duty either of every Masonic lodge to dissolve itself or of respectable Masons to repudiate all "vices, oaths, penalties and secrets." [34]

Throughout the winter of 1830–31, state conventions elected delegates to attend a national Anti-Masonic convention in Baltimore in September. One skeptic observed that the meetings, filled with delegates from the burned-over districts where Anti-Masonry had first ignited, resembled revivalist gatherings: "They all become fanatic or like all new converts manifest an extraordinary degree of Zeal—They break at once from all political ties & associations." "Disclaiming all association with Jacksonism and Clayism," with the Democrats and the National Republicans, Anti-Masons decided to build on their success in local elections and nominate candidates for president and vice-president of the United States. "The course we espouse," declared delegates at the Massachusetts Anti-Masonic convention, "has been driven by necessity to the BALLOT BOX."[35]

On September 28, on a motion from Thaddeus Stevens of Pennsylvania, delegates nominated William Wirt of Maryland for the presidency. But the nomination did not come easily. Stevens had zealously supported Supreme Court Justice John McLean, who toyed with the idea of accepting the nomination before finally turning it down. McLean's refusal, recalled William Seward of New York, "fell as a wet blanket upon our warm expectations." Stevens and Seward roomed together in Baltimore, and the two spent much of the night discussing the nomination. By morning, Stevens had agreed to support Wirt. An exhausted Seward wrote his wife, "If it were an agreeable subject, I would describe to you all the bustle, excitement, collision, irritation, enunciation, suspicion, confusion, obstinacy, foolhardiness, and humor, of a convention of one hundred and thirteen men, from twelve different States, assembled for the purpose of nominating candidates for President and Vice-President of the United States."[36]

The attorney general under James Monroe, Wirt was one of the most distinguished lawyers in the nation. Earlier in the year, he had defended a judge in a Senate impeachment trial and had argued before the Supreme Court the case of the Cherokee Indians, who claimed to be an independent nation free from the laws of Georgia. When the nomination came, Wirt was in the midst of a personal crisis, still mourning the death of his daughter from scarlet fever. "The charm of life is gone," he conceded in March. If running for president did not reinvigorate him, it did provide him with a field for action. In his letter of acceptance, he acknowledged surprise that he had been chosen, ratified the principles of the party, and confessed something that not everyone knew: he had been a Mason. Wirt said he had always regarded Masonry as "nothing more than a social and charitable club," and only

recently had come to be persuaded that it was a "political engine . . .
at war with the fundamental principles of the social compact." If anything, public confession and conversion made him that much more
appealing, and his candidacy went forward.[37]

Wirt's nomination received mixed reviews in the party press. "His
conversion to anti-masonry was remarkably sudden," snorted the *New
York Evening Post* (a pro-Jackson paper), "almost coeval with his nomination to the Presidency." Another editor accused the Anti-Masons of
hypocrisy and "sinister motives." National Republicans denounced Wirt
as ambitious and unscrupulous and joked that Anti-Masons offered him
the nomination only after trying everybody else, including Justices John
McLean and John Marshall, John Quincy Adams, Daniel Webster,
and Richard Rush. But the *New Jersey Journal of Commerce* (an anti-
Jackson paper) thought Wirt had "all the talents and all the qualifica-
tions necessary to make a splendid President." Wirt knew the price he
would pay for running: "I shall be laughed out, abused, slandered."
But he also knew who he was. "I am perfectly aware," he told his friend
Salmon Chase (who would seek the Republican nomination for president in 1860), "that I have none of the captivating arts and manners of
professional seekers of popularity. I do not desire them. I shall not
change my manners; they are a part of my nature. If the people choose
to take me as I am—well. If not, they will only leave me where I have
preferred to be, enjoying the independence of private life."[38]

Wirt had only two years to enjoy that life; he died in 1834. In the
election of 1832, he garnered fewer than thirty thousand votes, winning only Vermont and its seven electoral votes. For the most part, the
Anti-Masonic moment had passed. Some denounced Anti-Masonry
along with Masonry: "I renounce Anti-Masonry," proclaimed one
writer, "because anti-masons are doing precisely what they condemn
in the Masonic fraternity: namely, attempting to engross power and
office." One Mason associated Anti-Masonry with a leveling spirit
loose in the land, and he urged caution: "A strong and deep-moving
excitement is, at this time, shaking the whole earth; and, in a fearful
paroxysm, is madly grasping at us. In either hemisphere are observ-

able the strife of passion, and the thirst for aggrandizement and power, as well as the struggle for freedom and the searching for light. We see systems, institutions, and governments, honored and made venerable by time, and, to human view, fixed and changeless as the sun, in a moment swept away by the tide of popular power." Most voters silently agreed with one working-class advocate who thought it absurd to believe that "all evils which afflict human nature are of masonic origin." "To attempt to establish a political creed upon Anti-Masonry," he reasoned, was "like turning a sugar loaf upside down and expecting it to stand on the smaller end." "Twenty years hence," he predicted, "the citizens of these States will have half forgotten that there ever was such a thing in the world of politics as an Anti-masonic excitement."[39]

Seward left the convention realistic about Wirt's chances and the fate of Anti-Masonry. On the steamboat to New York, an accident occurred that moved him to deeper reflections than politics. A man fell overboard. "There was a fearful moment of uncertainty as to who it might be," confided Seward to his wife. "If every passenger on board the boat thought and felt as I did, he thought only of that person, nearest and dearest to himself, who was among the passengers. Tedious minutes elapsed until it was known. I cannot describe to you the intense, painful anxiety that bound in silence all the crowd, which looked upon the man, as he seemed to stand erect in the water, waiting, and waiting, and waiting for the boats to approach him. What a possession is human life, to be exposed to such hazards; and what must have been the solicitude of that poor mortal, while the boats were getting toward him! And yet, had he sunk beneath the waves, to rise no more, what would it have been but hastening for a few days, or months, or years, a catastrophe which is inevitable; and how very soon would the surface of human society, momentarily agitated by the event like the face of the waters disturbed by his struggle, have become smooth and borne no trace of the commotion!"[40]

Seward returned home safely and watched as the National Republicans, following the example of the Anti-Masonic Party, held a convention in Baltimore on December 12 and nominated Henry Clay for

president. The smooth-talking, slaveholding Kentuckian had served in
the House from 1811 to 1825, and as secretary of state under Adams.
One traveler described him as "tall and thin, with a weather-beaten
complexion, [and] small gray eyes." Elected to the Senate in November,
Clay had been implored to stand with the Anti-Masons. A fusion
of Anti-Masons and National Republicans seemed undefeatable
against a wobbly Jackson administration. But Clay refused to make any
public statement on the issue. "I tell them," he said, "that Masonry or
Anti-Masonry has, legitimately, in my opinion, nothing to do with politics."
Clay recognized that with Anti-Masonic support, which would
deliver New York, Pennsylvania, and Vermont, he would secure the
presidency, and he recognized that the two parties agreed on "every
thing the general Government can or ought to do." They differed only
on Masonry, but that difference was enough. Clay, seeing himself as
planet rather than satellite, felt "we ought to draw them to us, instead
of being drawn to them."

The National Republican convention concluded with an address to
the people of the United States. In reviewing Jackson's administration,
delegates proclaimed, "The political history of the Union for the last
three years exhibits a series of measures plainly dictated . . . by blind
cupidity or vindictive party spirit, marked throughout by a disregard
for good policy, justice, and every high and generous sentiment, and
terminating in a dissolution of the Cabinet, under circumstances more
scandalous than any of the kind to be met within the annals of the civilized
world." Citizens from every region should vote against Jackson
because of his "inconsistent and vacillating" positions. How, for example,
wondered the Republicans, could the president "be regarded at
the North and West as the friend of the Tariff and Internal Improvements
when the only recommendation at the South is the anticipation
that he is the person through whose agency the whole system is to be
prostrated?" A year earlier, voters were reminded, Jackson had vetoed
as unconstitutional the Maysville Road Bill, which would have provided
funds for construction of a highway in Kentucky, Clay's home
state. Jackson had also pledged himself against the Bank of the United

States, "this great and beneficial institution," six years before the issue
of renewal was even to emerge before Congress. If the president was
re-elected, warned National Republicans, "it may be considered certain that the Bank will be abolished." Jackson's behavior as president
seemed so tyrannical that, by 1834, the National Republicans
renamed themselves the Whigs, after the English party that had tradi-
tionally opposed the excesses of the monarchy.[41]

In addressing such issues as the tariff, internal improvements, and
the Bank, the convention identified a cluster of policies at the core of
the National Republican belief system, policies they believed would
carry them to the White House. A pro-Clay cartoon depicted the candidate as playing a card game against his leading political opponents.
His hand of three aces, which features the economic policies advocated by Clay, defeats William Wirt's Anti-Masonic card, John C. Calhoun's hidden hand of nullification and antitariff, and Andrew

8. "A Political Game of Brag" (Courtesy of the American Antiquarian Society)

Jackson's three kings of intrigue, corruption, and imbecility. At stake is the presidency of the United States. Supporters heralded Clay as the father of the "American system," a shorthand name for those measures endorsed by the party. Protective tariffs, National Republicans claimed, supported domestic industry against foreign imports; investments in roads, canals, and, most recently, railroads created a transportation infrastructure that promoted commerce; a national bank provided a uniform currency and regulated credit. As a consequence of these measures, all sections of the nation had prospered, and the United States had emerged as an international power.

The system, Clay believed, sustained both slaveholding and non-slaveholding states; as if to bolster his point, he even argued against introducing any schemes of gradual emancipation in Kentucky. Clay's first oration before the Twenty-second Congress, delivered over several days in February 1832, defended the economic principles on which he had staked his career: "This transformation of the condition of the country from gloom and distress to brightness and prosperity, had been mainly the work of American legislation, fostering American indus-try. . . . There is scarcely any interest, scarcely a vocation in society, which is not embraced by the beneficence of this system." The American system, he asserted, benefited not just a single state or a region but "the whole Union."[42]

By invoking the Union, Clay echoed the sentiments of another leading national republican, Daniel Webster, who was elected to the House from Massachusetts in 1822 and the Senate in 1827. Webster had gained fame as a lawyer and orator; when he was firing at full throttle, one observer noted, "his power is majestic, irresistible." On January 26, 1830, he reached the capstone of his career. A Senate debate with Robert Hayne of South Carolina had started over the sale of public lands and ended with a discussion of the tariff, slavery, states' rights, and the nature of the Union itself. The Constitution, he argued, was not created by the states but "made for the people, made by the people, and answerable to the people." Webster concluded with a paean to American nationalism: "When my eyes shall be turned to behold for the last time the sun in heaven, may I not see him shining on the broken and dishonored fragments of a once glorious Union; on States dissevered, discordant, belligerent; on a land rent with civil feuds, or drenched, it may be, in fraternal blood! Let their last feeble and lingering glance rather behold the gorgeous ensign of the republic, now known and honored throughout the earth, still full high advanced, its arms and trophies streaming in their original lustre, not a stripe erased or polluted, not a single star obscured, bearing for its motto no such miserable interrogatory as 'What is all this worth?' nor those other words of delusion and folly, 'Liberty first and Union afterwards'; but everywhere, spread all over the sea and over the land, and in every wind under the whole heavens, that other sentiment, dear to every true American heart,—Liberty and Union, now and forever, one and inseparable!" [43]

The speech made Webster a hero among National Republicans and a household name throughout the nation; its echoes would sound in an address delivered at Gettysburg more than three decades later. Always ambitious, the senator considered a run for the presidency. He thought it increasingly possible that Jackson would not be re-elected and believed the prospect of electing Clay "not promising." And although Anti-Masonic sentiment was gaining, Anti-Masonry as a political party did not offer "a principle broad enough to save the Country." The key, he felt, was to unite the Anti-Masons and National Republicans behind a candidate who, in the election of 1832, could secure New York and Pennsylvania. Webster undoubtedly thought of himself as that candidate, and his performance at a public dinner in New York on March 24 served to test political waters. [44]

Before 250 guests, the commercial and mercantile elite of New York, Webster spoke for an hour and a half. Once again, he defended the Constitution and the nation. He praised Hamilton, Jay, and Madison, the authors of *The Federalist Papers*, and he credited the principles of the American system for New York's emergence "as the commercial capital, not only of all the United States, but of the whole continent." Webster anointed America a place of "refuge for the dis-

tressed and the persecuted of other nations." But he warned that the
nation "can stand trial, it can stand assault, it can stand adversity, it
can stand every thing, but the marring of its own beauty, and the weak-
ening of its own strength. It can stand every thing but the effects of our
own rashness and our own folly. It can stand every thing but disorga-
nization, disunion, and nullification."[45]

One attendee, former Mayor Philip Hone, called the speech "patri-
otic, fervent, eloquent, imbued with no party violence, purely American; it was our country, our whole country, and nothing but our
country." Clearly, there was support for Webster, but, despite success
in New York, his presidential maneuverings sputtered. Fearful of
alienating Clay, he aborted plans to travel west to Ohio. He keenly
wished the opposition to Jackson could agree on a candidate, and he
sensed that a change in administration could *be done by us as a Union
Party*." But something about Webster provoked suspicion. A friend
compared him to a "thunder storm in July." When not animated by
debate, his deeply set eyes, "full, dark, and penetrating," made his
expression "cold and forbidding." The *New York Mirror* reported in the
fall that if you met him "in some solitary place" at dark you would not
know if he were "a demi-god or a devil." Webster ultimately stood loyal
to Clay, and the candidate of the National Republicans went forth with
a campaign motto provided by the senator from Massachusetts: "Clay,
Liberty and Union." Webster knew they would fail; he returned to
Washington at the end of the year believing that "Mr. Wirt's nomination has *secured* Genl. Jackson's reelection."[46]

National Republicans and Democrats differed fundamentally from
one another, and in 1831 the issues that divided them threatened to
eclipse the republic. The core distinction between the parties could be
expressed simply. Even the English visitor Thomas Hamilton could
parse it: a National Republican "is disposed to regard the United
States as one and indivisible, and the authority of the United government as paramount to every other jurisdiction. The Democrat considers the Union as a piece of mosaic, tasselated with stones of different
colours, curiously put together, but possessing no other principles of

cohesion than that of mutual convenience." For the one, the "United States" was singular. For the other, it was plural. Throughout the year, fissures between parties and within parties deepened, and it seemed as if none of the history of the nation since its founding had established any common ground. Writing in October, Webster reflected on what had already taken place and anticipated that "every thing is to be attacked. . . . Every thing is to be debated, as if nothing had ever been settled." "We live in an age of revolution," observed Clay. "There is a vague apprehension in the mind of the people," reported another senator as the year began, "that som[e] great misfortune is impending over the Country."[47]

ANDREW JACKSON'S ADMINISTRATION

Fault lines ran everywhere, and an especially active one cut through the White House. Andrew Jackson of Tennessee was the first candidate not from Massachusetts or Virginia to become president. He entered office in 1829 furious at the National Republicans who had stolen the previous election. (Jackson had the plurality of electoral votes and the popular vote, but the House gave the election to Adams, who received Clay's support.) The death of his wife, Rachel, in December 1828 left the president-elect bereft, and he never forgave the opposition for attacking her virtue during the campaign. (Rachel was married when she met Jackson, and accusations of adultery flew.) He had fought a duel in 1806 to protect her honor and carried a bullet in his chest for the rest of his life; he would wage battle again to protect her memory.

Jackson was the people's favorite, a military hero who presented himself as a common man, a self-made man. That he also had a reputation as a "roaring, rollicking, game-cocking, horse-racing, card playing, mischievous fellow" did not hurt among the people who flocked to the White House whenever given the chance. At a levee held in the spring of 1831, a visitor marveled at the diversity of the crowd: "The numerical majority of the company seemed of the class of tradesmen or farmers, respectable men, fresh from the plough or the counter, who, accompanied by their wives and daughters, came forth to greet their President. . . . There were tailors from the board, and judges from the bench; lawyers who opened their mouths at one bar, and the tapster who closed them at another;—in short, every trade, craft, calling, and profession. . . . There were sooty artificers, evidently fresh from the forge or the workshop; and one individual . . . who, wherever he passed, left marks of contact on the garments of the company."

Aged sixty-four, Jackson endured the gala as best he could. He stood in one of the rear apartments paying "one of the severest penalties of greatness; compelled to talk when he had nothing to say, and shake hands with men whose very appearance suggested the precaution of a glove. . . . He bore himself well and gracefully. His countenance expressed perfect good-humour; and his manner to the ladies was so full of well-bred gallantry, that having . . . the great majority of the fair sex on his side, the chance of his being unseated at the next election must be very small."

Visitors described Jackson as an aging man, careworn but still vital. Thomas Hamilton: "The countenance of General Jackson is prepossessing; the features are strongly defined, yet not coarse; and, even at his advanced age, the expression of his eye is keen and vivid. The manner of the President is very pleasing. . . . One sees nothing of courtly elegance, but, on the other hand, nothing which the most rigid critic could attribute to coarseness or vulgarity." Gustave Beaumont: "He is an old man of 66 years, well preserved, and appears to have retained all the vigour of his body and spirit. He is not a man of genius. Formerly he was celebrated as a duelist and a hothead; his great merit is to have won in 1814 the battle of New Orleans against the English. That victory made him popular and brought it about that he was elected president, so true is it that in every country military glory has a prestige that the masses can't resist, even when the masses are composed of merchants and business men." Henry Tudor: "His visage is long, covered with wrinkles, expressing a gravity and sedateness almost approaching to melancholy, and bearing the strongest marks of hard service and the wasting care to which the vicissitudes of his active life have exposed him."[48]

However weary Jackson may have appeared at times, political conflicts energized him, none more so than his ongoing battle with the vice-president, John C. Calhoun. The South Carolinian had served three terms in the House before James Monroe picked him as his secretary of war. As vice-president under Adams, Calhoun did little but disavow his earlier nationalist and protectionist politics and plot his ascendancy. By uniting with Jackson, he provided legitimacy to the general's campaign while positioning himself to take over for the sometimes feeble warrior, who had pledged to serve only one term. Described as ordinary-looking, "middle height, spare, and somewhat slouching in person," Calhoun was no ordinary man: "His mind is bold and acute; his talent for business confessedly of the first order; and, enjoying the esteem of his countrymen, there can be little doubt that he is yet destined to play a conspicuous part in the politics of the nation."

Events in the past, as much as actions in the present, opened a chasm between the men. At a dinner on April 13, 1830, to celebrate Jefferson's birthday, Jackson had offered a toast: "Our Federal Union; It must be preserved." Calhoun followed with his own toast: "The Union: Next to our liberty, the most dear." Several days later, Jackson received a letter from the Georgian William Crawford suggesting that Calhoun's opposition to the president long preceded their emerging differences on the nature of the union. In 1818, Jackson, pursuing the Seminole Indians, had invaded Florida, a Spanish province, and established military control. The House, led by Henry Clay, condemned the general's actions. But Jackson was led to believe that the Cabinet, particularly Secretary of War Calhoun, supported him. He now learned from Crawford, who had battled Calhoun politically for nearly a decade and was secretary of the Treasury under Monroe, that the secretary of war had proposed that "General Jackson should be punished in some form" for disobeying his orders. Jackson asked for an explanation and Calhoun squirmed in his response. He said he thought Jackson had long known what the Cabinet thought and, in any event, claimed to have been only a "junior member" of the administration. Though he confessed that "I was under the impression that you had exceeded your orders, and had acted on your own responsibility," Calhoun declared, "I neither questioned your patriotism nor your motives."[49]

The matter might have rested there, but Calhoun became obsessed with the timing and mode of the revelations. "The secret and mysterious attempts," he told Jackson, which had been made "by false insinuations for years to injure my character, are at last brought to light." He started writing letters seeking vindication. He queried William Wirt, who had been attorney general. He questioned John Quincy Adams, who had been secretary of state. And he pestered James Monroe for documents and recollections. The correspondents worried about revealing secret Cabinet discussions, but each told the vice-president what he already knew: censure of the general had been discussed, and even Crawford had thought Jackson should be condemned for his actions in Florida. After Monroe received a letter from John Rhea, a retired House Member from Tennessee, stating that, through instructions to him in 1818, the president had authorized Jackson to seize Florida and then ordered him to destroy the document, Calhoun launched a new series of inquiries. Rhea's letter turned out to be a hoax designed to vindicate Jackson, who thrived on his past military feats, at the expense of Monroe. "The deep gloom of Winter," wrote Calhoun in the midst of a severe January snowstorm, "over hangs the face of nature."[50]

For Monroe, the controversy only added to his woes. Financially, the ex-president was nearly bankrupt. He advertised for sale his twenty-five-hundred-acre estate in Albermarle County and sold his slaves to a Florida colonel for five thousand dollars. (The proceeds went to pay off a personal debt to John Jacob Astor.) In 1825, he had made a claim with Congress for reimbursement of unpaid salaries and personal expenses incurred while in the nation's service, expenses that dated to his mission in France during Washington's administration. He received partial settlement and now had his claim again before Congress. A bill for relief of the ex-president passed the House and Senate, but the thirty thousand dollars awarded did little to ease Monroe's situation. Physically, the seventy-three-year-old Virginian was in decline. A bad fall from his horse had left him motionless for twenty minutes and shaken for weeks. His wife had died the previous autumn, and Monroe relinquished his estate to live in New York with a daughter and son-in-law. On April 11, he wrote James Madison to say goodbye: "I deeply regret that there is no prospect of our meeting again, since so long have we been connected, and in the most friendly intercourse, in public and private life, that a final separation is among the most distressing incidents which could occur." In response, Madison chastised Monroe for abandoning Virginia and pretended that the two might embrace again.[51]

On April 27, John Quincy Adams visited Monroe in New York. What a contrast between the fortunes of the two ex-presidents. Adams had spent the two years since leaving the White House at leisure, attending public dinners, translating various psalms, and reading voraciously. At the moment, he was working his way through Jefferson's *Memoir*, and in his diary he composed a complex psychological portrait of his father's political antagonist: "a rare mixture of infidel philosophy and epicurean morals, of burning ambition and of stoical self-control, of deep duplicity and of generous sensibility." Adams's visit lasted half an hour, and he left shocked by the appearance of "the feeble and emaciated" man. "He is now dying," wrote Adams, "in wretchedness and beggary."

At half past three on July 4, James Monroe died. In death he achieved what he never had in life—comparison on equal terms to two of the Founders, Adams and Jefferson, who had both passed away on July 4, 1826. Commentators saw providential design behind this: "These are *really* wonderful things." During the summer, Monroe was the subject of numerous eulogies and orations. In Boston, the City Corporation invited John Quincy Adams to deliver an address and the former president could not refuse (he would repeat the task five years later, when Madison died). Through July and August, Adams struggled with the speech. On August 25, he traveled in the driving rain to the Old South Church. Before an audience "crowded to suffocation," Adams offered a eulogy with the only theme possible: the passing of the Fathers and the grave responsibility of the children to preserve what the older generation had created. In the sweltering heat and deepening darkness of the evening, Adams spoke for an hour and a half. Anyone listening closely, or someone examining the hundred-page eulogy published two weeks later, might have detected a defensive, even apologetic tone to the oration: had Monroe been born ten years earlier, he would have been a signer of the Declaration of Independence; Monroe's opposition to the ratification of the Constitution did not detract from his contributions; his administration offered no new policies.

The eulogy failed and Adams knew it: "As the sun went down, it grew so dark that it was becoming impossible for me to read my manuscript. I was forced to read so rapidly that my articulation became indistinct, and my voice and my eyes, both affected by the state of the atmosphere, were constantly threatening to fail me." Another visitor to the Old South Church, Ralph Waldo Emerson, confirmed Adams's fears: "There was nothing heroic in the subject, & not much in the feelings of the orator, so it proved rather spectacle than a speech."[52]

Calhoun expressed no remorse about disturbing Monroe in his final days. The vice-president's actions in February had not only added to the former president's anguish, but also hastened his own demise within Jackson's administration. On February 17, the *United States Telegraph* published the exchanges on the Seminole affair and later issued a fifty-two-page pamphlet, *The Correspondence Between General Andrew Jackson and John C. Calhoun*. Edited by Duff Green, the *Telegraph* had been the voice of the administration, but it now supported Calhoun; a new paper, the *Washington Globe*, edited by Francis Blair, spoke for Jackson. It was one thing for some of these letters to circulate privately and for rumors about their content to appear in the press; it was another for a government official to release them publicly, reveal "sacredly confidential" transactions, and jockey openly for position within Jackson's administration to further his own political standing. Webster confided to Clay that the correspondence "shows feelings & objects so personal—so ambitious—I may even say so *factious*, in some or all the parties, that it creates no small degree of disgust." In a preface addressed to the People of the United States, Calhoun claimed he sought to vindicate his character and prove himself worthy of his position, but he accomplished the opposite. Calhoun and Green, snorted Jackson, "have cut their own throats, and destroyed themselves in a shorter space of time than any two men I ever knew." [53]

The publication of the Seminole correspondence ended any "social intercourse" between the vice-president and president. The issue of social relations cut deeply in Jackson's White House. On January 1, 1829, John Eaton, Jackson's secretary of war and fellow Tennessean, married Margaret O'Neale Timberlake. Twenty-nine years old and a widow of only eight months, Peggy, according to rumor, had been Major Eaton's mistress. But Jackson blessed the union, pronouncing Mrs. Eaton to be "as chaste as those who attempt to slander her." His wife, Rachel, also hounded by false accusations of sexual impropriety, had just died. Here was a way to remain steadfast against the Washington gossip machine. The storm over Peggy Eaton, however, swirled out of control. Privately, politicians snorted, "Eaton has just married his mistress and the mistress of eleven doz. Others." Governor Floyd of Virginia described Peggy Eaton as "a woman destitute of virtue and of morals," adding, "I know myself that all is true which has been said of her." Margaret Bayard Smith, the doyenne of Washington society, called Peggy Eaton "one of the most ambitious, violent, malignant, yet silly women you ever heard of." When the Eatons paid a social call on the Calhouns and Floride Calhoun refused to return the courtesy, Jackson's Cabinet flew into turmoil.[54]

The "Eaton malaria" spread through the White House. In addition to the vice-president, the families of the secretary of the Treasury (Samuel Ingham), secretary of the navy (John Branch), and attorney general (John Berrien) avoided any social contact with the Eatons. Even Jackson's niece Emily Donelson, who had come to Washington after Rachel Jackson's death to serve as White House hostess, refused to have social relations with Mrs. Eaton. Only the postmaster general (William Barry) and, significantly, the secretary of state, Martin Van Buren, honored the president's wishes and interacted with Peggy Eaton. As a bachelor, Van Buren had no need to worry about the social rules that governed Washington high society. With each visit to Peggy Eaton, Van Buren endeared himself that much more to the president, just as, with each rejection of her, Calhoun further alienated the general. It did not take long for Jackson to see Calhoun as the source of dissension in his White House and Van Buren as the man who should succeed him.[55]

Jackson became preoccupied with tracing the source of all the rumors and refuting them. He wrote letters, conducted investigations, and called his Cabinet together to chastise them for their behavior toward "a virtuous and much injured Lady." Jackson overflowed with anger and lashed out in all directions. One minister, Ezra Stiles Ely of Philadelphia, received a stinging rebuke after he not only spread rumors about Mrs. Eaton but also suggested that Mrs. Jackson, when she was alive, had disavowed the woman: "Female virtue is like a tender and delicate flower; let but the breath of suspicion rest upon it, and it withers and perhaps perishes forever. When it shall be assailed by envy and malice, the good and the pious will maintain its purity and innocence, until guilt is made manifest—not by *rumors* and *suspicions*, but by facts and proofs brought forth and sustained by respectable and fearless witnesses in the face of day. Truth shuns not the light; but falsehood deals in sly and dark insinuations, and prefers *darkness*, because its deeds are evil."[56]

Never one to abandon a friend, Jackson staunchly defended the Eatons and began to imagine some larger, nefarious design behind the slanders and "most unfounded lies ever propagated." Culturally, he blamed the clergy for their moralistic exhortations and wondered "by what authority These ladies with their clergymen at their head has assumed for themselves this holy alliance and secrete inquisition to pass . . . upon the conduct of others." Politically, he at first saw a "wicked combination" led by Henry Clay. But, coterminous with the Seminole inquiry, he fixed on "the wicked machinations of Calhoun and his adherents" as plotting the destruction of the administration. "I believe him now one of the basest and most dangerous men living—a man, devoid of principle, and would sacrifice his friend, his country, and forsake his god, for selfish personal ambition," pronounced Jackson. Craving harmony in his Cabinet and reciting the scriptural pronouncement that "a House divided cannot stand," the president took action.[57]

On April 8, Jackson accepted John Eaton's resignation. Four days later, he acknowledged the "necessity" of Van Buren's also resigning. The Eaton scandal had paralyzed the Cabinet, and just as Jackson saw Clay and Calhoun behind the petticoat politics, the opposition claimed that Van Buren was secretly plotting for his own succession to the presidency. Shrewdly, Van Buren recognized that his departure from the administration would allow Jackson to purge the Cabinet of men loyal to Calhoun while strengthening his own position as Democratic candidate down the line. (Van Buren hoped to serve out his time as minister to Great Britain, but Calhoun, seeking revenge, cast the vote denying him confirmation and gloated, "It will kill him, sir, kill him dead.") Within a week Jackson secured the resignations of Ingham and Branch, Berrien resigned in June, and the president installed an entirely new Cabinet.

"A revolution has taken place in the Capitol of the United States," screamed the headlines. The reshuffling of the Cabinet shocked the nation and raised fears that the very structure of American government would be transformed. The resignations "constitute an epoch in the history of the United States," declared the *National Intelligencer*. Pro-administration papers applauded the move, arguing that it would allow the president to focus on issues of national importance, but anti-administration papers viewed it as tearing an irreparable hole in the ship of state: "The ship is sinking and the rats are flying!! The hull is too leaky to mend, and the hero of two wars and a half has not skill to keep it afloat."[58]

In Philadelphia, a promising young artist, Edward William Clay, seized the moment and drew a cartoon that provided an indelible image of Jackson under siege. He executed two somewhat different versions. In the first, "The Rats Leaving a Falling House," Jackson is shown slumped in his collapsing, thronelike chair. The Cabinet members, depicted as rats, scamper away while Jackson tries to prevent his secretary of state from escaping by stepping on his tail. All around, the pillars of government are collapsing and Jackson's "Altar of Reform," which swept hundreds out of government office, is shown to be guided over by a devilish imp. Jackson's spittoon and broken pipe lie at the dazed president's feet. John Quincy Adams—who was in Philadelphia, where the print first appeared in April—reported that two thousand copies were sold in a day and that ten thousand would be dispatched within a matter of weeks. The caricature, reported the *National Gazette*, "is now running, like wildfire, through the land."[59]

A version of the cartoon printed later in the year carried the title ",00001—The Value of a Unit with Four Cyphers Going Before It," a reference to Jackson's worthlessness in the eyes of opponents and a play on Jackson's insistence that he must make his Cabinet a harmonious unit. Newspapers called his Cabinet "the smallest figure ever known in political arithmetic." One editor gibed that the "rules of decimal arithmetic will not apply to the ex-Cabinet.—If report be true, they have dealt more in *Vulgar fractions*."[60] In this version, the president's crumbling chair is identified as Hickory, a reference to his nickname "Old Hickory." To the left, Van Buren reaches for the ladder of states that leads to the presidency, but Calhoun the terrier is there to stop him. Again, Cabinet members appearing like rats flee in all directions. Eaton says, "I'm off to the Indians," Berrien heads for Georgia, and Branch and Ingham are swept into the "rat hole of oblivion." A notice on the wall states, "Pollytickle mathewmatick taught here." Webster and Clay stand at the window and joke that Jackson "has nullifide the whole concern." "War! Pestilence! And Famin!," they assert, "is better than this."

Another popular lithograph, "Exhibition of Cabinet Pictures,"

9. Edward William Clay, "The Rats Leaving a Falling House" (Courtesy of the American Antiquarian Society)

10. Edward William Clay, ",00001—The Value of a Unit with Four Cyphers Going Before It" (Courtesy of the American Antiquarian Society)

11. "Exhibition of Cabinet Pictures" (Courtesy of the American Antiquarian Society)

offered a comprehensive condemnation of Jackson, who appears as an ape, a blind man, a jackass, and a grandmother. He is also the "sun" setting in a storm. The Cabinet library on the left contains numerous plays that refer to the Eaton scandals: "provoked husband," "she would if she could," "female stability," and "family quarrels." And a number of the pictures lampoon the power of petticoats. Jackson is shown washing one and slipping one on, and petticoats are even made part of the national seal.

Cartoons dramatized the political events of the day and sought with humor to alleviate public anxieties over the state of the union. By portraying cartoon images as works of art displayed in a museum, "Exhibition of Cabinet Pictures" subtly elevated the importance of the cartoonist's craft while making a mockery of Jackson's presidency. And newspapers increased their visibility, not to mention sales, as editors began not only to report the news, but also to make it. The appearance in print of confidential documents and undocumented rumors helped shape events in unexpected ways. John Quincy Adams lamented, "In our Presidential canvassing an editor has become as essential an appendage to a candidate as in the days of chivalry a squire was to a knight." Incendiary headlines became so commonplace that one publication even joked, "We should have prefaced this article with such phrases, in large capitals, as REVOLUTION AT WASHINGTON— EVACUATION OF THE DEPARTMENTS—MYSTIFICATION OF THE PEOPLE—NEW CABINET YET UNKNOWN—TENDER CORRESPON-DENCE." Here was a paradox at the heart of American politics: democracy meant telling all, but telling all, as in the Seminole and Eaton affairs, could threaten democratic government.[61]

Foreign visitors commented on the importance of newspapers in America—New York alone had forty-seven papers. "Nothing in America is perhaps more striking," observed James Boardman, "than the rapid and general diffusion of information through the community by means of newspapers." Tocqueville was struck by the contents of a poor farmer's cabin in Tennessee: "There one finds a fairly clean bed, some chairs, a good gun, often some books and almost always a newspaper, but the walls are so open to the day that the outside air comes in on every side." He deplored the "coarse insults . . . petty slanders . . . and impudent calumnies" that constituted the news, but he recognized that the papers' ubiquity served as a way of knitting together an expansive nation. "Newspapers penetrate to every crevice of the Union," noted Thomas Hamilton. "It is thus that the clamor of the busy world is heard even in the wilderness, and the most remote invader of distant wilds is kept alive in his solitude to the common ties of brotherhood and country."[62]

The government survived the Cabinet tempest, though several members refused to relent and began commenting openly in the papers. Eaton responded by challenging at least one of his colleagues to a duel and publishing a *Candid Appeal to the American Public*. Calling his lamentable associates "monuments of duplicity, ingratitude, and baseness," Eaton marveled at their inability to understand why, in attack-

ing the virtue of female character, "the sun of their political glory was
so suddenly shorn of its beams."

Jackson emerged reinvigorated, relieved at last to have regained
control over his house. He had been suffering from severe headaches
and physical exhaustion. His political opponents privately expressed
hope that the general might not live out the year. They even contemplated impeaching him, but feared generating still more sympathy for
a man whom the people "have not yet altogether ceased to idolize."
Jackson regained his spirit and his health, not to mention his political
balance. He continued to "long for retirement to the peaceful shade of
the Hermitage," his Tennessee estate, but he would not surrender his
office. The *Washington Globe* announced that the president would run
for re-election, and Jackson readied himself for a line of tumultuous
political storms that were enveloping the nation.[63]

STATE AND NATION

❋

INDIANS

The freezing rain of a February morning did not faze Chief Justice John Marshall as he trudged to the Supreme Court with his coat open and head uncovered. Edward Everett, riding to the Capitol in a hack, watched Marshall with wonder. The Massachusetts congressman, who was suffering from a "heavy and troublesome cold," paid half a dollar a day, as much as most workingmen earned, to be driven back and forth between the Capitol and his boarding rooms. "It makes me ashamed of myself," he confided, "to see the Chief Justice who is 75 years old trudging up to Court on foot. . . . Here I am, at the age of 37 obliged to drive up to the Capitol while the old Chief Justice walks."[1]

Marshall was not so vigorous as he may have appeared. Since the onset of his wife's illness, the chief justice had let himself go. William Wirt, who as attorney general appeared frequently before the Court, had commented on Marshall's unkempt appearance. He observed that one day the chief justice arrived in Court "badly shaved" and "with a quantity of egg on his underlip & chin." Associate Justice Joseph Story knew Marshall's condition better than most. Story entered the chief justice's chambers during the January term in 1832, only weeks after

Mrs. Marshall's death on Christmas Day, and found the great man cry-
ing. "The moment he relaxes from business he feels exceedingly
depressed, and rarely goes through a night without weeping over his
departed wife," reported Story. Throughout 1831, rumors spread that
the chief justice would soon retire, a possibility that many considered
a "national calamity." John Quincy Adams expressed his anxiety that,
with Marshall gone, Jackson would appoint some "shallow-pated wild-
cat . . . fit for nothing but to tear the Union to rags and tatters." "It
makes me melancholy to reflect," concluded one editor, "that such
men as *John Marshall* must grow old, become infirm and Die!"[2]

Marshall had sworn Jackson in as president, and he must have said
a silent prayer when the general vowed to "preserve, protect, and
defend the Constitution of the United States." Contentious issues
threatened the nation, and the fate of the Cherokee Indians at the
hands of the state of Georgia was one of them. Jackson hated Indians.
He had made his name fighting them, going to battle against the Creek
in 1813 and the Seminole in 1817. He never relinquished the belief
that the Indians desired only "to comit Murder with impunity," a fear
he expressed in 1793. In his First Annual Message to Congress he
declared that the presence of Indian tribes living independently within
state jurisdictions had become an acute problem. Jackson believed the
states had sovereign power to pass laws that applied to everyone residing within state boundaries, and that the national government had no
right to interfere. The president would not countenance independent
republics within state lines any more than he would approve separate
governments within national lines. The Indians living in the Southeast
would have to "submit to the laws of those States."[3]

Everyone knew what that meant. State laws in Georgia, Alabama,
and Mississippi abolished tribal units and powers, invalidated Indian
possession of lands, encouraged white settlement on Indian territory,
and denied Indians the right to vote or bring suit or testify. Georgians
seemed especially keen to control the territory occupied by the Cherokee Nation, an expanse of fertile ground on the state's northern border
with Tennessee. They had forced the Creek, Choctaw, and Chickasaw

off of millions of acres of land in the mid-1820s and now sought to do the same to the Cherokee, especially after the discovery of gold in the region. The Georgia General Assembly passed law after law asserting its own sovereignty over the entire state and circumscribing the rights of the Cherokee. A law went into effect on February 1 making it illegal for the government of the Cherokee to meet, compelling all whites (mostly missionaries) living among the Cherokee to take an oath of allegiance to the state, and creating a special unit, the Georgia Guard, to enforce all laws. Elias Boudinot, the editor of the *Cherokee Phoenix*, observed, "Cupidity and self-interest are at the bottom of all these difficulties—A desire to *possess* the Indian land is paramount to a desire to see him *established* on the soil as a *civilized* man."[4]

Boudinot was commenting on one of the ironies of the situation. The Cherokee had gradually repudiated elements of their own culture and embraced a program for "civilization" begun by George Washington. They became farmers, English-speakers, and Christians. One visitor commented, "They adopt in part the costume of Europeans; they have schools, and churches, and a printing press among them." In 1827, when the Cherokee ratified a constitution that proclaimed total sovereignty over their land and people, they had become too "civilized" for Georgia's leaders. Had they resisted missionary efforts, they would have been assaulted as savages; having embraced "civilization," they were condemned for zealously seeking to protect their identity and property. In the end, the "civilization" program provided the rationale for Indian removal. In relinquishing their own ways, Jackson claimed, the Cherokee doomed themselves to "weakness and decay," to an inability to fight off transgressors. Wishing to avoid the annihilation of the Cherokee, Jackson proclaimed, "Humanity and national honor demand that every effort should be made to avert so great a calamity." Just as free blacks were being pressured to abandon the South for lands in Africa, the only solution to the problem of the Indian presence, Jackson advised Congress, was to encourage "voluntary emigration" to territory west of the Mississippi.[5]

Responding to Jackson's message, Democrats introduced an Indian

Removal Bill that would authorize the president to provide land west of the Mississippi in exchange for tribal property in the East and would appropriate five hundred thousand dollars to carry out resettlement. The debate over the bill preoccupied Congress in 1830. Opponents of the measure—in the Senate, Theodore Frelinghuysen of New Jersey and Peleg Sprague of Maine; in the House, Henry Storrs of New York and Isaac Bates of Massachusetts—denounced Indian removal on historical, constitutional, and moral grounds. Since the adoption of the United States Constitution, they argued, there had been fourteen treaties signed with the Cherokee and each one had guaranteed the tribe "the remainder of their country forever," a promise that superseded any states'-rights claims. Furthermore, the Cherokee government could retain its independence and sovereignty, because it was not a state in the sense meant by the Constitution (Article IV, Section 3, proclaims, "No new State shall be formed or erected within the Jurisdiction of any other State") and it certainly was not a new state: "The emblems of [the Cherokee Nation] were sparkling in the sun, when those who now inhabit Georgia, and all who ever did, were in the loins of their European ancestry. . . . The Cherokees were the lords of the country in which they dwelt, acknowledging no supremacy but that of the Great Spirit, and awed by no power but his—absolute, erect, indomitable as any creatures on earth the Deity ever formed."[6]

"Removal is a soft word," observed Edward Everett, "and words are delusive." There was nothing at all voluntary about the measure; rather, if passed, the Removal Act would lead to the compulsory expulsion of some fifteen thousand Cherokee from their land. Everett denounced the Southerners for their ardent states'-rights stand and their indifference to the fate of the Southeastern Indians. He also exposed the true financial cost of the measure, putting the sum not at five hundred thousand dollars but at nearly twenty-five million. He concluded by addressing the conscience of Congress: "We are going . . . to take a population of Indians, of families, who live as we do in houses, work as we do in the field or the workshop, at the plough and the loom, who are governed as we are by laws, who raise their children to school, and who attend themselves to the ministry of the Christian faith, to march them from their homes, and put them down in a remote, unexplored desert. *We* are going to do it—the Congress is going to do it—this is a bill to do it."[7]

The Indian Removal Act passed the Senate by a vote of 28 to 19 and the House by a vote of 103 to 97. Jackson signed it on May 28, 1830. In his second address to Congress, he called the action "true philanthropy," because, in accepting the inevitability of the disappearance of the Indians, the nation could move forward. Who, Jackson wondered, could complain of a chance to move west at government expense and by doing so remove themselves from harm's way? Of course it was difficult to leave behind one's ancestral homeland, but "to better their condition in an unknown land our forefathers left all that was dear in earthly objects." If the "civilized Christian" could do so, certainly the "wandering savage" could do the same.

Opponents of Jackson and removal refused to abandon the issue. Throughout 1830, thousands of citizens signed numerous petitions opposing the Indian Removal Act. On February 7, 1831, Everett formally presented a memorial from his constituents praying for repeal of the act. He informed the House that he intended to speak on the following Monday, the day set aside for consideration of petitions and memorials. Jackson's supporters moved to silence Everett. Wilson Lumpkin of Georgia raised a series of procedural objections, but Everett's motion to refer the memorial to the Committee on Indian Affairs passed by a vote of 101 to 93. Despite suffering from a severe cold, Everett rose on February 14 to speak on the Indian question, "the greatest question which ever came before Congress, short of the questions of peace and war."[8]

Everett focused on Indian removal as an unconstitutional attack on the integrity of the American polity. "What is the union?" Everett inquired. "Not a mere abstraction; not a word; not a form of government; it is the undisputed paramount operation, through all the states, of those functions with which the Government is clothed by the Constitution." Jackson and the state of Georgia had disrupted those operations. By refusing to uphold legal and binding treaties, the executive and the state were guilty of the very crime currently being threatened by South Carolina with regard to the tariff: nullification. The president's place, averred Everett, was not to decide on the constitutionality of law, only to abide by it. And Georgia's place was not to declare all Indian treaties unconstitutional, only to follow them until they were revised by Congress. More than the fate of the Cherokee rested upon these deliberations; the fate of the Union did as well. Speaking two days after the atmospheric phenomenon that had closed Congress early in the day, Everett warned, "If we proceed in this path, if we now bring this stain on our annals, if we suffer this cold and dark eclipse to come over the bright sun of our national honor, I see not how it can ever pass off; it will be as eternal as it is total."[9]

With the president, Congress, and the states aligned behind removal, the Cherokee delegation in Washington decided to bring the issue to the Supreme Court. Taking the advice of Webster and Clay, they retained William Wirt as counsel for the Cherokee Nation. A talented orator and experienced legal tactician, Wirt took the case because he found the legal questions fascinating, had little sympathy for Andrew Jackson, and was paid a handsome fee. Shortly after passage of the Removal Act, he told John Ross, chief of the Cherokee Nation, "Your case is a great and urgent one." Wirt wrote immediately to George Gilmer, governor of Georgia, suggesting that the Court be allowed to settle the "difference of opinion" on Indian sovereignty; Gilmer responded by denouncing Wirt as an advocate of nationalist power against the "friends of liberty" who sought to preserve the authority of the state. Knowing the letter would make its way to Chief Justice Marshall, Wirt also wrote to Dabney Carr, a judge on the Virginia Court of Appeals. When Marshall told Carr that he had followed the debate over Indian removal and wished "the executive and legislative departments had thought differently on the subject," Wirt had the signal he was hoping for.[10]

Believing it an insult for "a sovereign and independent state . . . to become a party, before the Supreme Court, with a few savages, residing on her own territory," Georgia decided to ignore a writ of error commanding the state to appear on the second Monday in January to show cause why a judgment had been rendered against one George Tassel, a Cherokee who was convicted and sentenced to death by a Georgia court for murdering an Indian within Indian territory. Tassel claimed he was exempt from the jurisdiction of the Georgia courts and applied to the Supreme Court to review the matter. But Governor Gilmer refused to take part, telling the Georgia legislature that cooperation would "eventuate in the utter annihilation of the state governments." On Christmas Eve, 1830, in defiance of Marshall's order, Georgia executed Tassel, thus making the writ a moot issue. The "intemperate and indecorous proceedings" distressed Justice Joseph Story, who saw a general scheme at work "to elevate an exclusive State sovereignty upon the ruins of the general government."[11]

On March 5, Wirt and his co-counsel, John Sergeant—a leading National Republican, chief counsel for the Bank of the United States, and, by year's end, Henry Clay's running mate—moved for an injunction from the Supreme Court to restrain Georgia from executing and enforcing its laws against the Cherokee. The Court granted the request and soon heard arguments from Sergeant and Wirt in the case of *Cherokee Nation v. Georgia*; no counsel appeared for the respondent. On Saturday, March 12, Sergeant addressed the bench for several hours. In a presentation described as "cold and dry," he detailed two principal legal arguments. First, the Supreme Court had original jurisdiction under Article III, Section 2, which extended judicial power to all cases arising under treaties. Second, treaties, precedents, and legal authorities established that the Cherokee were an independent foreign state: they controlled a territory, they had fixed boundaries, they had laws and government, and they were parties to treaties that recognized their rights as a nation. In sum, they met all the criteria offered by political philosophers for the definition of a state: it has "affairs and interests; it deliberates and takes resolutions in common; and becomes a moral person, having an understanding and a will peculiar to itself; and is susceptible to obligations and laws."

Sergeant emphasized that it mattered little whether the Cherokee were inferior or dependent: a weak state is still a state, much as an amputee is still a man. The laws of Georgia had jeopardized the Indian right of self-government and right to property. The Cherokee Nation now came before the Court to address not an abstract question or a political issue but a legal problem—the protection of its rights as a foreign state against Georgia's encroachment.

On Monday, Wirt addressed the Court. He covered many of the legal points made by his colleague, but in even more exhaustive fashion. The difference was not in degree of detail but in passion of argument. He implored the Court to uphold the conscience of the nation: "Are we so lost to character as to . . . make the tacit admission, that we hold ourselves bound by our engagements only so long as we can be compelled to fulfill them? . . . If such be the point of degeneracy to which we have already sunk since the age of Washington, farewell to the honor of the American name." He begged the Court to strike a blow against the racism of the age: "It is not the tincture of a skin by which the rights of these people are to be tested. We are beginning to recover from our mistake on this ground, with regard to another unfortunate race. Let us not create for ourselves, and place in the hands of a just God, a new scourge of a similar description." He demanded that the Court act without regard to whether the president would enforce its decision: "If the injunction shall be awarded, there is a moral force in the public sentiment of the American community which will, alone, sustain it, and constrain obedience. . . . For, if the judiciary is struck from the system, what is there of any value that will remain. Sir, the government cannot subsist without it. It would be as rational to talk of a solar system without the sun."

In a soft voice, with the darkness of late day enveloping the Court, Wirt concluded: "The existence of this remnant of a once great and mighty nation is at stake, and it is for your honours to say, whether they shall be blotted out from creation, in utter disregard of all our treaties. They are here in the last extremity, and with them must perish forever the honor of the American name. The faith of our nation is fatally linked with their existence, and the blow which destroys them quenches forever our own glory: for what glory can there be of which a patriot can be proud, after the good name of his country shall have departed? We may gather laurels on the field and trophies on the ocean, but they will never hide this foul and bloody blot upon our escutcheon. 'Remember, the Cherokee nation' will be answer enough to the proudest boasts we can ever make."[12]

Wirt's speech left many in tears, but few observers believed he had succeeded in turning a question of state power into one of national honor. John Quincy Adams, who attended both days of oral arguments, thought that the "weight of the State will be too heavy for them [Sergeant and Wirt]. The old vice of the confederacies is pressing upon us—anarchy in its members. Whenever a State does set itself in defiance against the laws or power of the Union, they are prostrated. This is what the States having Indian tribes within their limits are now doing with impunity, and all the powers of the General Government for protection of the Indians, or the execution of the treaties with them, are nullified."[13]

The Cherokee Nation did not have long to wait for the Court's decision. On March 18, the final day of the session, Marshall read the majority opinion, two other justices offered concurring opinions, and Justice Story joined Justice Smith Thompson in a dissent. Though moved by the plight of the Indians, Marshall ruled that the Cherokee could not, "with strict accuracy, be denominated foreign nations." He relied on the wording of the commerce clause (Congress had the power to "regulate commerce with foreign nations, and among the several states, and with the Indian tribes") as evidence that the Indians were distinguishable from foreign states. Wirt had anticipated this argument and ingeniously suggested that this clause employed the word "foreign" only in a geographic sense as related to markets, not in a political sense related to sovereignty. Marshall, who had no rival when it came to ingenious solutions to seemingly intractable legal problems, found the Cherokee to be neither a foreign state nor a subject tribe but, rather, a "domestic, dependent nation." As a result, their case could not be brought before the Court.

Compared with the concurring opinions, Marshall's was a model of brevity and sympathy. William Johnson of South Carolina and Henry Baldwin of Pennsylvania rejected the petitioners' claims in the strongest terms. Johnson thought it unlikely that the word "state" could possibly apply "to a people so low in the grade of organized society as our Indian tribes generally are. . . . [They are] wandering hordes, held together only by ties of blood and habit, and having neither laws or government, beyond what is required in a savage state." Baldwin, a Jackson appointee to the Court, who in two years would suffer from a nervous breakdown, went even further. He refused to recognize the plaintiff at all and protested against any sort of judicial activism that might undermine the "full dominion" of the "sovereign power of the people of the United States" over their territory.

The decision left Marshall uneasy. Publicly, his opinion had hinted that the Court might consider a more limited case that focused on Cherokee property rights. Privately, he encouraged Smith Thompson and Joseph Story to write a dissent. The dissent, of course, would not alter the holding of the Court, but it could influence future rulings. Thompson, with Story concurring, argued that the Cherokee were a foreign state and that the Court held original jurisdiction. Even more directly than Marshall, Thompson announced that the Court could not rule on abstract questions, only on questions in which a law was in operation and threatened specific rights of person or property. As an example, Thompson cited the Georgia law authorizing the governor to take possession of gold and silver mines located in Cherokee territory. Privately, Story placed the tragedy in human terms. "I never in my whole life was more affected by the consideration that they and all their race are destined to destruction," he confided to his wife. "I feel, as an American, disgraced by our gross violation of the public faith towards them. I fear, and greatly fear, that in the course of Providence there will be dealt to us a heavy retributive justice."[14]

Months would pass before the dissent became widely known and Cherokee supporters could rally public opinion and plan another assault on Georgia's laws. Until then, Jacksonians and Southerners offered their constituencies a slanted interpretation of the Court's decision: "The Court has decided in favor of the views of the Executive. . . . A war of extermination was to be waged by the Union against the State of Georgia, to protect some ideal notions of Indian sovereignty; and the President was to be *forced* into these measures by the Supreme Court and the excitement produced on the public mind. . . . The Court has nipped in the bud this mad scheme of political ambition."[15]

Shortly after the decision, the Cherokee delegation to Washington, headed by John Ridge, called on Andrew Jackson. Months later, some Democratic newspapers reported that Ridge had asked Jackson if "he was angry with them," to which Jackson replied that he was only sorry they had been deluded by their friends. Ridge responded to the story, which was designed to humiliate the Cherokee. "Sooner than ask the President if he was angry with me," wrote Ridge, "I would cut my tongue out of my mouth." Rather, Jackson expressed surprise that the Indians would go to court. Ridge answered, "As a statesman and a warrior we do not believe you would blame the Cherokees for the efforts they have made to maintain their rights for liberty."

Jackson lapsed into anecdote and reminded the delegation of the once mighty Catawba, who "took some of the Cherokee warriors prisoners, threw them in the fire, and when their intestines were barbecued, ate them—now they [the Catawba] were poor and miserable, and reduced in numbers, and such will be the condition of the Cherokees, if they remain surrounded by the white people." A politician from Georgia was announced at that point, and the delegation rose to leave. As they departed, Jackson said, "You can live in your lands in Georgia if you choose, but I cannot interfere with the laws of that state to protect you."[16]

Even as Jackson and Ridge spoke, events in Georgia were unfolding that would lead to another Supreme Court case. The evangelical impulses of the Second Great Awakening had led organizations such as the American Board of Commissioners for Foreign Missions to redouble their efforts among the Indians. On March 13, Samuel Worcester, a thirty-three-year-old Congregationalist missionary to the Cherokee, was arrested along with several other missionaries for violating a recently enacted Georgia law that prohibited the residence of whites in Indian territory, with the exception of government employees. In a Gwinnett County courtroom, Judge Clayton upheld the Georgia law but released the defendants on the grounds that they qualified as agents of the federal government. Governor Gilmer, intent on banishing the antiremoval missionaries from the territory, arranged with Jackson-administration officials to have Worcester removed from his position as postmaster at New Echota and to disavow any relationship between the government and the missionaries. In July, the state rearrested Worcester for refusing to leave Cherokee territory. In September, he, physician Elizur Butler, and nine others were convicted and sentenced to four years at Milledgeville Penitentiary.

The American Board of Commissioners for Foreign Missions hired Wirt and Sergeant and appealed the convictions to the Supreme Court. Beginning on February 20, 1832, the counsel replayed the arguments they had offered nearly a year earlier; once again, no one appeared for the state of Georgia. *Worcester* v. *Georgia* was an easier case to argue. Marshall had already indicated his desire to rule again on the Georgia laws; there were no jurisdictional issues, since this was a direct appeal from the decision of a state court; and public opinion in the climate of evangelical enthusiasm was particularly exercised by "the degrading manner in which the missionaries of the cross have been arrested, conducted in chains to trial, and consigned to the penitentiary." Story gave more than a hint of how the Court would rule when he wrote his wife that Wirt's argument was "uncommonly eloquent, forcible and finished." "I blush for my country," he concluded, "when I perceive that such legislation, destructive of all faith and honor towards the Indians, is suffered to pass with the silent approbation of the present Government of the United States."[17]

Chief Justice Marshall, recovering from surgery and from the death of his wife, whispered the Court's decision. The Cherokee Nation, he ruled, "is a distinct community, occupying its own territory, with boundaries accordingly described, in which the laws of Georgia can have no force, and which the citizens of Georgia have no right to enter, but with the assent of the Cherokee themselves, or in conformity with treaties and acts of Congress." Story felt proud. "The Court has done its duty," he boasted. "Let the nation now do theirs. If we have a government, let its command be obeyed; if we have not, it is as well to know it at once, and to look to consequences."[18]

Story, of course, knew what the nation knew—that the Court was powerless to enforce the decision. Jackson gloated that the ruling "has fell still born." At first, the Cherokee rejoiced over the decision, but soon even their supporters advised them to sign a treaty and voluntarily move west. With Jackson's re-election nearly certain, public political support for the Cherokee cause began to erode. And with South Carolina threatening nullification of a federal law, the president needed Georgia far more than he ever needed the Indians. For sixteen months, Worcester and Butler languished in jail. They refused to concede any wrongdoing or ask for a pardon. At last, they wore down and wrote the new governor, Wilson Lumpkin. Without repudiating their principles, they informed him that they would no longer pursue their case against the state. In January 1833, they left the penitentiary. That month, even the American Board of Commissioners for Foreign Missions, who had been zealously antiremoval, suggested that the Cherokee come to terms with the government.

Two factions emerged. John Ross, the chief of the Cherokee, encouraged resistance and opposed abandoning ancestral lands. Major Ridge, a Cherokee leader who had fought with Jackson against the Creek in the War of 1812, his son John Ridge, and his nephews Elias Boudinot and Stand Waite, advocated signing a treaty. Ross and Ridge were both wealthy slave owners acting for what each thought was in the tribe's best interest, but the division between them would divide the Cherokee for decades. Jackson recognized Ridge's minority faction and, in Ross's absence, negotiated the Treaty of New Echota in 1835. The Senate ratified it by one vote. The vast majority of Cherokee opposed the treaty. When, after two years, fewer than two thousand had left, President Van Buren decided to compel removal.

Soldiers rounded up the Cherokee, placed them in camps, and sent them west in a series of forced marches that have come down to us as the "Trail of Tears." Victimized by unscrupulous furnishing agents, extreme climates, and the rigors of making an overland journey to unknown territory, more than four thousand Indians died. They died of dysentery and pellagra, cold and hunger, brutality and despair. Both the rich and the poor suffered, especially women and children. Among the many victims was John Ross's wife, Quatie, who in a snowstorm gave her blanket and her life to a freezing child. Prior to joining the Cherokee on the trail west, the Baptist missionary Evan Jones commented on the catastrophe that was unfolding: "Most of their faces, I fear, we shall not see again till the great day when the oppressor and the oppressed shall appear before the tribunal of the righteous judge. I have no language to express the emotions which rend our hearts to witness their season of cruel and unnecessary oppression. For if it be determined to take their land and reduce them to absolute poverty, it would seem to be mere wanton cruelty to take their lives also."[19]

At the same time that the Cherokee appealed to the courts to preserve their homeland, a group of Indians in Illinois resorted to arms. In the spring, members of the Sauk tribe crossed to the east side of the Mississippi and returned to their ancestral village at Rock Island. Authorities believed that, through treaties signed in 1804, 1816, and 1825, the tribe had relinquished its rights to these lands. Settlers petitioned for protection from marauding Indians who "are Burning our fences destroying our crops of Wheat now growing by turning in all their Horses[.] They Also threaten our lives if we attempt to plant corn and say they will cut it up & That we have Stole their Lands from them and they are determined to exterminate us provided we don't leave the country." In May, the governor informed William Clark—the superintendent of Indian affairs, who, nearly thirty years earlier, had traveled with Meriweather Lewis to Oregon and back—that he was calling out the militia "to protect those citizens, by removing said Indians, peaceably, if they can: but forcibly, if they must. Those Indians are now, and so I have considered them, in a state of actual invasion of the State."[20]

Clark immediately wrote to the commanding officer of the Western Department of the United States Army, Edmund Gaines, and informed him that, though most Sauk leaders had agreed to move to a new village on the Iowa River, west of the Mississippi, two bands of Indians, "after abandoning their old village . . . returned again in defiance of all consequences." Gaines and six companies of infantry boarded a steamboat for Rock Island, prepared to use force to drive the Indians across the river.

Upon his arrival, Gaines found that the Indians were not "in a state of actual hostility," and he called for a council with the chiefs and braves of the tribe. Keokuk, a fighter opposed to the band who had reoccupied Rock Island, was present, along with many other leaders. The house was nearly full when those Sauk in question arrived. They approached the meeting place "singing a war song, and armed with lances, spears, war clubs and bows and arrows, as if going to battle." But at the doorway, the leader, Black Hawk, paused. He wanted the room cleared of everyone except a few other Indian leaders. After all, he was the main reason for the gathering. When Gaines complied, Black Hawk entered.[21]

Black Hawk was born in 1767, and he led his life at the tribal village of Saukenak. At age fifteen, he scalped a member of the rival Osage and established himself as a warrior. Year after year, the men hunted for food and raided rival tribes while the women cultivated several hundred acres of fertile land that extended to the Mississippi River. His head plucked free of hair except for a scalp lock at the top, Black Hawk's name and appearance converged in his oval face and aquiline features. Even at age sixty-four, he looked stern and muscular.[22]

Major General Gaines addressed Black Hawk: "Your great Father at Washington is so much displeased with your conduct, that he will no longer suffer you to remain on the Rock River lands, & I have only to add that you must move off those lands."

Black Hawk answered that his people "were unanimous in their desire to remain in their old fields—That they wished to raise their corn & would do it peaceably, as they had no evil at heart against the whites; but there the Great Spirit had placed them long ago & now they had no desire to leave their homes."

Gaines became angry. "The Black Hawk," he declared, "has

received bad counsel & he has given bad counsel to his braves." "Who is he," he wondered, "that he should lead his people into difficulties? I have never heard of him as a Chief. . . . The world is wide enough for all of us: this is our part of it, & that [pointing west] is yours."

Black Hawk responded: "You asked, 'Who I am'—I am a Sauk; my fathers were great men, & I wish to remain where the bones of my fathers are laid. I desire to be buried with my fathers; why then should I leave their fields?"

Although his question remained unanswered, within several weeks Black Hawk consented to move across the river. The chiefs, especially his rival Keokuk, supported the migration, and the military forces arrayed against the tribe were formidable. On June 25, in anticipation of an assault by Illinois militia, Black Hawk and his followers deserted Saukenak during the night, a necessary action that left the warrior feeling humiliated. Once Gaines promised to provide provisions to get the tribe through the winter, Black Hawk signed the Articles of Agreement and Capitulation. "I touched the goosequill to this treaty," he recalled, "and was determined to live in peace."

But peace was not to be. Rumors spread that Illinois settlers were desecrating Indian graves. The Sauk felt the pinch of diminishing supplies of corn, and they became increasingly agitated over having been forced to flee their ancestral village. Believing that earlier treaties were fraudulent, and trusting the words of the prophet White Cloud, who envisioned the support of other tribes and even the British, with whom the Sauk fought in the War of 1812, Black Hawk, in the spring of 1832, recrossed the Mississippi.

The war to which his name was given lasted a few months. At first, Black Hawk and his several hundred followers confounded the efforts of the army of several thousand. Andrew Jackson became so dismayed that he dispatched General Winfield Scott to the region, but the cholera epidemic traveled west along with the soldiers and prevented them from having any impact on the course of the war. The raids and skirmishes went back and forth. At one point, some Indian scouts tried to surrender, but in the haze of mixed communications and suspicions they were killed when soldiers opened fire. On August 2, 1832, the war ended when forces slaughtered more than a hundred Indian men, women, and children at the Battle of Bad Axe. The next day, William Clark received word that "the Inds. were pushed literally into the Mississippi, the current of which was at one time perceptibly tinged with the blood of the Indians who were shot on its margin & in the stream." Two weeks later, Black Hawk, dressed in a new white deerskin outfit, surrendered.[23]

The prisoner was chained and transported down to Jefferson Barracks, near St. Louis. The lieutenant in charge was Jefferson Davis, whom Black Hawk praised as a "good and brave young chief." Also serving in the detail was Lieutenant Robert Anderson, who would one day become a national hero in the North by refusing to surrender Fort Sumter to a Confederate government headed by Davis. The lesson that allies could become enemies was one that Black Hawk knew all too well.

Incarcerated in St. Louis, Black Hawk received visitors who were curious to see the warrior and his fellow prisoners. One traveler who spent time with the Sauk was the artist George Catlin, who had arrived in St. Louis in 1830 "with the determination of reaching, ultimately, every tribe of Indians on the Continent of North America, and of bringing home faithful portraits of their principal personages, both men and women." Like so many men of his generation, Catlin had studied to become a lawyer, but he abandoned the courts for the canvas and set out to make his reputation and fortune with his paintbrush. He imagined the creation of a traveling, changing "*Gallery unique*, for the use and instruction of future ages," and he passed most of the decade among the tribes of the West. Catlin painted a portrait of Black Hawk in which the aged warrior appears dignified but despondent. The Sauk prisoners would soon be transported east, where they would be imprisoned in Virginia and then released to return to their new home west of the Mississippi.[24]

In the fall of 1831, while making plans for a journey up the Missouri River, Catlin met Pigeon's Egg Head, also known as Wi-jun-jon. The Assiniboine warrior was part of a delegation headed for Washington to visit Jackson. Catlin painted him in his "classic and exceedingly beautiful" native costume: "His leggings and shirt were of the mountain-goat skin, richly garnished with quills of the porcupine, and fringed with locks of scalps, taken from enemies' heads. Over these floated his long hair in plaits, that fell nearly to the ground; his head was decked with the war-eagle's plumes—his robe was of the skin of the young buffalo bull, richly garnished and emblazoned with the battles of his life."[25]

The following spring, Catlin and Wi-jun-jon met again on the steamboat traveling to the Yellowstone, and the Assiniboine's story, expressed in both word and image, served as the artist's cautionary tale about the fate of the Indians. Once in the East, Wi-jun-jon "travelled the giddy maze, and beheld amid the buzzing din of civil life, their tricks of art, their handiwork, and their finery; he visited their principal cities—he saw their forts, their ships, their great guns, steamboats,

12. George Catlin, *Black Hawk, a Prominent Sauk Chief* (Courtesy of the National Museum of American Art, Smithsonian Institution, Gift of Mrs. Joseph Harrison, Jr.)

13. George Catlin, *Pigeon's Egg Head (The Light) Going to and Returning from Washington* (Courtesy of the National Museum of American Art, Smithsonian Institution, Gift of Mrs. Joseph Harrison, Jr.)

balloons, &c. &c." He returned a changed man, and Catlin eventually painted a portrait, *Pigeon's Egg Head (The Light) Going to and Returning from Washington.* He went east a warrior and returned west a dandy, exchanging his native costume for a blue military outfit laced with gold and epaulettes, and donning a high-crown beaver hat, stiff-lace collar, white gloves, and high-heeled boots that made him "step like a yoked hog." Wi-jun-jon held an umbrella in one hand and a fan in the other, and from his pockets protruded flasks of whiskey. "In this fashion," reported Catlin, "was poor Wi-jun-jon metamorphosed, on his return from Washington; and, in this plight was he strutting and whistling Yankee Doodle, about the deck of the steamer winding its way up the mighty Missouri, and taking him to his native land again."

Wi-jun-jon's return to his people ended in tragedy. After he arrived home and "passed the usual salutations among his friends, he commenced the simple narration of scenes he had passed through, and of things he had beheld among the whites; which appeared to them so much like fiction, that it was impossible to believe them, and they set him down as an imposter." Wi-jun-jon fell into disgrace and drunkenness. As he unraveled, so did his outfit, until all that was left was his umbrella, which he always held in his hand. The stories he told about gaping multitudes and fabulous cities and "curious and wonderful machines" earned him a reputation among his people not only as a liar, but as a conjurer whose medicine was potent and evil. At last, a member of the tribe fitted the muzzle of his gun with an iron projectile made out of a pot handle and, while Wi-jun-jon was talking to a trader, came up behind the storyteller and "blew out his brains."

Civilization had destroyed the Indian not only by turning him to foppery and whiskey but by revealing scenes that, to the Indians of the West, could not possibly be true, though they were. Catlin drew out the moral for his listeners, readers, and viewers: "Thus ended the days and the greatness, and all the pride and hope of Wi-jun-jon, the Pigeon's Egg Head, a warrior and a brave of the valient Assinboins, who travelled eight thousand miles to see the President, and all the great cities of the civilized world; and who, for telling the *truth*, and *nothing but the truth*, was, after he got home, disgraced and killed for a wizard."

Catlin was not the only traveler to experience and document the fate of the North American Indians. On Christmas Day, on a steamboat heading down the Mississippi from Memphis to New Orleans, Alexis de Tocqueville recorded the "truly lamentable" scene of a group of

Choctaw being boarded for a journey to Arkansas: "The Indians came forward toward the shore with a despondent air; they first made the horses go, several of which, little accustomed to the forms of civilized life, took fright and threw themselves into the Mississippi, from which they could be pulled out only with difficulty. Then came the men, who, following their usual custom, carried nothing except their weapons; then the women, carrying their children attached to their backs or wrapped up in the blankets that covered them; they were, moreover, overburdened with loads that contained all their riches. Finally, the old people were led on. There was among them a woman of a hundred and ten years of age. I have never seen a more frightening figure. She was naked, with the exception of a blanket that allowed one to see, in a thousand places, the most emaciated body that one can imagine. She was escorted by two or three generations of grandchildren. To leave her country at that age to go seek her fate in a strange land, what misery! . . . There was, in the whole of this spectacle, an air of ruin and destruction, something that savored of a farewell that was final and with no return; no one could witness this without being sick at heart."

"The Americans of the United States," concluded Tocqueville, "more humane, more moderate, more respectful of law and legality, never bloodthirsty, are profoundly more destructive, and it is impossible to doubt that within a hundred years there will remain in North America, not a single nation, not even a single man belonging to the most remarkable of the Indian races."[26]

BANK OF THE UNITED STATES

The Indians were not Jackson's only enemy. With equal fervor, he sought to destroy the Bank of the United States. The Southeastern tribes and the Bank may seem like random pursuits, but for Jackson they were united in one crucial way: both stood as impediments to the interests of the states.

Congress chartered the First Bank of the United States in 1791. As envisioned by Alexander Hamilton, the Bank regulated the supply of currency by issuing bank notes redeemable in gold or silver, collected taxes, and served as the depository for all government funds. Private investors controlled the Bank, which was rooted in Philadelphia with branches located in other cities. The charter expired in 1811, and in 1816 a Second Bank of the United States, chartered for twenty years, began operations and started opening branches in major cities across the United States.

From the start, the Bank had its opponents. Local banks and state governments feared the centralizing, monopolizing powers of the Bank of the United States. Especially in the South and the West, where preferences ran to gold and silver rather than paper currency, local authorities dreaded the power of the Bank to control credit and currency and to engage in speculative practices. States began taxing branches of the Bank and challenged the constitutionality of the institution. The Bank fought back, and in *McCulloch* v. *Maryland* (1819), Justice Marshall declared that the states could not tax a branch of the federal government and that Congress, under the implied-powers clause, had the authority to create the institution. In 1821, the Bank moved into an opulent building, modeled after the Parthenon, with Doric and Ionic pillars imported from Italy. Two years later, Nicholas Biddle, a member of Philadelphia's social elite and a Pennsylvania state legislator, became president of the Bank and oversaw its expansion. In 1831, the bank issued nineteen million dollars in notes and had transactions of nearly fifty million in bills of exchange. Supporters praised it for providing a sound national currency, for efficiently handling deposits and transfers, and for supplying credit.

Jackson, from personal experiences as a land speculator that turned him against paper currency, and from political principles that made him hostile to remote, centralized authority, continued to oppose the Bank. Choosing to ignore John Marshall's ruling, he declared in his First Annual Message, "The constitutionality and the expediency of the law creating this bank are well questioned by a large portion of our fellow-citizens, and it must be admitted by all that it has failed in the great end of establishing a uniform and sound currency." A memo from an adviser informed Jackson that the bank was not only unconstitutional but also "dangerous to Liberty." It concentrated power in the hands of a few men who used their influence to create and destroy wealth, its stock was owned largely by foreigners, and it strengthened the national government at the expense of state governments. Again, in his Second Annual Message, on December 6, 1830, Jackson averred that "nothing has occurred to lessen in any degree the dangers which many of our citizens apprehend" from the Bank. He thought it should be reorganized and "shorn of the influence which makes that bank formidable."[27]

Events in 1831 would prove decisive for the fate of the Bank. Biddle eyed the coming storm, observing in January, "The President aims at the destruction of the bank." Throughout the year, arguments against the bank issued forth on a regular basis. An essay by George Bancroft, published in the *North American Review*, an influential journal of politics and opinion that generally sustained the doctrines of the National Republicans, dismayed bank supporters. Bancroft, a Democrat and a historian, suggested that "the body politic might enjoy excellent health even without the National Bank. . . . The sun would still rise and set, and the day be spent in its usual business, and merchandise be bought and sold, and bills of exchange be negotiated, even without a machine so vast" as the Bank of the United States. In another widely circulated pamphlet, a Boston merchant condemned the Bank as an "engine of influence" contrived by Hamilton's "monarchical party" to maintain influence and create private fortunes. The writer attacked the *McCulloch* decision and denounced the Bank as a monopolistic aggrandizement of power that was anathema to the democratic principles of the republic: "The Bank charter ought to have been pronounced unconstitutional by the Supreme Court. . . . If the principles laid down in deciding the *McCulloch* case are to prevail, the Constitution may mean any thing that Congress and the Supreme Court may choose to make it mean. . . . A monopoly is such an odious measure for pillaging the people—such a violation of natural right, that in this state of the world it will hardly be tolerated even in the most despotic countries."[28]

Selected voices in the Northeast, where the Bank had its most ardent supporters, raised suspicions about the institution, but a voice from the West launched a full-scale political assault. Born in North Carolina, Thomas Hart Benton acquired land in Tennessee before settling in Missouri. He gained influence as a newspaper editor and was soon elected as a senator. Because of his love of hard currency and hatred of paper money, opponents awarded him the derisive sobriquet "Old Bullion." On February 2, Benton rose in the Senate and blasted the Bank as "an institution too great and powerful to be tolerated in a government of free and equal laws." He denounced Biddle's Bank as embodying "a system of centralism, hostile to the federative principle of our Union, encroaching upon the wealth of the States, and organized upon a principle to give the highest effect to the greatest power." The Bank, by controlling the flow of currency, created and destroyed fortunes, made "the rich richer, and the poor poorer." It was no bank of the federal government, as the name might suggest, or even of the states, "but chiefly of private individuals, foreigners as well as natives." The Bank, Benton thundered, was "dangerous and pernicious to the Government and the people."[29]

The National Republicans, for whom the Bank served as a central component of any vision of American growth, still controlled the Senate, and when Webster asked for the yeas and nays, Benton's resolution against rechartering the Bank was defeated. But the rhetorical stakes had been raised, and throughout the year supporters issued encomiums for the Bank. Although Benton had used the language of class conflict in denouncing the Bank, Stephen Simpson, in his *Working Man's Manual*, defended the institution. The Bank, he thought, had healed the nation of its economic illness after the War of 1812, when panic gripped the country. The Bank "is the physician of our country: it has restored it to a sanative and vigorous state; and let us not prove ungrateful or unwise, by forfeiting its diploma, and despising its prescriptions." Simpson argued that the intentions of the framers should not matter in the debate over the constitutionality of the Bank: "Garments adapted to the limbs of a pigmy, would but ill suit the motions and colossal frame of a giant." Sounding more like the National Republican he became in 1831 when he closed down the *Mechanics' Free Press* and started the *Pennsylvania Whig* in opposition to Jackson, Simpson insisted that the Bank's accumulation of capital was not to be feared but, rather, "instead of creating a monied aristocracy, it opens wide the door to the diffusion of capital, and promotes equality of fortune, competition in business, and republican habits."[30]

A more authoritative voice in favor of the Bank was Albert Gallatin's. Newly appointed president of John Jacob Astor's National Bank, Gallatin had served as secretary of the Treasury under Jefferson and Madison. It was Gallatin who, as a congressman from Pennsylvania, proposed the creation of a standing committee on finance, the influential Ways and Means Committee. The Bank of the United States used Gallatin's *Considerations on the Currency and Banking System* as a promotional pamphlet, though Gallatin—unlike Webster, who was on retainer—refused any payment from Biddle. Both experience and theory, urged Gallatin, demonstrated the pivotal role of the Bank of the United States. The Bank provided a uniform currency, eased the government's fiscal operations, afforded security in all transactions, and provided stability in times of crisis. The country could no more get along without a national bank than could a farmer without a barn. The issue came down to one of nationalism versus localism, and Gallatin defended a national bank in preference to the proliferation of state banks that had followed the dissolution of the First Bank of the United States. State banks offered no security, failed frequently, suspended specie payment regularly, were often improperly administered, and destroyed the uniformity of currency. The complaints of state banks that the Bank of the United States checked their activities bemused Gallatin, who pointed out, "It was for that very purpose that the bank was established." Comparing the resources of state banks with the Bank of the United States, Gallatin concluded that they had no legitimate claim of excessive restraint or abuse on the part of the Bank of the United States. Simply put, the Bank had proved itself indispensable to the political economy of the nation.

Jackson remained impervious to arguments in favor of the Bank, but the dissolution of his Cabinet and appointment of a new secretary of the Treasury held out some promise of a compromise. Louis McLane, a former chairman of the Ways and Means Committee and minister to England, was a friend of Biddle's and a supporter of the Bank. In an attempt to resolve the looming controversy over recharter, he proposed saving the Bank by selling the government's stock in the institution (some seventy thousand shares, worth eight million dollars) and applying the proceeds toward paying off the national debt of twenty-four million. Jackson seemed intrigued by the idea and understood that, with the public debt retired, the administration could reduce tariff duties and in so doing neutralize the nullifiers in South Carolina. Asserting that McLane's proposal still left him "free and uncommitted," Jackson praised his secretary of the Treasury. McLane told Biddle that the president had agreed to a plan that would preserve the Bank. McLane had proved so successful that a draft of Jackson's annual message made almost no mention of the Bank and even suggested that the issue should be left to Congress to decide. Attorney General Roger Taney objected that citizens would think that the president had reversed himself on the issue. The revised message delivered to Congress simultaneously reasserted the "opinions heretofore expressed" while leaving the subject to "an investigation of an enlightened people and their representatives."

Bank supporters were thrilled. McLane's own annual report unabashedly supported rechartering the Bank, and Jackson seemed amenable to an agreement that would allow the institution to survive. To be sure, McLane's report outraged opponents of the Bank, who accused the president of vacillating. Jackson defended himself against the accusation that he had changed his views. Two weeks after delivering his annual message, he wrote, "I have uniformly on all proper occasions held the same language in regard to that institution: that it has failed to answer the ends for which it was created, and besides being unconstitutional . . . it is on the score of mere expediency dangerous to liberty." The matter might have rested here, with rhetoric flying but a tacit agreement in place to allow, in due course, a discussion of the rechartering of the Bank. But Biddle made a fateful decision that assured the result he most dreaded. Rather than take cover, he decided at year's end to apply early for recharter.[31]

After the fact, Biddle undoubtedly spent many an anxious day reflecting on his decision in December to seek renewal for the Bank's recharter. As of November, the information before him suggested that he should wait until after the election of 1832. McLane personally told Biddle that forcing the issue of recharter now would be perceived by the president as a political maneuver aimed at derailing his re-election, and for that reason alone he would veto it. Others warned Biddle not to press Jackson into a corner, especially since he seemed to be wavering in his opposition to the Bank. "If you apply now," McLane warned, "you assuredly will fail,—if you wait, you will as certainly succeed."[32]

Others, however, encouraged Biddle to act. A representative from Virginia predicted that Jackson's re-election was "as certain as his life" and that his influence over Congress would only increase. Why not apply now, when Calhoun, the vice-president, George McDuffie, the chair of the Ways and Means Committee, and McLane, the secretary of the Treasury, all supported recharter? Henry Clay argued that "if *now* called upon he would not negative the bill." And Daniel Webster urged that "*it is* expedient for the Bank to apply for the renewal of its Charter without delay." They believed that Jackson would not veto a recharter bill in an election year but he would once re-elected.[33]

Biddle should have known better. The men advising him all hated Jackson and were seeking to turn the upcoming election into a contest. McLane had worked hard to gain a compromise and warned repeatedly that the president would take a premature application for recharter "as an act of hostility," and would veto it "even if certain that he would thereby lose the Election." But Biddle ignored the warnings and, in January 1832, supporters in the Senate and House moved for the recharter of the Bank of the United States.[34]

For six months, anti-Bank Democrats assailed the institution and pro-Bank forces defended it. Supporters of recharter undoubtedly thought they had clinched the argument over constitutionality when they circulated a letter from James Madison, the last of the framers, in which he supported the Bank and declared that a veto from the executive would violate "all the obligations derived from a course of precedents amounting to the requisite evidence of a national judgment and intention." Opponents, however, held the father of the Constitution to his original opinion, expressed in 1791, when he opposed the Bank of the United States as unauthorized. The oscillating arguments grew familiar and stale, but the passions intensified. Declaring it a "hydra-headed monster," Jackson told Van Buren, "The Bank . . . is trying to kill me, but I will kill it." He was true to his word. In early summer, Congress passed a bill for recharter. Jackson responded with the most powerful weapon in his presidential arsenal: on July 10, 1832, he vetoed the bill.[35]

In killing the bank, Jackson offered justifications that terrified his political opponents. His veto message repudiated the doctrine that the Supreme Court decided issues of constitutionality. Arguing that the

14. "The Downfall of Mother Bank," 1833 (Courtesy of the American Antiquarian Society)

executive as well as Congress had as much obligation and right as the judiciary to determine constitutional questions, Jackson declared that the "authority of the Supreme Court must not be permitted to control the Congress or the Executive." Jackson condemned the Bank not only as unconstitutional, but also as corrupt and antirepublican. Appealing to nationalistic urgings, he denounced the Bank as an instrument of foreign domination. "Every impulse of American feeling admonishes that it should be purely American," he declared. The powers of the Bank were "dangerous to the Government and country." They exacerbated inequality and favored the rich over the poor, the powerful over the weak. By adding artificial distinctions of titles, gratuities, and exclusive privileges to the natural ones that already existed, the Bank, through the government, made "the rich richer and the potent more powerful," leaving "the humble members of society— the farmers, mechanics, and laborers"—the victims of governmental injustice. The Bank invaded the rights of common citizens and the rights of states: "In thus attempting to make our General Government strong we make it weak. Its true strength consists in leaving individuals and States as much as possible to themselves—in making itself felt, not in its power, but in its beneficence; not in its control, but in its protection; not in binding the States more closely to the center, but leaving each to move unobstructed in its proper orbit."[36]

For only the tenth time, a president had employed the veto; almost never before had it been used for an issue of national importance, and never was it justified in this way. The framers had envisioned a delicate balance of power between Court, Congress, and executive. If Marshall had earlier in the century bolstered the Court by developing the doctrine of judicial review, Jackson now sought to strengthen the executive, not only by denying the Court an exclusive right to judge constitutional matters but by declaring that the president could freely decide questions of state on any grounds he saw fit. Jackson's veto breathed the language of equality, yet made the presidency more autocratic; it celebrated the American nation, but seemed to give comfort to those who favored the local over the national, state government over federal government. The veto "has all the fury of a chained panther biting the bars of his cage," proclaimed Biddle, who pretended to be delighted with the extremism of it because he hoped the act would bring Jackson down: "It is really a manifesto of anarchy—such as Marat or Robespierre might have issued to the mob of the faubourg St. Antoine: and my hope is that it will contribute to relieve the country from the dominion of these people."[37]

Jackson's veto of the recharter of the Bank, and subsequent removal of government deposits, destroyed the institution and led his opponents to coalesce into a new political organization, the Whig Party. But Biddle's judgment that Jackson's actions would cost him reelection proved as faulty as his decision to apply early for rechartering. The Democratic press celebrated the president as a slayer of monsters, and the only votes the veto cost him were those he was not going to receive anyhow. Jackson's opposition to the national bank, however, inevitably encouraged those opposed to other national policies. In emphasizing the prerogatives of states over the federal government, the veto message further emboldened Southerners, particularly South Carolinians, who felt aggrieved by the tariff policy of the federal government and demanded relief from what they viewed as excessive duties on imports. The conflict over free trade versus protective tariffs was the single most contentious political issue of the day. It divided state against nation and, through the doctrine of nullification, led the country toward the brink of dissolution.

NULLIFICATION

"The Tariff is the great subject upon which the eyes of the public are turned," declared a North Carolina Superior Court judge at the end of the year. Indeed, from the beginning of the republic, the tariff question had generated considerable controversy. The Tariff of 1789, introduced by James Madison, raised concerns over whether the Constitution allowed the government to impose tariffs for any reason other than revenue. If such a tariff were intended, for example, to protect the growth of American industries by placing duties on imported items, it might stand outside of congressional authority. In 1790, even before Alexander Hamilton submitted his Report on Manufactures advocating a protective tariff, one proponent of free trade warned that such a tariff would lead to "a dissolution of the Union."[38]

The Tariff of 1789 passed, as did tariffs in 1816 and 1824. Not only were tariff rates increasing, but so too was the variety of products included for protection: woolens, iron, lead, glass, hemp, and salt. Southerners felt particularly aggrieved. The tariff seemed to protect Northern industries at the expense of Southern agriculture. Cotton growers in particular feared that, in retaliation for a tariff, English manufacturers would reduce their imports from the South and develop alternative markets. Furthermore, tariffs meant increased prices for the variety of consumer goods purchased by Southerners. The Tariff of 1828 raised rates even higher, toward 50 percent of the value of imported goods, and Southerners condemned it as an "abomination." The price of cotton had plummeted from thirty-one cents per pound in 1818 to eight cents in 1831. Ignoring other factors, such as the simultaneous increase in production (from four hundred thousand bales to over a million), Southerners blamed their economic woes on the tariff, which seemed to act as a form of indirect taxation on the South for the benefit of the North. It also seemed to pose an assault upon slavery. After all, the slave economy produced cotton for export, and any measure that affected the price of the staple had an impact upon the stability of the institution. Furthermore, in the context of slave unrest and antislavery activism, Southerners increasingly worried that the power to impose tariffs and the power to attack slavery were one and the same.

Thomas Hamilton, visiting from England, noted that the Tariff of 1828 "inflicted a deep wound on the stability of the Union. The seeds of dissension among the different States had long been diffused, and now began to exhibit signs of rapid and luxuriant growth." Doubly odious to Southerners was the lack of respect accorded their position against the tariff. On February 2, the novelist Catherine Sedgwick happened to attend a session of the House in which members debated reducing the duty on salt. "Some Southern members spoke with great vehemence," she noted, "but nobody on the floor paid any attention to them. They spoke of their oppression, of throwing themselves on the Sovereignty of the States, of being goaded to rebellion, of the time being near when 'vengeance should stalk about those halls.' It was melancholy to see such feelings aroused among our countrymen, and more painful to see them quite disregarded."[39]

In opposition to the tariff, Southerners advanced the doctrine of nullification. Godfrey Vigne defined the term for readers of his *Six Months in America*: "A nullifier is a person who holds that the federal constitution is merely a compact or league between the several states; and that each state has a right to decide for itself concerning the infractions of that league by the federal government, and to nullify and declare void an act of the federal congress within its limits." With passage of the tariff of abominations in 1828, talk of nullification ignited, and Southern statesmen, especially in South Carolina, kept the fire blazing. Declaring that "the principles of free trade are the principles of human liberty," James Hamilton, a rice planter who would serve as governor of South Carolina from 1830 to 1832, denounced the tariff for making the Palmetto State a decaying wilderness, whereas once it had been a bustling empire. The only way to offset the political power of "the despotic majority that oppresses us," Hamilton proclaimed, was to build upon the reserved rights of the states to nullify an act of Congress. No less an authority than Jefferson, in the Virginia and Kentucky Resolutions of 1798, proclaimed that, when the federal government assumes "powers that have not been delegated, a nullification of the act is the rightful remedy." In Hamilton's hands, Jefferson's words became an even stronger expression of states' rights: "That the several States who formed the Constitution being sovereign and independent, have the unquestionable right to judge its infractions; and that NULLIFICATION by those sovereignties of all unauthorized acts, done under colour of that instrument, is the *rightful remedy*."[40]

The South Carolina legislature adopted an *Exposition and Protest* against the tariff. Though it was published anonymously, by the following year rumor had it that John C. Calhoun, the newly elected vice-president from South Carolina, had authored the manifesto. In the *Exposition and Protest*, Calhoun argued that, constitutionally, the power of Congress to pass protective tariffs was neither expressly granted nor necessary and proper for putting its powers into effect. The effect of the tariff was to divide the nation into sections. In any discussion of it, Calhoun announced, "it will be impossible to avoid . . . the use of sectional language." Quite simply, he argued, the tariff favored Northern manufacturing interests at the expense of Southern agricultural producers and transferred wealth toward one region and away from another. "We export to import," explained Calhoun, and tariffs, which raised the prices on imported goods in order to protect nascent Northern industries, cost Southerners dearly. The effect "is to compel us to purchase at a higher price" goods from both domestic and foreign markets "without receiving a corresponding increase of price for what we sell." "We are not permitted to consume the fruits of our labor," declared Calhoun, but "through an artful and complex system, in violation of every principle of justice they are transferred to others."

Having emphasized the economic effects of the tariff, Calhoun went on to discuss how the protective system acted "to corrupt the government and destroy the liberties of the country." Government, he thought, must balance the various interests of its constituents regardless of size or strength. If it failed to do so, if it succumbed to the principle of majority rule, it could not preserve liberty. "An unchecked majority, is a despotism—and government is free, and will be permanent in proportion to the number, complexity and efficiency of the checks, by which its powers are controlled." One such check, the *Exposition* insisted, was "the constitutional right of the States to interpose in order to protect their powers." "Interposition" was another word for "nullification," and South Carolina threatened to use this power to protect itself against the tariff, which it viewed as "unconstitutional, oppressive, and unjust." "The time is coming," warned one Southern editor, "when the true theory of this Constitution is to be brought to its test. If it fails, then clouds and darkness rest upon us. The Union itself may pass under one of the deepest Eclipses which has ever obscured it."[41]

"Carolina fever," as one observer labeled nullification, was infectious and potentially fatal to the survival of the Union. Statesmen such as James Madison labored to find a remedy. Madison, eighty years of age in 1831, was the last surviving oracle of the nation's founding. Time and again writers solicited his opinion on constitutional questions, and time and again, although describing himself as "decrepit and feeble," he wrote lengthy letters explicating the meaning of the Constitution. Acknowledging that "doubts and difficulties should occur in expounding" upon the document, Madison defended the constitutionality of the tariff. Article I, Section 8, gave Congress the power to "lay and collect taxes, duties, imposts, and excises" and "to regulate commerce with foreign nations." That power was intended not only to raise revenue but also to impose duties so as to encourage the development of American manufactures. Besides, "as a cause of the general sufferings of the country . . . the tariff . . . has been vastly overrated." Increased production led to reduced crop prices just as the availability of inexpensive Western lands depressed property values. The tariff was not to blame.[42]

Madison not only defended protective tariffs as constitutional, but also denounced nullification as an "absurdity" and a "heresy." "Who could, at that day, have foreseen some of the comments on the Constitution advanced at the present," he lamented. In a published letter, he explained that the United States government was neither a consolidated nor a confederated entity but a mixture "formed by the States— that is, by the people in each of the States, acting in their highest sovereign capacity. . . . It cannot be altered or annulled at the will of the States individually." The Constitution, he explained, was "adopted as a whole" and could only be altered by the votes of three-fourths of the states. Madison repeatedly sought to "rescue the resolutions of Kentucky in '98–'99, from the misconstruction of them," and to defend their author, Jefferson, from being portrayed as the intellectual father of nullification. That Jefferson "ever asserted a right in a single State to arrest the execution of an act of Congress," shrieked Madison, "is countenanced by nothing known to have been said or done by him." It bewildered him that South Carolinians argued that the Virginia Resolutions of 1798 furnished a precedent for the idea that a single state could nullify an act of the United States when such a notion was contradicted by proof from the time and never countenanced by the state, then or now. "In *every* instance in those proceedings," testified Madison, "where the *ultimate* right of the States to interpose is alluded to, the *plural* term *States* has been used; the term State, as a single party, being invariably avoided."[43]

Madison's defense of the tariff and opposition to nullification did not stop those who tried to use the Founding Father to justify their purposes. Opponents of federal authority even claimed that Madison supported the right to secede from the Union, a step beyond nullification. The exasperated Virginian wrote in response, "I know not whence the idea could proceed that I concurred in the doctrine. . . . Take the linch-pins from a carriage, and how soon would a wheel be off its axle." The idea that disunion was preferable to union perplexed him: "If the States cannot live together in harmony under the auspices of such a Government as exists, and in the midst of blessings such as have been the fruits of it, what is the prospect threatened by the abolition of a common Government, with all the rivalships, collisions, and animosities inseparable from such an event?"[44]

Whatever Madison, a former president, thought, it was the opinions of Jackson, the current president, that mattered. But disappointment awaited any South Carolinian who hoped that Jackson would oppose the tariff because he had declared the Bank of the United States unconstitutional and vetoed the Maysville Road Bill, which would have appropriated federal funds to construct a road in Kentucky, on the grounds that it would lead to "the destruction of state rights." Jackson, the hero of the Battle of New Orleans, was an ardent nationalist when it came to the progress of the country, and he had consistently supported protective duties. Voting as a senator in favor of the Tariff of

1824, he explained that, as long as it "embraces the design of fostering, protecting, and preserving within ourselves the means of national defense and independence, particularly in a state of war, I would advocate and support it." As South Carolina's opposition to the Tariff of 1828 intensified, Jackson never wavered from supporting its constitutionality ("the States have delegated their whole authority over imposts to the General Government without limitation or restriction"). As president, he called for a "judicious" and "expedient" modification of tariff rates, but he defended the government's policy against attack.[45]

Jackson believed that the reduction of duties would "annihilate the Nullifiers as they will be left without any pretext of Complaint." "If they attempt disunion," reasoned Jackson, "it must be because they wish it, and have only indulged in their vituperations against the Tariff for the purpose of covertly accomplishing their ends." Jackson had always made it clear that, though he would oppose "all encroachments upon the legitimate sphere of State sovereignty," he would defend the preservation of the union at all costs. When the attorney general for South Carolina declined to bring suit against two merchants who refused to pay duties on imported goods, Jackson considered impeaching him for malfeasance and condemned "all who are engaged in this act of intended Treason against our Government. . . . *The union shall be preserved.*" Jackson justified his decision to run for re-election on the belief that "it is *now* necessary for the preservation of the Union." In February, he explained to Robert Hayne, senator from South Carolina, that he never believed "that a state has the power to nulify the Legislative enactments of the General Government." "In all Republics," he declared, "the voice of a majority must prevail; oppose it, and disagreement, difference and danger will certainly follow. [A]ssert that a state may declare acts passed by congress inoperative and void, and revolution with all of its attendant evils in the end must be looked for and expected."[46]

Discussions of the tariff and nullification led commentators to ponder whether the United States could survive as a nation. Embedded in these issues ran the fault lines along which the republic would either develop or crumble: federal versus state power, the meanings of the Constitution, the future direction of the nation, and the tensions between majority rule and minority dissent. The traveler Thomas Hamilton invited readers to "look for a moment at this Union. In Florida and Louisiana they grow sugar; in Maine there is scarcely sun enough to ripen a crop of maize. The people of these States are no less different than the productions of their soil. They are animated by no sentiment of brotherhood and affinity. Nature has divided them by a distance of two thousand miles; the interests of one are neither understood nor cared for in the other. In short, they are connected by nothing but a clumsy and awkward piece of machinery, most felicitously contrived to deprive both of the blessing of self-government. What is gained by this? A certain degree of strength, undoubtedly, but not more than might be produced by an alliance between independent States, unaccompanied by that jealousy and conflict of opposing interests, which is the present curse of the whole Union."

Not only were Americans unattached to the Union, thought Hamilton, they were barely attached to their immediate region: "An American is not a being of strong *local* attachments, and the slightest temptation of profit is always strong enough to induce him to quit his native State, and break all the ties which are found to operate so powerfully upon other men." No wonder that in a matter of ten years, observed J. M. Peck, author of a best-selling guide for emigrants to the West, "what was then frontier, is now thrown into the middle of States and Territories." Under such conditions of mobility, restlessness, and rootlessness, few observers believed that a nation such as the United States could remain knitted together.[47]

Tocqueville also had his doubts about the republic's survival. Time and again he observed that Americans had little attachment to the country as a whole. In one conversation he told a citizen, "Your country is composed of little, almost entirely separate nations." "That is even truer than you realize," replied the informant. "Not only does each State form a nation, but each town in the State is a little nation. Each ward of a town is a little nation and has its own particular interests, government, representatives, in a word its own political life."

Among Americans as a people, Tocqueville observed, "restless-ness of character seems to me to be one of the distinctive traits." A for-mer American diplomat explained: "The land never stays in the hands of the one who clears it. When it begins to yield a crop, the pioneer sells it and again plunges into the forest. It would seem that the habit of changing place, of turning things upside down, of cutting, of destroy-ing, has become a necessity of his existence." The American, thought Tocqueville, cares only for himself: he is "devoured by the longing to make his fortune; it is the passion of his life; he has no memory that attaches him to one place more than another, no inveterate habits, no spirit of routine; he is the daily witness of the swiftest changes of for-tune, and is less afraid than any other inhabitant of the globe to risk what he has gained in the hope of a better future." America, he declared, presented "the spectacle of a society marching along all alone, without guide or support, by the sole fact of the cooperation of individual wills. In spite of anxiously searching for the government, one can find it nowhere, and the truth is that it does not, so to speak, exist at all."[48]

Tocqueville would take the undigested interviews and insights of his journey in 1831 and transform them into a penetrating analysis of an American democracy characterized by individualism, self-interest, and solitude. He observed that "the Union has never shown so much weakness as on the celebrated question of the tariff." The reason it aroused such intense political passion, he believed, was that "tariffs favor or harm, not opinions only, but very powerful material interests." Beaumont noted that "the sole interest which absorbs the attention of every mind is *trade*. It's the *national passion*." "Money is the god of the United States," he proclaimed. The "passion to get rich," wrote Tocqueville, "leads and dominates all the others." No wonder, then, that the tariff debate might prove fatal to the nation.[49]

The inflammatory arguments over protection troubled Tocque-ville, and he was equally disturbed by a call on the part of opponents of the tariff for a free-trade convention to condemn the government's policy. Tocqueville initially saw such conventions as an assault upon the operations of legitimate government and an expression of the sovereignty of the people run amok. He believed that popular conventions challenged the rule of law and threatened public order. But by the time he returned to France and completed *Democracy in America*, he had changed his mind. Voluntary associations and political conventions, he came to believe, tied together otherwise disconnected citizens and served as a check by minority interests upon the power of majorities.

The Free Trade Convention met in Philadelphia between September 30 and October 7. The idea for the convention had emerged only three months earlier, when Henry Sedgwick of Massachusetts and New York issued a call for such a gathering. "There is a danger," he warned, "that the restrictive system, under the delusive name of the American system may be fixed upon the nation as its permanent policy. . . . The country is in a state of thick darkness upon this subject of almost vital importance." Carried by the press from Maine to New Orleans, the proposal generated excitement across the nation. When the convention opened at the Musical Fund Hall, more than 150 delegates from fifteen states gathered to discuss ways of "procuring the repeal of the Restrictive System." Among the delegates were Albert Gallatin from New York, Thomas Dew from Virginia, and Thomas Pinckney from South Carolina.

Though the delegates agreed that the tariff was oppressive, other issues threatened to divide them. Initially, they could not decide whether to vote as states or individuals. To vote as states would equalize the disparity in representation. For example, more than forty delegates came from South Carolina, whereas eighteen came from Massachusetts. But because the effects of the tariff were sectional in nature, delegates feared that voting by state would place local interests above the general principle of free trade that they had come to reaffirm. Furthermore, a collective vote would deny the opportunity of members within a state delegation to voice their own opinions, thus reproducing within the convention the very tyranny of the majority to which they objected. This issue alone took up much of the first day, until a delegate reminded the body that they need not continue to debate the question of voting by individual or state, because "this body was not a Congress, but a voluntary meeting." With that, they unanimously elected Philip Barbour of Virginia the president of the convention and moved on to drafting an "Address to the People of the United States."

The text of the address, however, also caused consternation. Delegates disagreed on whether or not Congress had the power to pass protective tariffs. Two South Carolinians argued vehemently that the unconstitutionality of the tariff was the "chief objection among his constituents. They can no where find, in the Constitution, an express authority given to Congress by the people of the States, to encourage manufactures by taxation." But Albert Gallatin strenuously objected and declared he could not vote for the address if it included a statement objecting to the tariff as unconstitutional. The problem, he insisted, was not constitutionality but "the effect of the Tariff on different sections of the country, . . . its unavoidable tendency to demoralize the community, and gradually to alienate the affections of a whole section of these United States." The motion to strike out that part of the address that referred to constitutional issues was defeated, 159 to 35.

The brief address reiterated arguments that were becoming familiar. Referring to the nation as a confederacy, the document explained that the Free Trade Convention brought together "numerous, respectable, and intelligent" citizens "to consider the grievances which they suffer under the existing Tariff of duties." As advocates of free trade, delegates affirmed "the unquestionable right of every individual to apply his labor and capital in the mode which he may conceive best calculated to promote his own interest." They deprecated protective tariffs as a "system of taxation, which is unequal in its operation, oppressive, and unjust." Delegates also challenged the right of the government to create such a system: "They do not doubt—they utterly deny—the constitutional power of Congress to enact it." The tariff system, which was "grossly, fatally unwise and impolitic, since it is subversive of the harmony of the Union—which is in violation of the principles of free government, and utterly at variance with the spirit of justice and mutual concession, . . . such a system, if persevered in, must alienate our affections from each other, engender discontents and animosities, and lead, inevitably, and with a force which no human power can resist, to the most awful of calamities."[50]

By the end of October, a rival convention of those who supported the tariff met in New York. Calling themselves the Friends of Domestic Industry, several hundred delegates from thirteen states gathered in the Hall of the Quarter Sessions. The leaders of the convention included Alexander Everett from Massachusetts, James Tallmadge from New York, Mathew Carey from Pennsylvania, and Hezekiah Niles from Maryland. Everett, the brother of Representative Edward Everett, edited the *North American Review* and was a staunch defender of the principles of protection against those of laissez-faire. Tallmadge had gained national attention in 1819 when he proposed an amendment, passed in the House but defeated in the Senate, to forbid slavery in Missouri. Carey's renown as an editor and writer dated back to the Revolution, and he continued to issue a steady stream of essays supporting American manufactures and denouncing free trade and nullification. Niles used his position in Baltimore as editor of *Niles' Weekly Register* to promote economic nationalism in the upper South. One participant likened the delegates at the Free Trade and Tariff Conventions to dueling forces representing sectional interests: "The assembling of the Free Trade Convention at Philadelphia, may be regarded as the first movement of the Free Trade *Army* upon the enemy's country. The Tariff Convention at New York was the rally of the Northern Forces upon finding their territory invaded."[51]

The "Address of the Friends of Domestic Industry" defended protective tariffs as constitutional. They warned that the abolition of tariffs and embrace of free-trade principles would lead the nation toward "ruin and despair." It has been "the constant interpretation of the Constitution" that Congress has the power to use tariffs not only for revenue but for the protection of domestic industrial enterprises. The earliest legislation of the government avowed such measures, and every president and Congress since has reaffirmed them. It confounded the delegates that some Americans professed that such a power did not exist: "It is not only against the words of the Constitution, against the manifest design of the nation in establishing it, against the uniform sense of Congress in passing laws under it, against the practice of forty years, never stayed nor suspended, against the opinion of every tribunal in the country . . . but it is also against the entire conviction of a vast majority of the people themselves, that these new and what we think dangerous opinions, are now brought forward as the true doctrines of the constitution."[52]

As a matter of political economy, compared to constitutional authority, protective tariffs were equally unimpeachable. The tariff "constitutes the American System. It invites the application of American capital to stimulate American industry. It imposes a restriction, in the form of an impost duty, on certain products of *foreign* labour, but so far as relates to *American* capital, or *American* labour, it simply offers security an inducement to the one, and gives energy and vigour to the other." Within a nation, free trade provides great advantages. But between foreign nations "there is no free trade—there never was—there never can be." Noting that the cry of oppression came predominantly from the South, the address argued that it was not the tariff but the acquisition of fertile lands that had depreciated Southern property values. Furthermore, the Southern "aversion to manufactures has engendered, of late, bitter local prejudices in parts of those states in which they do not flourish." Simply put, defenders of the tariff believed that Southern economic problems would have been alleviated had the region manufactured goods instead of specious arguments against the tariff.

Neither the Free Trade nor the Domestic Industry Convention ever referred to nullification, but the word hovered over the nation like dark clouds on a summer's day. Even as plans went forth for these conventions, which were intended to provide a forum for reasoned discussion and public remonstrance and an opportunity for minority opinions to be voiced, some South Carolinians took strides toward disunion. On May 19, at a public dinner, Representative George McDuffie delivered a blistering speech, "a red hot thunder and lightning speech of six hours length," that denounced the tariff and defended nullification. McDuffie, who had once espoused a doctrine of American nationalist growth and carried a bullet near his spine from a duel over the issue a decade earlier, now proclaimed that nullification "flows from a higher source" than the Constitution. He denounced as "unequal," "oppressive," "unjust," and "iniquitous" a system of taxation that reduced the South to "colonial vassalage." He feared not for personal liberty but for property rights, which the revenue power of the federal government assailed by imposing tariffs that were "ruinous to our interests, in order to build up the prosperity of other States at our expense." The prosperity of the North and the decay of the South, McDuffie thundered, resulted from a federal tax on cotton that was equal to "one third of our incomes," and this very tax was "transferred as a bounty to Northern labour and . . . Northern industry." Denouncing the government as "an upstart, mercenary aristocracy of absentee landlords" who imposed a "heartless and irresponsible tyranny," McDuffie demanded the interposition of some power to relieve Southerners from their oppression.

That power, offered McDuffie, was nullification: "The people of South Carolina are subject to the laws of Congress, provided they be authorized by the Constitution; but with no propriety of language can it be said that the State, the sovereign State of South Carolina is subject to Congress, or to any human power." McDuffie mocked those who cried, "The Union, the Union, the Union is in danger." The "phantom of disunion, civil war, and fraternal bloodshed" was conjured up by tyrants seeking to maintain power. "The idea of bloodshed and civil war, in a contest of this kind," thought McDuffie, "is utterly ridiculous. How would the war commence? Who would begin it, and what would be the occasion or the pretext of using arms? I confess I am utterly at a loss to imagine." And if the Union were in danger, whose fault was it, that of the oppressor or the oppressed? "The Union, such as the majority have made it," concluded McDuffie, "is a foul monster, which those who worship, after seeing its deformity, are those worthy of their chains." Likening South Carolina's position to that of the

colonies as a "glorious example before us," McDuffie inquired, "Shall
we be terrified by mere phantoms of blood, when our ancestors, for less
cause, encountered the dreadful reality? Great God! Are we the
descendants of those ancestors; are we freemen; are we men?"[53]

It was not only what McDuffie said but how he said it. His manner
demanded attention. He "hesitates and stammers; he screams and
bawls; he thumps and stumps like a mad man in Bedlam," offered one
observer. Charleston and Washington were abuzz after McDuffie spoke.
It seemed that the state was moving decidedly toward nullification, and
for Democrats who wished to challenge Jackson for the presidency,
such a doctrine meant political suicide. Duff Green, who as editor of
the *United States Telegraph* once supported Jackson but now opposed
the administration, denounced the speech as "unexcusable folly and
deliberate madness" and condemned nullification as a word "more
odious to me than any other in our Language." He thought its extremism "has done more than Daniel Webster & Henry Clay could do to
confirm the tariff & elevate Clay." Green warned Calhoun that if he
had any hopes of challenging Jackson "you [must] seize the first occasion to separate yourself" from McDuffie's remarks. Calhoun understood that people "cannot view the doctrine of nullification as it exists
in South Carolina in any other light than as a revolutionary measure."[54]

The vice-president knew that the time had come to state his position publicly. Isolated within the administration, he denounced the
president as "too ignorant, too suspicious & too weak to conduct our
affairs successfully" and acknowledged that "every connection personal & political" with Jackson "is rescinded." Jackson, for his part,
goaded Calhoun to declare himself. In a letter to a South Carolina
unionist group, he warned against "distinguished citizens . . . pursuing
a course of redress through any other than constitutional means." Privately, Calhoun affirmed, "Our State right doctrines ought to be man-
fully supported." "Whether I am a nullifier, or not," he wrote in May,
"will depend on the meaning to be attached to the word. If it means a
disunionist, a disorganizer or an anarchist, then so far from being in
favour of nullification, I am utterly opposed to it. . . . But, if the term

means one, who believes that the General Government originated with the people of the States . . . and that the Constitution is in fact a compact between the States in that character, and that, as parties to it, they have the right to interpose to arrest the violation of the compact, in cases of palpable and deliberate violations of it, then am I, to the full extent, a nullifier & always have been."

Driven by presidential ambition, cornered by McDuffie's speech, and propelled by his position as South Carolina's leading statesman, Calhoun placed in the *Pendleton* (South Carolina) *Messenger* a statement of his views on nullification. Throughout early August, newspapers reprinted the vice-president's letter. Writing from his home at Fort Hill, Calhoun finally, inevitably, and fatally defended the doctrine of which he was part progenitor: "The Constitution of the United States is in fact a compact, to which each state is a party . . . and . . . the several States or parties, have a right to judge of its infractions, and in cases of deliberate, palpable, and dangerous exercise of power not delegated, they have the right, in the last resort, to use the language of the Virginia resolutions '*to interpose for arresting the progress of the evil, and for maintaining within their respective limits, the authorities, rights and liberties appertaining to them.*' This right of interposition, thus solemnly asserted by the State of Virginia, be it called what it may, State right, veto, nullification, or by any other name, I conceive to be the fundamental principle of our system, resting on facts historically as certain, as our Revolution itself, and deductions, as simple and demonstrative, as that of any political, or moral truth whatever."[55]

Planters such as James Hammond, who supported nullification, believed that Calhoun's essay made "everything as clear as a sunbeam," but the light it cast fell unevenly across the nation. Try as he might to justify nullification by invoking Jefferson, by calling it different names, by presenting it not as revolutionary or anarchical but as "the only solid foundation of our system, and of our Union," Calhoun had crossed a line, one that divided South from North and, in 1831 at least, South Carolina from the rest of the region. Georgians, unwilling to alienate a president who supported their efforts to rid the state of the Cherokee, refused to support nullification. And Virginians, though divided regionally and led by Governor Floyd—who supported nullification, despised Jackson, and carried South Carolina in the presidential election of 1832—remained "anti-tariff, anti-Bank, and anti-Nullification." Calhoun's paeans to union and nation could not mask the obvious truth that nullification meant disunion. "To commit the administration of this government to the hands of a *nullifier*," thought a contributor to the *United States Gazette*, "would be to send the lamb to the wolf to be nursed." "The doctrine in all its parts is so adverse to my convictions," wrote John Quincy Adams, "that I can view it in no other light than as *organized civil War*." Henry Clay boasted that the vice-president's "late exposition has nullified him" from consideration as the Anti-Masonic candidate. And Jackson, quick to revel in his antagonist's demise, recognized what Calhoun's "nullification exposé" meant: it "has destroyed his prospects forever."[56]

JULY 4, 1831

On July 4, 1831, the Boston Sabbath School Union held a celebration of the fifty-fifth anniversary of American independence at the Park Street Church. The choir introduced a new song that day. Untitled, it contained five verses; over time, only the first took hold:

> My country, 'tis of thee,
> Sweet land of liberty,
>   Of thee I sing:
> Land where my fathers died,
> Land of the pilgrims' pride,
> From every mountain-side
>   Let freedom ring.

Country and liberty. Land and freedom. Here were the terms of the equation, but few agreed on their order or relationship.

15. S. Bernard, *View Along the East Battery, Charleston* (Courtesy of the Yale University Art Gallery, Mabel Brady Garven Collection)

In Charleston, the States Rights and Free Trade Party gathered to celebrate the occasion and reaffirm their commitment to nullification. They met at the customs house, and a large procession moved through the streets toward the home of General Charles Cotesworth Pinckney, where the ladies of the city presented a banner. On the one side of the satin banner was the Arms of the State. On the other, a palmetto tree with STATES RIGHTS inscribed on the trunk. Bales of cotton and barrels of rice were piled at its base. The states'-rights motto inscribed in gold encircled the image: "Millions for defence, not a cent for tribute."

At the Circular Church, Senator Robert Hayne delivered the day's oration. The audience, remarked one observer, was "delighted and enchanted throughout—now deeply affected by his pathos—now roused and animated by his impassioned ardor." Hayne denounced the tariff and the American system as a form of indirect taxation upon the South "that comes not upon us like the strong-man armed, at noon-day, but steals on the wings of the wind, and, like the 'pestilence walking in darkness,' infuses the fatal poison into our veins, and seals our destruction, before we are even aware of its approach." Of the eight million dollars per year in exports from South Carolina, he estimated that the state paid three million dollars in duties to the federal government. And why was this money taken from the pockets of Southern planters? Not "because the Government wants money . . . but because it is deemed expedient that *Northern manufactures* should be made profitable at the expense of *Southern industry*." The Tariff Party, Hayne argued, refused to dismantle the American system and even threatened force against South Carolina should the state exercise its right to nullification. But "ours is a government, not of force, but of opinion, and every one feels that the only secure basis of the Union, are the affections of the people, founded on a conviction of the justice of the government, and the perfect equality of its dispensations," and the people are not "to be held in bonds of iron, or forced into harmonious action, by violence and blood-shed." "When nullification shall be our only means of deliverance from the oppression," observed Hayne, "who is there that would not be a *nullifier?*"[57]

Hayne's oration concluded at half past three, at which time numerous toasts and additional speeches were offered: "South Carolina in '76 and '31—Though divided among ourselves, we triumphed over our oppressors in '76, and will triumph now." "The South Carolina Doctrines—Identified with our dearest interest, happiness, prosperity, and liberty—They *must* be maintained." "May no true-hearted son of South Carolina submit to be slaves 'while the earth bears a plant, or the sea rolls its waves.' "

The day's remarks hit the same chords over and over: speakers denounced the tariff as unconstitutional; they defended nullification as historically grounded; they decried Southern exploitation at the hands of Northerners; they devoted themselves to liberty over union. The States Rights and Free Trade Party also made explicit an argument against the tariff that expressed the deepest fears of the planters gathered on July 4: if the federal government had the power to impose protective tariffs, then who was to say they did not have the power to interfere directly with the institution of slavery? One nullifier proclaimed: "If the frightful evil of Disunion and Secession shall come upon me, it will not be because I desire these things, but because they will be forced upon me by the unrelenting tyranny of the Federal Government. . . . It is impossible for any son of the South, to look with complacency, into the Pandora's Box of evils, which a Consolidated Government would inflict on this Southern Country. The destruction in store for the foreign commerce which feeds us—the regulation of our internal industry by a majority who have great local interests to promote and which cannot be sustained but at the expense and ruin of the South—the fires which Northern fanaticism is every where enkindling to subvert our *peculiar local* policy, and which has already extended to the Halls of Congress—these are calamities which, to my mind at least, are most appalling." One slaveholder made the point even more directly: "If Congress has a right to fix such a system as that upon us, then has it a right to do any thing it pleases. Then has it a right to emancipate our slaves, and, after having destroyed the value of our property, to force us to change entirely the whole character and current of our avocations and pursuits."[58] Nullification represented more than straightforward opposition to the tariff or assertion of states' rights; it provided a rationale for defending the Southern way of life until the bloody end.

Southerners had reasons to be concerned. Already, Garrison's *Liberator* and Walker's *Appeal* had made them anxious over outside interference with slavery. Already, petitions against slavery were flooding Congress, and colonization schemes as a means of gradually ending slavery were winning support. Within two months, Nat Turner would rebel and rumors of insurrections across the South would place slaveholders on high alert. But if nullification meant resisting the power of the national government to interfere with slavery, it also meant creating an atmosphere of lawlessness that incited the slaves. For some Southerners, insurrection and nullification, in resisting legally constituted authorities, formed mirror images of one another. Calling Nat Turner's revolt "a melancholy commentary on nullification," one Virginian Republican condemned Southern Democrats who advocated the

doctrine. Garrison too saw connections. If nullification meant separation, then, because of the threat of insurrection, it also meant destruction: "A separation from the Union, by any one or by all of the slave
states, would be like cutting their hold on existence." The real problem in the South was not economic policies. "Does the tariff, or the system of internal improvements, generate her diseases?" he asked. "No,"
he answered, "the canker that is upon her vitals—the curse that is
blighting her fields—the plague that is retarding the increase of her
population—*is slavery—and nothing but slavery.*" A writer to the
United States Gazette, hoping that Southerners would recognize their
need for the protection of the federal government, believed, "The
slave-holding states will not, after the recent outrages in Virginia, and
the more alarming rumours, be quite so eager to cut loose from the
states North of the Potomac; and that nullification fever may have
received a check from which it will not very suddenly recover."[59]

Some South Carolinians, wanting to preserve their relationship
with the federal government, refused to place nation and state in opposition to each other. On July 4, members of the Union and States Rights
Party gathered at the First Presbyterian Church. These citizens, while
also denouncing the tariff, opposed nullification and insisted that
union and states' rights were not incompatible objectives. "If the nullifier is right," wrote one citizen, "then the framers of the constitution
were guilty of designedly introducing the element of *civil war*, into an
instrument, the very object of whose creation, was to avoid this evil."
For Charleston's Unionists, "the question to be decided now is—
whether or not we shall suffer DISUNION and CIVIL WAR." It was delu-
sory to believe in nullification as a peaceful remedy; rather, most
regarded it as revolutionary. "If the hearts of some who are now exciting the people to madness, were exposed to public view," wrote one
resident of Abbeville under the pseudonym Madison, "I much fear that
more love of *self* than *country* would be found there. . . . Let the conflict once commence; let blood once be shed, and the Union is gone;
and I would as soon expect to see a planet start madly from its sphere,
and roll beyond the verge of creation, as to see republican and free
institutions springing from the ashes of our present system."[60]

In his oration on the Fourth of July, Representative William Drayton reminded the audience, "In our efforts to rescue ourselves from what we feel to be oppressive legislation, we should not transcend those means which are constitutional, among which cannot be included the interposition of a State to nullify an Act of Congress and thus, whatever the motive, necessarily involve us in a contest with the General Government." It bemused him that supporters of nullification defended the doctrine as constitutional: "A state cannot be *in* the Constitution and *out* of it, at the same time." And it irked Drayton that a single state would have the arrogance to dictate to its sister states: "Is it republican, is it rational, that a single State should be able to control twenty-three States?" Without question, states maintained their sovereignty, but there "are but two constitutional modes by which a State can prevent the encroachment of the General Government on the rights of the States—*an amendment to the Constitution and a reference to the Judiciary.*" If an amendment failed, and the courts ruled the law constitutional, then the only means of redress was resistance by force or withdrawal from the Union.

What, Drayton wondered, would be the outcome of secession, even if accomplished peacefully? "Have we the means of retaining our independence? Does history furnish the solitary example of any nation having preserved its independence, without the physical power to secure it?" he asked. He could not bear to "contemplate the spectacle of the now free and brave—with their national banner torn—its stars shooting madly from their sphere—marching to the funeral of their own liberty by the lurid glare of the torch of discord."

More than likely, rather than peaceful secession, armed conflict with the federal government would ensue. "The interposition of the veto of the State could not be a *peaceful remedy*, unless the President should fail to perform his duty," and Jackson, Drayton reminded the audience, was not one to back down. Nullification meant revolution and, if it was invoked, South Carolina would not escape "the direst of all calamities, intestine war. In such a struggle, victors are victorious without honor—the vanquished defeated, without sympathy. Amidst intestine feud, all the kindly feelings of the human heart would be eradicated, and for them would be substituted those burning and savage passions, which embroil the domestic fire-side—which pour rancours into the bosom of friends—which convert the excitements of honorable rivalry into deadly personal hatred. Then . . . might we witness the spectacle of brother armed against brother, of parent against child, and of the child against his parent."[61]

A thousand miles north, at the Fourth of July celebration in Quincy, Massachusetts, John Quincy Adams also warned of civil war. The day began early for the former president, who had a procession of visitors. As the town band, infantry company, Committee of Arrangements, and citizens marched toward the meeting house, Adams felt the scorch of a blazing sun. "I never experienced atmospherical heat more intensely than from the time I left my house in the morning till my return to it after dinner," he noted in his diary. In an oration that lasted an hour and a half, Adams defended the pre-eminence of the Union: "The Declaration of Independence was a manifesto issued to the world, by the delegates of thirteen distinct, but UNITED colonies of Great Britain, in the name and behalf of their people. It was a united declaration. Their union preceded their independence." But "our happy but disputatious Union" has suffered at various times from the fever of heated politicians who proclaimed "the *sovereign* power of any one state of the confederacy to nullify any act of the whole twenty-four States." The "hallucination of State Sovereignty" led to the creation of an impotent confederation government, a "bloodless corpse." The Constitution saved the Union, and the powers reserved were powers "reserved to the people, and which never have been delegated either to the United or to the separate States." But there never was such a thing as "an absolute, irresistible, despotic power, lurking *somewhere* under the cabalistic denomination of *sovereignty*."

Such, however, was the import of nullification, "a word which contains within itself an absurdity, importing a pretended right of one State in this Union, by virtue of her *sovereignty*, to *make* null and void, which it presupposes to be null and void before." "Philosophically, politically, morally considered," shrieked Adams, who strained his voice as he spoke, nullification "is an inversion of all human reasoning; it cannot be conceived without confusion of thought; it cannot be expressed without solecism of language, and terms of self-contradiction. . . . Stripped of the sophistical argumentation in which this doctrine has been habited, its naked nature is an effort to organize insurrection against the laws of the United States." A tempest, warned Adams, was forming, and though it might serve only to purify the atmosphere, it threatened desolation. As he concluded, he outlined the consequences of nullification: "It strips us of that peculiar and unimitated characteristic of all our legislation—free debate. It makes the bayonet the arbiter of law; it has no argument but the thunderbolt. It were senseless to imagine that twenty-three States of the Union would suffer their laws to be trampled upon by the despotic mandate of one. The act of nullification would itself be null and void. Force must be called in to execute the law of the Union. Force must be applied by the nullifying State to resist its execution. . . . The blood of brethren is shed by each other. The scaffold and the battlefield stream alternately with the blood of their victims. Let this agent but once intrude upon your deliberations, and Freedom will take her flight for heaven. The Declaration of Independence will become a philosophical dream, and uncontrolled, despotic sovereignties will trample with impunity, through a long career of after ages, at interminable or exterminating war with one another, upon the indefeasible and unalienable rights of man."[62]

In time, the threat of force arrived. Despite the efforts of Southern Unionists, nullifiers gained control of the South Carolina legislature, and on November 24, 1832, passed an Ordinance of Nullification against the Tariff Acts of 1828 and 1832. Some nullifiers hoped that, despite unambiguous pronouncements, the president, a native son of South Carolina, would somehow endorse their position. Given his disregard of the Supreme Court in *Worcester* v. *Georgia*, some commented that "the *old man* seems to be more than half a Nullifier himself."[63]

Such wishful thinking vanished like the morning fog. On December 10, 1832, Jackson responded with a Nullification Proclamation in which he declared "the power to annul a law of the United States, assumed by one State, *incompatible with the existence of the Union, contradicted expressly by the letter of the Constitution, unauthorized by its spirit, inconsistent with every principle on which it was founded, and destructive of the great object for which it was formed.*" Declaring that "disunion by armed force is *treason*," Jackson threatened to use whatever means necessary to save the country. Preparations for armed conflict accelerated. Robert Hayne, now governor of South Carolina, called for a volunteer force of ten thousand men; South Carolina's Unionists informed the president that eight thousand men stood ready to heed a call to arms. Only with the passage of a compromise tariff in 1833 that significantly lowered duties did the conflict abate. Along with the new tariff, Congress passed a Force Bill that authorized the use of federal troops to enforce compliance with tariff laws. South Carolina repealed its nullification ordinance but, in a final truculent act, nullified the Force Bill. The union had passed "under one of the deepest Eclipses which has ever obscured it," but the tensions between state and nation continued to cast shadows and darkness.[64]

MACHINES AND NATURE

✳

RAILROADS AND REAPERS

"A rail-road! You never travelled on a rail-road! Then you have yet to witness one of the noblest triumphs of human ingenuity." It was November, and Robert Dale Owen, editor of the *Free Enquirer*, could hardly contain himself. He had left New York City on a journey, and just outside of Albany, he boarded a car on the recently opened Mohawk and Hudson railway line. As he arrived, he found "the steam engine already smoking, and six or eight stages—*cars* they are usually termed though scarcely differing except for their wheels from ordinary stages—ready to receive passengers." The engine initially "set off without its train (as one would walk a race horse about, before starting) to get up its steam." On its return, six nine-seated cars were attached, "and the next minute we were off at the rate of twenty miles an hour, whistling past surrounding objects pretty much in the same style as if mounted on a fleet horse at full gallop." The party traversed the entire line of twelve and a half miles in less than twenty-five minutes. "No one," concluded Owen, "can enter a rail-road car for the time, and thus find himself conveyed with perfect ease and safety, without feeling, that a new era in the annals of locomotion has commenced. . . . That, in twenty years from this time, the entire Union will be intersected with rail-roads, it needs not the spirit of prophesy to foresee; but how immense the advantages, mental and moral perhaps as well as physical, which may thence result, it is not easy to predict."[1]

"RAIL-ROAD MANIA" is "epidemic," declared editors across the nation. One passenger compared a railway journey to "sailing on dry land," and expressed no surprise that "there is *Railroad fever* abroad in the land; for whoever see the operation of railroad travelling . . . cannot but be infected with this contagious fever." James Alexander reported, "Rail-roads were the universal topic of conversation in all parts of the country." Railroad travel made plausible what had previously seemed impossible. "The increasing facilities for journeying from one portion of our great republic to another," imagined one writer, "will soon cause extended space, or remote distance, to be a matter scarcely worth taking into consideration." "The Americans are indeed a locomotive people," concluded a contributor to one newspaper, and the time was approaching when a young man would "sleep one night in Penobscot, the next in Cincinnati, the third in Charleston, the fourth in Philadelphia, and the fifth in a remote corner of Lake Winnipeg!" The new form of travel "annihilated time and space by its celerity" and overthrew in a day "notions which have been received from our ancestors, and verified by our own experience. . . . The world has received a new impulse." But as remarkable as that seemed, railroads too would become outmoded: "Mounting the air by means of steam balloon (no improbable conjecture), man will circumnavigate the globe in less time than it takes this paper to travel to Ohio. . . . The sun will be partially eclipsed by the *flights* of men."[2]

Railroad developments occurred so quickly that someone sheltered from the news for several weeks could miss an entire phase of its history. Only three months before Owen's journey, William Seward traveled on the Mohawk and Hudson line. He boarded the car and, while he was waiting, "a fine large gray horse was attached to it, by shafts, exactly like those of a one-horse wagon." The horse drew the stage car "through hills and over valleys," and after four miles stopped to drink.

A new horse replaced the gray, and the journey of twelve miles was completed in eighty minutes. By November, a horseless engine was in place and railroad lines around the country had placed orders for steam locomotives. Steam power had already transformed river travel, but "rail roads, associated with steam power," predicted *Niles' Weekly Register*, "are about to accomplish a much greater revolution in the *future* affairs of men and nations, than steam, itself, has yet brought about in the *present* condition of things."[3]

Appropriately, the engine on the Mohawk and Hudson line was named the *Robert Fulton*. Built in England by Robert Stephenson, whose early designs made the Liverpool and Manchester Railroad a model for what was possible with steam locomotion, the *Robert Fulton* did not work so well on the hilly American landscape as it had on flat British soil. The engine often derailed, and its low steam pressure kept it from hauling heavy loads over steep grades. But American manufacturers learned about steam engines by literally taking them apart and putting them back together again. In October 1830, Robert Stevens, the president and chief engineer of the Camden and Amboy Railroad, sailed for England to purchase a locomotive for the new line. He made his way to Stephenson and Company in Newcastle-on-Tyne and placed an order for an engine that would come to be known as the *John Bull*. Completed on June 18, the *John Bull* was tested, disassembled, and shipped to Philadelphia, where it arrived in August. The engine cost about four thousand dollars; a tariff on British locomotives added 25 percent to the price. The engine body, boiler, wheels, axles, and four crates of parts reached Bordentown, New Jersey, on September 4, and Isaac Dripps, a twenty-one-year-old steamboat mechanic who worked for Stevens, faced the task of putting it together. There were no drawings. There were no instructions. Dripps and his assistants worked for ten days, assembling and reassembling, adjusting and improvising. Finally, they filled the boiler, lit the flame, opened the throttle, and cheered as the *John Bull* lurched into motion.

On Saturday, November 12, Stevens invited politicians and local dignitaries to ride the *John Bull* along the test track. One participant described the event: "They had a coach that held thirty passengers attached to the steam car and ran one and a quarter miles in two minutes and twenty-two seconds. This they repeated a great many times, as there was a great assemblage of people there and all wanted to ride. The legislature was invited and attended in a body, and a great many of the best people in New Jersey. Robert Stevens conducted the machinery itself. It was a fine performance and gave great satisfaction."[4]

Sometime during the fall, Matthias Baldwin inspected the *John Bull*. Baldwin, an evangelical Presbyterian and Whig supporter, had earlier in the year designed a one-fourth-scale working model of a locomotive engine. Placed at the Philadelphia Museum, the engine drew two cars with four passengers each around a track every evening. Throughout the summer, lines at the museum formed early. Baldwin turned his energies toward building a full-size locomotive engine. Named *Old Ironsides*, it first ran in November 1832 on the Philadel-

16. "Railroad Depot at Philadelphia" (Courtesy of the Library Company of Philadelphia)

phia, Germantown, and Norristown Railroad. Here was the beginning of the Baldwin Locomotive Works, which dominated engine design and production in the nineteenth century.[5]

What started as novelty soon became ubiquitous as legislatures and various commercial interests across the nation promoted the construction of railroad lines. States held railroad conventions. Investors sent stock prices soaring. Shares of the Camden and Amboy, for example, rose from twenty-three to seventy dollars before the *John Bull* even arrived. The fever spread south as well as north. In Richmond, the principal engineer called the railroad system "the triumph of the age—the ultimate effects of its introduction are incalculable." The South Carolina Canal and Rail-Road Company began construction on a route from Charleston to the west bank of the Savannah River, below Hamburg (now part of North Augusta, South Carolina), a distance of 133 miles. Hoping to make Charleston "one of the chief Atlantic cities for the Imports and Exports of 'the Great West,' " the directors celebrated the railroad as evidence of "a spirited determination . . . to shake off the imputation that South Carolina neither possesses the means, enterprise, or capability, of bettering her condition." Even in New Orleans, known as the "wet grave" because water rose so close to the surface that holes had to be drilled into coffins to keep them sunk, the Pontchartrain Railroad connected the city with the lake five miles to the north.[6]

The most ambitious railroad line in the country, the Baltimore and Ohio, had been chartered in 1827. At the laying of the first stone on July 4, 1828, ninety-one-year-old Charles Carroll, the last surviving signer of the Declaration of Independence, turned the earth and proclaimed, "I consider this among the most important acts of my life, second only to my signing the Declaration of Independence, if even it be second to that." The first line of twelve miles to Ellicotts Mills opened in 1830. On January 4, the B & O announced a contest. The directors offered a prize of four thousand dollars for a four-wheel, coal-burning locomotive that weighed no more than three and a half tons yet could draw fifteen tons at fifteen miles per hour. Their goal was to develop "a supply of Locomotive Steam Engines of *American manufacture*." A year before, Peter Cooper, a wealthy manufacturer and inventor, had "rigged up" the *Tom Thumb*, a one-ton locomotive, and ran it successfully. That it lost a race to a horse-drawn car did little to diminish the enthusiasm for steam power. The B & O received five entries. One exploded during its trial run. Another vibrated so badly that pieces of the machine went flying. Phineas Davis's *York* captured the prize, and in July the engine carried five loaded cars the length of the line. By December, when the extension to Frederick, Maryland, opened, a passenger could travel sixty-one miles west of Baltimore by railroad.[7]

Two decades later, the line neared its final destination, the Ohio River at Wheeling. Nationally, about a hundred miles of rail had expanded into sixty-five hundred miles of iron road. Little got in the way. Sharp curves and severe inclines, which required less blasting and digging, kept construction costs down and challenged engineers to design ever more powerful, dependable engines. Viaducts leaped rivers and chasms. Lanterns allowed engines to run at night, and cow-catchers, attached to the front of the engine, kept the tracks cleared of cattle and people. Andrew Jackson, who often voiced disdain at the rage for internal improvements, yielded to the "onward spirit of the age" when, in 1833, he boarded the B & O and became the first president to ride the rails. That same year, a prisoner of Jackson's government, Black Hawk, saw the railway line and expressed surprise that so much labor and money would be spent simply to make a good road for travel. "I prefer riding on horseback," he concluded.[8]

As Black Hawk's remark suggests, the railroad was not without its critics. Labor activists condemned the railroad corporations as yet another example of a general movement toward greater inequality of wealth. George Henry Evans favored the chartering of the New York and Harlem Rail Road, but protested that the aldermen received grants of stock in return for their support. "We already have too many laws to favor *capitalists*," he snorted. Amos Gilbert concluded: "Rail roads, canals, and every other facility, whether for growing, manufacturing, or transporting the products of labour, would unquestionably be of benefit, if society were rightly constructed; if all were sharers and equal sharers in the benefit. That they are not is not attributable to the improvements themselves, but to an unequal, unnatural, anti-social system which excludes the great mass from any share in the advantages."[9]

Recognizing the huge profits accruing to railroad corporations, workers urged that they were entitled to generous compensation for the arduous work of clearing land, quarrying stone, and laying rails. At the end of June, Irish laborers, dismayed at having not been paid and disgusted by a ban on whiskey, refused to continue working on a nine-mile section of the B & O. The supervisor summoned a sheriff who was greeted "by the workmen to the number of 135 marching with their stone hammers and other tools, with a handkerchief on a pole for a flag. . . . One of them seized the reins of the Sheriff's horse and refused to let him proceed, and all were totally regardless of his authority and injunctions." The workers bashed, broke, and burned the iron, stone, and wood. Only with the arrival of the militia, and the eventual payment of the workers, who earned three to four dollars a week, was harmony restored.

Others worried that thousands would squander their savings by investing in railroad schemes. "The railroad mania," warned one writer, "will divest many of our citizens of their prudence, and involve them in absurd and ruinous expenditures on railroads, where the scarceness of the population, or physical obstacles, render them inexpedient." "The tendency of our countrymen," he lamented, "is towards excess in every speculation which presents the chance of profit." Where wealth created, it also destroyed, and one investor's opportunity was another's ruin. The railroad not only pitted worker against capitalist, but corporations against one another. Though orators such as Henry Clay might talk about turnpikes, canals, and railroads as equal components of a transportation revolution, proponents of one form of internal improvement frequently battled proponents of another. The rapid emergence of the railroad posed a threat to the supporters of canals, who, with the opening of the Erie Canal in 1825, envisioned an arterial system of waterways for the nation. Railroad advocates argued that railroads were less expensive to construct, faster, safer, healthier, and more convenient than canals. Canals required more land than railroads and relied on animal power. Their still waters spawned disease. It was doubtful that a canal could negotiate the altitudes of the Allegheny Mountains, but a railroad could. And severe weather would not keep locomotives frozen in place.[10]

Some politicians gave careful thought to railroads versus waterways as a means of development before choosing one over the other. In 1831, a twenty-one-year-old pioneer built a flatboat on the Sangamon in Illinois and explored the river. The following year, proud of his service as a captain in Black Hawk's War, he ran for election to the Illinois legislature. He praised railroads as "a very desirable object" that served as a "never failing source of communication, between places of business remotely situated from each other," but he lamented the great expense of constructing a railroad line and recommended to the voters that the state devote its resources to improving the navigation of the Sangamon. Abraham Lincoln lost that first election; years later a railroad would carry him to Washington and take his body back home.[11]

Like Lincoln, other statesmen took sides. On the same day Charles Carroll turned the earth for the B & O, President John Quincy Adams broke ground for the Chesapeake and Ohio Canal. The competing ventures had already begun suing, seeking injunctions to prevent one another from acquiring right of way along a narrow stretch of the Potomac. The railroad won two initial decisions, but on December 30, the Court of Appeals, with one prorailroad justice absent because of illness, found for the canal and allowed them to proceed with construction along the contested area from the Point of Rocks to Harpers Ferry. William Wirt was among the attorneys for the C & O; Roger Taney and Daniel Webster for the B & O. Eventually, the legislature passed a bill effecting a compromise. Each had to narrow its width so that both ventures could be accommodated along the narrow pass. In addition, a fence would separate the steam engines from the horses who pulled the boats. But the competition between the two corporations remained keen, and each wished fervently for the other's destruction.[12]

As the contest between the C & O and B & O illustrated, development entailed conflict between vested interests. In March, the Supreme Court first heard arguments in a case, *Charles River Bridge* v. *Warren Bridge*, that in many ways defined the changing features of the economic and legal landscape. In 1785, the Massachusetts legislature issued the Charles River Bridge Company a charter to construct a bridge between Boston and Charlestown. In return for building the structure, the company received the right to collect tolls for several decades. But in 1828, the legislature gave a charter to the Warren Bridge Company to erect a new bridge, less than one hundred yards away from the Charles River Bridge. The question before the Court was whether the old charter implicitly conferred an exclusive right to the Charles River Bridge Company that could not be taken away without just compensation, and whether the state's actions constituted a violation of the contract clause of the Constitution, which forbade states to pass laws that impaired the obligation of contracts.[13]

For Justice Joseph Story, the decision was clear. The original charter implied a monopoly that gave the Charles River Bridge Company an exclusive right, and by granting a charter to a competing company, the legislature violated its contractual agreement, overstepped its authority, and threatened to impede future investments by failing to support the original proprietors. But despite writing "a very elaborate opinion extending over sixteen folio sheets," Story could not move the Court toward a decision. The case was continued and reargued, and by the time it was finally decided, in 1837, the Court had changed as much as the nation. John Marshall was gone, replaced by Roger Taney, whom one observer described as "a gaunt, ungainly man," but whose words were "so clear, so simple, so admirably arranged . . . you never thought of his personal appearance." Jackson had made two other appointments as well. Story remained, bitter that he had been bypassed for chief justice, and the draft opinion of six years earlier now formed the basis for a dissent: "I stand upon the old law, upon law established more than three centuries ago, in cases contested with as much ability and learning, as any in the annals of our jurisprudence, in resisting any such encroachments upon the rights and liberties of the citizens secured by public grants. I will not consent to shake their title deeds by any speculative niceties or novelties."

Seeing novelties as necessities, Taney and the majority ruled in favor of the Warren Bridge proprietors. To uphold the implied monopoly of the Charles River Bridge charter, he argued, would be against the interests of the public, would favor one group over another merely because they had the good fortune to arrive first, would restrain competition, and would impinge on the rights of the state to exercise its own legislative authority. "Let it once be understood that such charters carry with them these implied contracts," he argued, "and you will soon find the old turnpike corporations awakening from their sleep, and calling upon this Court to put down the improvements which have taken their place. The millions of property which have been invested in railroads and canals upon lines of travel which had been before occupied by turnpike corporations will be put in jeopardy. We shall be thrown back to the improvements of the last century, and obliged to stand still until the claims of the old turnpike corporations shall be satisfied and they shall consent to permit these States to avail themselves of the lights of modern science, and to partake of the benefit of those improvements which are now adding to the wealth and prosperity, and the convenience and comfort, of every other part of the civilized world."[14]

Winners and losers. Development would take place, but who would pay and who would profit? Courts faced these issues repeatedly in cases having to do not only with charter rights, but also with such legal questions as eminent domain (the power of the state to confiscate land), just compensation, and negligence. Time and again they found ways to use the law as an instrument to promote competition and development. They also struggled to sort through competing patent claims. Among the "practical and ingenious improvements" that received patents in 1831 were a platform scale for weighing heavy objects, wheels for railroad cars, a process for making coke from anthracite, and a way of manufacturing gas for illumination. More than sixty patents were

THE TESTING OF THE FIRST REAPING MACHINE NEAR STEELE'S TAVERN. VA. A.D. 1831.

17. "The Testing of the First Reaping Machine Near Steele's Tavern, Va. A.D. 1831," n.d. (Courtesy of the Chicago Historical Society)

issued for various kinds of threshing machines, but one machine, tested on July 25, proved as revolutionary as the steam engine.[15]

About a mile from the family's Virginia farm in the Shenandoah Valley, Cyrus McCormick tested his reaping machine. Only twenty-two at the time, McCormick experimented in the blacksmith shop and emerged with a machine that promised to cut grain across a six-foot swath under any conditions. On the day of the trial run, McCormick family slaves held the reins of the horse to keep it from jolting at the whirring sound of the blades. One observer later described the device: "The cutting was done by a straight blade with a sickle edge, which received a vibratory motion from a crank, the grain being supported at the edge of the blade by stationary pieces or points of wood projecting before it. On one side of the Machine the gearing was attached by cog wheels which operated the crank, driven by one main wheel running upon the ground and supporting one side of the Machine—the crank being attached to a blade by a connecting piece. From the frame work that supported the wheels, a pair of shafts were extended forward to which a horse was attached that pulled it—and the side of the Machine extending into the grain was supported by a small wheel." McCormick rapidly made improvements and patented it in 1834. Reporters exclaimed that, "besides the great savings of labor it effects, which is estimated by intelligent farmers at fifty per cent, it takes off the grain with far less waste than the ordinary modes."[16]

In time, the mechanical reaper transformed American agriculture and McCormick became known as "the liberator of agriculture." The machine made the Midwest, Old Northwest, and Great Plains into the most productive agricultural land in the world. It freed farmers from the soil, sending laborers to the factories of the industrial age and others to lands still uncleared. Its cutting power was so great that some say it even helped snip the chains of the enslaved who, in Gustave Beaumont's observation, served as the "agricultural machinery" of the slaveholders. Within two decades, the reaper would be described as "that wonderful machine . . . seen moving quietly and steadily on, and laying the harvest-field bare at the rate of an acre to the hour, in place of what was formerly seen, the farmer toilfully cutting up the stalks with a sickle, and depositing them on the ground by the armful." The mechanical reaper, everyone agreed, served as an "effective and beneficent agent of human progress."

The success of the reaper led to conflicts over its patent. In 1848, another inventor, who claimed to have devised the machine first, challenged the extension of McCormick's patent. The Senate Committee on Patents examined the history of the device and concluded that McCormick's invention and testing of the reaper in the harvest of 1831 gave him priority. McCormick brought suit for patent infringement, and in 1854 his attorney, William Seward, won the case with an argument that highlighted sectional rivalries: "The defendants stigmatize the plaintiff as a Virginian, and his machine as a Virginia humbug. . . . A citizen of Connecticut, a Northern man, enriched the Southern States by devising and delivering to them an automoton, which picked the seeds from the cotton boll and prepared the clean fibre for the spindle. Courts and juries in those States denied him the redress to which he was entitled for unlawful violation of his patented rights. South Carolina, to her lasting honor, vindicated her character by bestowing a munificent donation upon the inventor out of the public treasury. A Virginian has returned to us in the form of an automoton-reaper, the benefit which Eli Whitney conferred on the South. That automoton is the slave of Cyrus H. McCormick. He created the automoton and the law made it his slave for fourteen years, only nine years of which period have elapsed. The defendants have appropriated that slave to their own use. I appeal to you as just and magnanimous citizens to restore it to its owner."[17]

In depicting machinery and slavery as indistinct, Seward failed to grasp the tension his analogy created with his own political views. Seward detested slavery but, like many Americans, he worshipped technology, so much so that he fell easily into thinking about the machine as an ideal slave. He was not alone. "The engine," wrote one enthusiast, "has no feeling. It can neither smart under the lash, nor be galled by yoke or harness. No cruelty, neglect, or exposure can occasion to it one of those tortures which mercy, with bleeding heart, weeps when she sees inflicted on a beast. . . . Who can estimate the suffering which the Steam Engine is destined to save, through all coming time, to man and the inferior animals? Countless labors are to be performed, and, if lifeless machines did not perform them, living creatures must." Machines would liberate humans to pursue other endeavors: "The consequent saving of the most valuable of all earthly possessions—time— is equivalent to a new lease on life—a prolongation of the usual terms of human existence." "Machinery seems likely to do everything," proclaimed one editor, "and man will soon have nothing to think of but lay his head on a basket of peaches generated by heat, and fix his eye on a cherry tree from which the fruit will be pulled by a steam engine."[18]

Some went further. Machines were not a substitute for men; men were merely advanced machines. In *The Results of Machinery*, a paean to technology published on both sides of the Atlantic, Charles Knight argued, "The most stupid man that ever existed is, beyond all comparison, a machine more cunningly made by the hands of the Creator, more perfect in all his several parts, and with all his parts more exquisitely adapted to the regulated movement of the whole body, less liable to accidents and less injured by wear and tear, than the most beautiful machine that ever was, or ever will be invented."

But if the machine had its promoters, it also had its detractors. Rather than freeing workers from labor, technological advances might make humans slaves to the machine. A "furious hostility to machinery" led workers on both sides of the Atlantic to sabotage the mechanical inventions that put them out of work. By performing with greater efficiency and less expense the tasks of many men, machines displaced labor; instead of marking progress, they became a "grievous curse" to the laboring classes. "Machinery," observed one writer, "substitutes bodies of iron, with souls of steam, to do the work of living men." Whereas some activists, such as Stephen Simpson, urged that "all MACHINERY and IMPROVEMENTS constitute in themselves an immense stock of industry, and add immeasurably to the national wealth," others alleged that "machinery gathers men together in large masses, confines them in unhealthy apartments, ruins their health, contracts their minds, and depraves their morals; that its wages, like the wages of sin, is death,—moral, intellectual, physical death."[19]

The new machines of the age seemed to violate nature. They literally cut through and across the face of the land and made possible construction and production on an unimaginable scale. For some, annihilating time and space was not to be welcomed but dreaded, a rupture from the established rhythms of life. "If machinery was used simply in following nature," urged the author of a work on poverty, "it would be a blessing; but while nature has to follow it, and is distanced in the contest, it is the means of destroying harmony and producing every degree of suffering and misery."[20]

TOCQUEVILLE AND BEAUMONT

"The fact remains that I think I am more than ever a human machine." Tocqueville was back in Paris after nearly a year traveling in America, and he felt overwhelmed by the task that lay ahead, writing a report on the penitentiary system. He and Beaumont had stayed true to their promise and visited Sing Sing, Auburn, Charlestown, Wethersfield, Eastern State, and several other jails and penitentiaries. He sat in an immense easy chair, his thick notebook balanced on his knees, a writing stand perched next to him. With "eyes half-closed, I wait for the spirit of the penitentiary system to appear to me," he reported. Despair was part of Tocqueville's makeup, and it hit with particular force once he returned from the excitement and challenge of his American journey. In October, from Hartford, he had written a friend, "The great point of this life is to forget as much possible that one exists." Faced with figuring out America, he had largely managed to succeed in the enterprise amid a swirl of travels and dinners and conversations. But now, alone with his notes, he was all too aware of his existence.[21]

The term he used to describe his self-imprisonment—human machine—applied equally well to the goals of the penitentiary system, which aimed to "reduce the inmate to a silent working machine." The means applied to do so were enforced silence, solitary confinement, and regular labor. Thinking about the American penal regime, Tocqueville wondered, "Can there be a combination more powerful for reformation than that of a prison which hands over the prisoner to all the trials of solitude, leads him through reflection to remorse, through religion to hope; makes him industrious by the burden of idleness, and which, while it inflicts the torment of solitude, makes him find a charm in the converse of pious men, whom otherwise he would have seen with indifference, and heard without pleasure?" No doubt the impression this regimen made on the prisoner ran deep. But whether or not it was durable, Tocqueville was unsure. The penitentiaries of New York, Massachusetts, and Pennsylvania certainly marked an advance over what he saw in the South, where, at the prison in New Orleans, he encountered "men thrown in pell-mell with swine, in the midst of excrement and filth, . . . they are chained like wild beasts; they are not refined but brutalized." But his research also yielded more than enough material "to prove that the penitentiary reforms and that it does not reform; that it is costly and cheap; easy to administer and impracticable."[22]

In their visit to Sing Sing, Tocqueville and Beaumont first began to speculate about the power of association and communication in society. They noted that thirty officers watched over nine hundred prisoners in an open field. Why, they wondered, were "these nine hundred collected malefactors less strong than the thirty individuals who command them?" The answer was that "the keepers communicate freely with each other, act in concert, and have all the power of association; while the convicts, separated from each other, by silence, have, in spite of their numerical force, all the weakness of isolation." And yet "an act of simultaneous determination" on the part of the prisoners "would infallibly set them at liberty." Tocqueville developed his ideas about the power of association and made it a cornerstone of his understanding of American society. He also seemed to recognize how tenuous the balance was between order and liberty, structure and chaos: "As long as the machinery is in good order, the discipline prevailing in their prisons will be a thousand times better than that of any in Europe. But there cannot be a half-revolt there. So the system at Sing-Sing seems in some sense like the steamships which the Americans use so much. Nothing is more comfortable, quick, and, in a word, perfect in the ordinary run of things. But if some bit of the apparatus gets out of order, the boat, the passengers and the cargo fly into the air."[23]

Tocqueville's metaphor emerged from his experiences. In only a month, he had already experienced delays and groundings along the Hudson. On November 26, Tocqueville and Beaumont nearly drowned on the Ohio River when, near midnight, their steamboat, the *Fourth of July*, struck a rock at the Burlington Bar, between Pittsburgh and Wheeling. The vessel, "driven by the current and all the forces of steam, smashed itself like a nutshell on a rock in the middle of the Ohio." The cry of "we sink" "resounded immediately; the vessel, the gear, and the passengers started in company for eternity." The water rushed quickly into the boat and began to fill the cabins. An eerie silence filled the air as the two hundred passengers solemnly awaited death in the freezing, ice-choked river. Tocqueville and Beaumont "grasped each other's hand in farewell." But "suddenly the boat stops sinking; its hull is hanging on the very reef that broke it." Until they were picked up by another boat, the two remained "planted in the middle of the river like prisoners on a hulk."

Tocqueville and Beaumont survived the sinking and continued on their travels. They had come to America to study the penitentiaries and came away "doubtful whether one could succeed in *reforming* criminals." They had come to understand the "mechanism of republican government" and discovered that "no central idea seems to govern the movement of the machine." They had come to study American society and encountered a society of nations "without roots, without memories, without prejudices, without routines, without common ideas, without a national character," yet contented and linked together, paradoxically, by self-interest ("the passion for making a fortune carries away and dominates all others") and restlessness ("in the midst of the universal movement that surrounds him, the American could not stay still"). The travelers had come as well to explore the American wilderness.[24]

"We have no word to render the idea that the English express by the word wilderness," Beaumont informed his sister. "Here the natural state of the earth is to be covered with woods; that's the state of wild nature, and this untamed wilderness, as sovereign, still dominates the regions into which civilization has only penetrated in the last forty or fifty years." "The entire country is still nothing but one vast forest," proclaimed Tocqueville. But, to conquer the wilderness, Americans assaulted the woods with "all the energy of civilized man." "With us," remarked Beaumont, "one cuts wood to use it; here it's but to destroy it. Prodigious efforts are made to annihilate it." Tocqueville agreed: "What one calls clearing the land here is cutting a tree at three feet from the ground. The operation completed, they work the ground and sow it. It results that in the midst of the finest harvests one perceives by hundreds the dead trunks of the trees which formerly beautified the land." "There is therefore in America a general feeling of hatred against trees," concluded Beaumont.

The assault upon the wilderness meant for Tocqueville that, "by a strange inversion of the ordinary order of things, it is nature that changes, while man is unchanging." He was thinking about the ongoing transformation of the land and the structure of American character: "The same man may give his name to wilds that none has traversed before him; he has been able to fell the first tree in the forest, and build in the midst of solitude a planter's house round which first a hamlet was formed, and which is now surrounded by a huge city. In the short space between birth and death he has seen all these changes, and a thousand others like him have been able to do so. In his youth he has lived among tribes who now live only in history; during his life rivers have changed or diminished their course, the climate is different from what it was before, and all that is still in his imagination only a first step in an endless career."

Nature succumbed over and over to the unchanging American characterized, above all else, by an obsessive desire for change: "Often born under another sky, placed in the middle of an ever moving picture, driven himself by the irresistible torrent that carries all around him along, the American has no time to attach himself to anything, he is only accustomed to change and ends by looking on it as the natural state of man. Much more, he feels the need of it, he loves it, for instability instead of causing disasters for him, seems only to bring forth wonders around him."

This American love of instability, leading deeper and deeper into the forests, had brought extinction to the Indians. Beaumont felt he could not express the "emotion we experience in traversing this half-wild, half-civilized country, in which fifty years ago were to be found numerous and powerful nations who have disappeared from the earth, or who have been pushed back into still more distant forests; a country where are to be seen, rising with prodigious rapidity, new peoples and brilliant cities which pitilessly take the place of the unhappy Indians too feeble to resist them." On July 4, in Albany, Tocqueville reflected, "The European is to the other races of man what man in general is to the rest of animate nature. When he cannot bend them to his use or make them indirectly serve his well-being, he destroys them and makes them vanish little by little in front of him. The Indian races are melting in the presence of European civilization like snow in the rays of the sun."[25]

Tocqueville and Beaumont were eager to experience "nature vigorous and savage," to probe the "dark forest." On July 8, they traveled northeast from Fort Brewerton in New York and, a mile and a half from their host's home, found a path that opened into the forest. Soon the travelers found themselves "in the middle of one of those deep forests of the New World whose sombre savage majesty strikes the imagination and fills the soul with a sort of religious terror." They marveled at the trees, generations of which succeeded one another through "uninterrupted centuries." They contemplated the way "a thousand different plants," covered and cornered by the "immobile corpses" of dead trunks, "press in their turn towards the light." Sometimes, Tocqueville and Beaumont happened to come upon an immense tree that the wind had torn up by the roots. But because the forest floor was so crowded, its branches remained balanced in the air, like pitchforks perched upon haystacks. They walked for hours, hearing nothing more than the sounds of rustling leaves and snapping branches beneath their horses' hooves. The companions remained silent, their "souls filled with the grandeur and the novelty of the sight."[26]

The forest walk only whetted their appetites. On July 19, Tocqueville and Beaumont left Buffalo on a two-week journey that carried them to Detroit, Pontiac, and Saginaw, a journey in which they experienced the "joy of advancing at last into the wilds." On the first day, the travelers had their initial encounter with Indians, and the experience left them deeply disturbed and disappointed. Tocqueville expected the Indians of romantic literature, "savages on whose face nature had stamped the marks of the proud virtues which liberty brings forth." But instead he encountered what he viewed as small, thin, dark people with deformed mouths and ignoble faces. Their manner of dress repulsed him. The Indians wore European clothes, but not as civilized people should: "Some dressed themselves in blankets; the women with breeches and hats; the men in women's clothes." Tocqueville described their movements as "quick and jerky, their voices shrill and discordant, their glances restless and savage." It was easy at first glance, he confessed, to "mistake each of them for some wild beast of the forest."[27]

Near Oneida Castle, an Indian village, Tocqueville and Beaumont came across a group of Indians. One young man lay motionless by the side of the road, groaning in despair. Tocqueville watched as, now and again, Indians passed by, rolled the body over, felt for a heartbeat, and then moved on. A young Indian woman approached the debilitated man. He thought it was perhaps a wife or sister, and he expected that at last help had arrived. "All my life I shall remember" what happened next, Tocqueville wrote: "She looked at him attentively, called his name aloud, felt his heart and being assured that he was alive, tried to shake him out of his lethargy. But seeing that her efforts were useless, she burst out in fury against the inanimate body lying in front of her; she struck his head against the ground, twisted his face in her hands, and kicked him with her feet. As she gave herself over to these acts of ferocity, she uttered inarticulate and savage cries which I think I can still hear echoing in my ears."

On their return to town, Tocqueville and Beaumont told several people about the Indian. They even offered to pay the costs of an inn for the fallen man. But townsfolk told them not to bother, that the Indian was drunk and sleeping it off in the middle of the road. Others seemed to realize that in all likelihood this man would die if left unattended, but Tocqueville thought he could read on their lips the thought, "What is the life of an Indian?" The general feeling of indifference led him to issue a stinging indictment: "In the midst of this American society, so well policed, so sententious, so charitable, a cold selfishness and complete insensibility prevails when it is a question of the natives of the country. . . . This world here belongs to us, they tell themselves every day: the Indian race is destined for final destruction which one cannot prevent and which it is not desirable to delay. Heaven has not made them to become civilized; it is necessary that they die. Besides I do not want to get mixed up in it. I will not do anything against them: I will limit myself to providing everything that will hasten their ruin. In time I will have their lands and will be innocent of their death."

The travelers continued on their way. By the end of their "fortnight in the wilds," they came to realize that it would be a mistake to judge all Indians by what they observed in Buffalo. They arrived in Detroit and soon thereafter left for Pontiac. They wanted to reach Saginaw, "the last point inhabited by Europeans to the northwest, . . . an advanced station, a sort of observation post, which the whites have established in the midst of the Indian tribes." Concerned about crossing Chippewa land, Tocqueville and Beaumont asked a trader who lived in a log house whether they had anything to fear. " 'No, no,' he said, 'for my part I should sleep more soundly surrounded by Indians than by whites.' " The comment startled Tocqueville, who recorded that this was the first positive view of Indians he had heard since arriving in America. He would hear something similar days later from a European settler who proclaimed that he would "rather live among [Indians] than in the society of the whites."

But it was not only what others told them that changed their minds; their experience with several Chippewa compelled them to confront their fears and rethink, at least temporarily, their ideas about Indians as savages. On their way through the forest, they turned at one point to admire the view and spotted an Indian following them. He ran, said Tocqueville, without making more noise than a wolf. The man's physical appearance was striking. "Large and wonderfully well proportioned," he had shining black hair that fell to his shoulders, and his face was painted with black-and-red stripes. The Chippewa was armed with a knife and a carbine, and he carried two dead birds in his left hand. Fearing an attack, Tocqueville and Beaumont hurried forward, but the Indian followed: "We slow down. He slows down. We run. He runs without making the slightest noise." At last, the travelers tried to speak to the "silent and mysterious being." And then, eye to eye, neither displaying hostile feelings, the Indian smiled and Tocqeville's vision of an entire race shifted. "An Indian in serious mood and an Indian smiling, are two entirely different beings," he reflected. Talking through signs, the travelers gave the Indian some brandy and a coin; in return he gave them his birds, each one pierced by a single bullet.[28]

With night falling, the travelers pressed on toward the Flint River.

They briefly became separated, and Tocqueville shouted Beaumont's name. But he heard nothing; only "the same silence of the dead reigned in the forest." At last, the sound of barking dogs brought them together at a log house on the river, where they spent the night and secured two Indian guides, boys aged eighteen and fourteen, to lead them through the wilderness to Saginaw. Tocqueville felt powerless and knew his fate rested in their hands. What he had always thought of as the natural order, civilized Europeans on top of savage Indians, was now reversed. Describing himself, Tocqueville realized that, "plunged into deep darkness, reduced to his own resources the civilised man walked like the blind, incapable not only of being his own guide in the labyrinth that surrounded him, but even of finding the means to sustain life. It is in the heart of the same difficulties that the savage triumphs; for him the forest obscured nothing; he felt at home there; he walked with his head high, guided by an instinct more sure than the navigator's compass."

But this new and unfamiliar role of follower to leader would again be reversed in a way that further humanized for Tocqueville the life of the Indian. After hours of strenuous running, trying to outdistance the setting rays of the sun because Tocqueville refused to heed the guide's advice to stop but bribed him with a wicker-covered bottle to continue, the Indian leader, Sagan Cuisco, "was suddenly seized with a violent nosebleed." Fearful that the Indians would lead no longer, Tocqueville and Beaumont dismounted and allowed the guides to ride horseback. And so, through the darkening forest, two "half-naked men solemnly seated on an English saddle" rode while the Europeans in traveling clothes and boots "laboured along on foot in front of them." Darkness came, and "nothing but the occasional flight of a firefly through the woods traced a thread of light in their depths." "Too late we realized how right the Indian's advice had been," conceded the European.

Tocqueville's experiences with the Chippewa in the forests of the Northwest did not stop him from describing Indians as savages and barbarians; those were the only words he had as antonyms for civilization and refinement. But he came to recognize the error of imagining that the Indian envied the European's lot. Instead, for a moment at least, he envied them. "Sleeping in his cloak in the smoke of his hut," observed Tocqueville, "the Indian looks with mistrust at the European's comfortable house; he for his part prides himself on his poverty, and his heart swells and rejoices at the thought of his barbarian independence. He smiles bitterly as he sees us plagueing our lives to get useless wealth. What we call industry, he calls shameful subjection. He compares the workman to an ox laboriously tracing out a furrow. What we call the comforts of life, he calls children's playthings or women's affectations. He envies us nothing but our weapons. When a man can find cover at night in a tent of leaves, when he can find enough to light a fire to keep off the mosquitoes in summer and cold in winter, when his dogs are good and the country full of game, what more can he ask from the eternal being?"[29]

Tocqueville and Beaumont returned to Detroit and, on August 1, boarded the steamboat *Superior* for a journey to Green Bay. Tocqueville left the forest knowing that, in time, the Indian way of life was doomed by ever-advancing settlements, and that nature itself would succumb to the conquering forces of American expansion west. He thought that at Saginaw he had reached the ultimate point of the westward push, but even as he turned eastward, the American Society for the Encouraging of the Settlement of the Oregon Country advertised for emigrants willing to journey to a place "where the fertility of soil, the healthfulness of climate, the good market for every product of earth or of labor, and the enjoyment of free and liberal government, will conspire to make life easy and the settlers happy."[30]

Tocqueville's journey into the wilderness had proved all his expectations mistaken. He had imagined that the farther away from civilization one traveled, the more backward society became, "a vast chain descending ring by ring" from the patrician in the town to the savage in the wilds. But he discovered that "nothing is true in this picture." Instead, he found an ever-extending circle, not a spiraling chain. Everyone everywhere was the same. "In America," Tocqueville observed, "there is one society only . . . made up everywhere of the same elements. . . . The man you left behind in the streets of New York, you will find again in the midst of almost impenetrable solitude: same dress, same spirits, same language, same habits and the same pleasures." The country consisted of a "nation of conquerors . . . which shuts itself up in the solitudes of America with an axe and a newspaper, . . . a restless, calculating, adventurous race which sets coldly about deeds that can only be explained by the fire of passion, and which trades in everything, not excluding even morality and religion."

Not only were Tocqueville's ideas about society mistaken, his vision of nature was as well. In Europe no forest excluded the sounds of civilization, but in the wilds of America silence reigned, "a stillness so complete that the soul is invaded by a kind of religious terror." In Europe nature seemed tamed and curtailed, but nature in America brought together the forces of life and death in a "competition" and a "struggle" that placed "the elements perpetually at war." Tocqueville's brief references to struggle and survival, competition and creation, suggest the words of another traveler who, across the Atlantic, was preparing for a voyage that would forever change the way humans thought about natural history: on December 27, Charles Darwin set sail on the *Beagle*.

On his last night in Saginaw, Tocqueville heard rumblings from the east. Unable to sleep, he left his hut and felt the wind rustling the trees. The forest floor began to shake as lightning illuminated the sky. He heard "deep groans and lingering wails," the "fearsome voice of the wilds." The storm broke at midnight, and he stood in the rain surrounded by the "endless echo" of a "burst of thunder . . . in the solitudes" of the forest. Planted in the deep virgin woods, Tocqueville felt the future. "The facts are as certain as if they had already occurred," he wrote. "In but few years these impenetrable forests will have fallen." Americans, he observed, were incapable of appreciating "great trees and the beauties of solitude." Rather, they scrambled to "break through almost impenetrable forests, to cross deep rivers, to brave pestilential marshes, to sleep out in the damp woods . . . if it is a question of earning a guinea." "We are perhaps the last travelers who will have been allowed to see it in its primitive splendour," reflected Tocqueville, "so great is the force that drives the white race to the complete conquest of the New World."[31]

Though he could not see it, Tocqueville himself was part of that force. As he traipsed across America, his rifle was never far from his side. Indians often expressed admiration for his weapon, which "could kill two men in one second and be fired in the fog." Tocqueville explained through his guide that the gun had been made "on the other side of the great water." He once gave a demonstration for an Indian chief, and then asked for one of his feathers, a sign that the leader had killed a Sioux. "I will carry it to the land of the great warriors," boasted Tocqueville.

The two Frenchmen took special joy in hunting birds and found frequent opportunities to use their weapons. Once, out of boredom, Tocqueville killed "red, blue, yellow birds, not to forget the most brilliant parrots" he had ever seen. Several Chickasaw Indians accompanied him that day outside of Memphis, and though the act "hardly raised us in the esteem of our allies," Tocqueville confessed that it "had the merit of amusing us thoroughly." There were many moments in Tocqueville's journey that he would never forget, and this was one of them. More than two decades later, he referred to Beaumont as the companion with whom he had hunted the parrots at Memphis. At the time, Beaumont viewed matters a bit differently. His friend, he thought, "was carrying on a war to the death against the American birds."[32]

JOHN JAMES AUDUBON AND CHOLERA

For Tocqueville and Beaumont, the birds of North America offered a colorful sidelight to their journey. But another traveler, who set sail from England in August with gun and sketchbook in hand, made the birds his only focus. He would kill them not only for sport, but also in the interests of nature and art. John James Audubon arrived in New York on September 3 and journeyed south to Washington, Norfolk,

Charleston, and the Florida Keys before heading north again, spending more than a year in Boston, and returning to England in 1834. He had come to draw the birds of the Southern states, to gather subscribers for *Birds of America*, and to promote *Ornithological Biography*, an extended work of prose that provided information about the birds in the drawings and which would ultimately expand to five volumes. Though born in Haiti in 1785, Audubon had lived in Kentucky between 1807 and 1811 and became an American citizen. It was in England, however, that he found support for his work; the artist lived in Great Britain even though it meant making repeated crossings to study the birds.

Like so many travelers, Audubon endured terrible seasickness. In *Men and Manners in America*, Thomas Hamilton, who arrived in England just as Audubon was departing, summarized the miseries of the transatlantic voyage: "At its worst, it involves a complication of the most nauseous evils that can afflict humanity,—an utter prostration of power, both bodily and mental,—a revulsion of the whole corporeal machinery, accompanied by a host of detestable diagnostics, which at once converts a well-dressed, and well-favoured, gentleman, into an object of contempt to himself and to those around him." "A long voyage," Audubon confessed, "would always be to me a continued source of suffering, were I restrained from gazing on the vast expanse of the waters, and on the ever-pleasing inhabitants of the air that now and then appear in the ship's wake. The slightest motion of the vessel effectually prevents me from enjoying the mirth of my fellow passengers, or sympathizing with them in their sickness. When the first glimpse of day appears, I make my way on deck, where I stand not unlike a newly hatched bird, tottering on feeble legs."[33]

Audubon's work appeared at a moment when the study of birds was in vogue, and his drawings turned interest into obsession. "We remember a time," mused the editor of *Blackwood's Edinburgh Magazine*, "when the very word Ornithology would have required interpretation in mixed company; and when a naturalist was looked on as a sort of out-of-the-way but amiable monster. Now, one seldom meets with man, woman, or child who does not know a hawk from a handsaw." The explanation for such intense passion seemed simple enough: "All objects of nature are capable of exciting intense interest in the mind of man, the moment he begins to look upon them as fragments of the vast and wondrous machinery of which he himself forms a part." And of all the animals, suggested Thomas Nuttall in his *Manual of the Ornithology of the United States and Canada*, none were "more remarkable in their appearance and habits than the feathered inhabitants of the air. They play around us like fiery spirits, elude approach in an element which denies our pursuit, soar out of sight in the yielding sky, journey over our heads in marshalled ranks, dart like meteors in the sunshine of summer, or seeking the solitary recesses of the forest and the waters, they glide before us like beings of fancy."[34]

It was no accident that Audubon became the most celebrated naturalist of the day. He worked hard at cultivating influential contacts, promoting his drawings and writings, and managing the business aspects of his work. He envisioned a family enterprise in which his sons would take over and the name Audubon would become synonymous with the study of birds. He also denounced his competitors, even if they were documenting species other than birds. Some reviewers linked Audubon's enterprise with George Catlin's attempt to preserve images of the Western Indian tribes before they all disappeared. One writer said he was "proud of such men as Audubon and Catlin—of native artists who are diffusing accurate knowledge of natural objects, in the land of their birth, by means of the elegant creations of the pencil." But Audubon ridiculed Catlin's work as "trashy"; in response, Catlin might have pointed out that at least his portraits brought no harm to his subjects.[35]

In the way he looked, through the stories he told, and especially by the drawings he made, Audubon presented himself as hailing from the forests themselves. He did all he could to cultivate his image as the "American woodsman." He embodied the part, with shoulder-length hair "yet unshorn from the wilderness," tattered leather coat, frayed blanket, and a large knife hanging at his side. Once, he was mistaken for an itinerant preacher and, asked to say grace, did so with "fervent spirit." But if Audubon was a missionary, he cast himself as a missionary from the wilderness into civilization, not the other way around. "I received light and life in the New World," he testified, and "when I hardly yet learned to walk, and to articulate those first words, always so endearing to parents, the productions of nature that lay spread all around, were constantly pointed out to me. They soon became my playmates. . . . I felt that an intimacy with them, not consisting of friendship merely, but bordering on phrenzy, must accompany my steps through life." "Self-nursed, self-ripened, and self-tutored among the inexhaustible treasures of the Forest," Audubon emerged from the woods and offered birds as salvation.

In a story told in *Ornithological Biography*, he expressed his despair at being trapped in the forest by a violent storm that destroyed his shed and extinguished his fire, a storm that "seemed to involve the heavens and the earth in one mass of fearful murkiness, save when the red streaks of the flashing thunderbolt burst on the dazzled eye." Only at dawn, with the sounds of the wood thrush, did he feel safe: "How fervently, on such occasions, have I blessed the Being who formed the wood thrush, and placed it in those solitary forests, as if to console me amidst my privations, to cheer my depressed mind, and to make me feel, as I did, that man never should despair, whatever may be his situation, as he can never be certain that aid and deliverance are not at hand."[36]

What separated Audubon from other naturalists and artists was that the birds he captured on paper appeared as if they were still alive. "We must look upon them as scenes from nature," declared one admirer, "not merely as representations of birds." "To paint like Audubon," thought another, "will henceforth mean to represent Nature as she is." Those who viewed Audubon's drawings felt transported into nature. At an exhibition of his watercolors in England, one visitor reported, "The spectator imagined himself in the forest." The birds were all life-size, and the colors rich and vibrant. Audubon depicted the birds not as static, isolated objects, but with "attitudes and pos-

tures . . . in motion or rest, in their glee and their gambols, their loves
and their wars, singing, or caressing, or brooding or preying, or tearing
one another to pieces. The trees, too, on which they sat or sported, all
true to Nature, in bole, branch, spray, and leaf; the flowering—shrubs
and the ground flowers, the weeds and the very grass, all American. So
too the atmosphere and the skies—all transatlantic." Audubon's drawings provided the illusion of nature observed and undisturbed and
allowed viewers to indulge themselves in the belief that they had journeyed into the wilderness, although they never left the safety of civilization.[37]

The first volume of *Birds of America* contained a hundred plates
with pages three feet three inches long and two feet two inches wide.
Audubon issued five plates at a time, and each set cost about ten dollars, a week's wages for a skilled worker. Its expense, lamented one
reviewer, "puts it beyond the means of any but the richest." Describing it as "the handsomest octavo ever got up in America," the *United
States Gazette* celebrated *Birds of America* as "the most magnificent
illustrations of natural history that has ever been produced." In saying
so, the paper, published in Philadelphia, took Audubon's side in a
controversy that left the artist embittered. The leading American
naturalist before Audubon was Alexander Wilson, whose *American
Ornithology* appeared in nine volumes between 1808 and 1814. Wilson had come to America in 1794 and settled in Philadelphia, where
he became a prominent figure in the literary and scientific community
of the city. Although Wilson had died in 1813, those who cherished his
memory felt that the praise of Audubon's drawings constituted an
implicit attack on Wilson's. For example, one reviewer remarked that
in no case did the birds of Audubon's prints "appear before us in the
stiff and formal attitudes in which we find them in other works,
perched upon an unmeaning stump or stone." Another observed that
in his descriptions of birds Audubon "does not appear as the dry, sys-
tematic naturalist, the manufacturer of the barbarous Latin jargon,
after the manner of the old school."[38]

In retaliation, some defenders of that old school attacked

Audubon's prints as unnatural fiction rather than natural history. They took particular aim at a drawing in which Audubon showed a family of mockingbirds defending their nest from a rattlesnake. Rattlesnakes, they chortled, did not and could not climb. Perhaps the naturalist confused the rattlesnake with the moccasin, which was known to climb plants after prey. The picture may have told a moving story, but the story was a lie. Seeking to keep Audubon from election to the American Philosophical Society, they circulated a report that speculated about other instances in which the ornithologist invented facts and chastised Audubon for propagating fantasy rather than history.

The newly published *Monthly American Journal of Geology and the Natural Science* came to the artist's defense. A colonel of the United States Topographical Engineers confirmed that rattlesnakes did indeed climb. Audubon responded to the accusations against him with disdain, proclaiming, "Rattlesnake *do clime Trees!!!*" and suggesting that his detractors ought to leave the city more frequently. "It has now been made notorious, that numerous respectable individuals, whom duty, or the love of adventure, have led into the wilds of our country, have often seen snakes—and the rattlesnake too—in trees," commented Audubon. He described his critics as passing "their lives in stores and counting houses," and observed that they "ought not to contradict these facts, because they do not meet with rattlesnakes, hissing and snapping at them from the paper mulberries, as they go home to their dinners." In the end, the American Philosophical Society not only elected Audubon to membership, the institution subscribed to *Birds of America*. "My Enemies are going down hill very fast," exulted Audubon.[39]

The naturalist did not linger in Philadelphia. By early October, he was in Richmond, "a rather flat Country bounded as is always in America by Woods, Woods, Woods!" He met with Governor Floyd, who thought Audubon "accomplished and sensible," and reported to his wife that "the negro disturbances are quite at an end and the famous Genl. Nat is supposed to have drowned himself." Audubon pressed on to Charleston, and took lodgings at a boardinghouse where he paid ten and a half dollars for three meals and two nights. Always preoccupied with money, he had set out in search of less expensive lodgings when he was introduced to Reverend John Bachman, who invited Audubon to stay at his house. "Could I have refused his invitation," Audubon asked his wife rhetorically. "No!—it would have pained him as much as if grossly insulted. We removed to his house in a crack."

Audubon settled in with the Bachmans for three weeks. He was accompanied by two assistants, Lehman, who completed the drawings by filling in the scenery, and Henry, whose responsibility was skinning and preserving the specimens. He loved his time in Charleston, where the city's elite showered him with "attention, Kindness, and hospitality." "The Papers here have *blown me up* sky high," he reported. "I am the very pet of every body," he boasted, "and had I time or Inclination to visit the great folk I might be in dinner parties from now until Jany next." But Audubon had hunting to do, and he was reluctant to become drawn into political issues. "Politics run high with the Tariff men," he noted, and quickly added, "Further I know not." He did express delight, however, that his connections helped assure passage of an act that would allow for "the free entry of my Works in America." "The Birds of America," wrote one enthusiast, must be "permitted to come in without duty, and free as the animated beings of which they are the beauteous resemblances."[40]

On November 8, Audubon set out on a trip to Cole's Island, twenty-five miles south of Charleston. Accompanied by Bachman and a neighbor, and rowed by four slaves, the party reached the island by midday. Audubon was in search of the long-billed curlew, and at nightfall he spied his prey: "As the twilight became darker, the number of Curlews increased, and the flocks approached in quicker succession. . . . Not a single note or cry was heard as they advanced. They moved for ten or more yards with regular flappings, and then sailed for a few seconds . . . their long bills and legs stretched out to their full extent." The curlews, Audubon warned, "are extremely wary. . . . Some one of the flock, acting as sentinel, raises his wings, as if about to fly, and sounds a note of alarm. . . . At times, a single step made by you beyond a certain distance is quite enough to raise them, and the moment it takes place, they all scream and fly off." Still, he found the bird "in general easily shot," and in the contest between the army of curlews and Audubon's troops, the birds, which sold for twenty-five cents a pair at the Charleston market, had little chance.[41]

Audubon's drawings vibrate with life, but to achieve the effect the naturalist slaughtered thousands of birds. He reveled in his role as hunter and sportsman as much as in his other capacities. "Out shooting every day—skinning, drawing, talking ornithology," he exulted. Once he saw a "Hawk of great size entirely *new*," and thought that the next day he "may perhaps kill him." It took dozens of birds for Audubon to capture one on paper, especially since the colors of the feathers faded rapidly after death unless quickly skinned and preserved. "Shot a vast quantity of birds, without meeting with any thing new," he reported from Charleston. Henry was kept busy; in Charleston, he skinned over two hundred birds, including "upwards of 20 Carion Crows & Turkey Buzzards." When the birds were sparse,

18. John James Audubon, *Long-Billed Curlew*, in *Birds of America*, Plate CCXXXI, Robert Havell, engraver, 1834 (Courtesy of the National Gallery of Art, Washington, D.C., gift of Mrs. Walter B. James)

Audubon became irritable. "You must be aware," he informed the editor of the *Monthly American Journal*, "that I call birds few when I shoot less than one hundred per day."[42]

One bright December morning in East Florida, he and several "negro servants" went in search of birds. "I was anxious to kill some 25 brown Pelicans to enable me to make a new drawing of an adult male bird," Audubon reported. Suddenly, he came upon several hundred pelicans "perched on the branches of mangrove trees, seated in comfortable harmony." Audubon studied the sleeping birds, "examined their countenances and deportment well and leisurely, and, after all, levelled, fired my piece, and dropped two of the finest specimens I ever saw." He only regretted that a mistake in reloading his gun prevented him from shooting "one hundred of these reverend sirs."

Audubon's relentless pursuit of prey reached its apogee a little over a year later in Boston. Called to the museum to inspect a live bird, he found himself staring at a golden eagle. "As I directed my eye toward its own deep, bold and stern one, I recognized it at once," he exclaimed. Audubon purchased the eagle for $14.75 and carried it back to his residence. He studied "the captive . . . , watched his eye, and observed his look of proud disdain." In the eagle's eye, Audubon saw humanity, and he acknowledged that "the eye of Birds is like that of man." For perhaps the only time in his life, he weighed releasing a specimen rather than destroying it. "At times I was half inclined to restore to him his freedom," admitted the naturalist, "that he might return to his native mountains; nay, I several times thought how pleasing it would be to see him spread out his broad wings and sail away toward the rocks of his wild haunts; but then, reader, some one seemed to whisper that I ought to take the portrait of the magnificent bird, and I abandoned the more generous design of setting him at liberty, for the express purpose of shewing you his semblance." For the eagle to survive, it had to die.

So Audubon set out to kill the captured eagle. He tried suffocating the bird with the fumes of burning charcoal. Placing the blanket-covered cage in a small room, Audubon set a pan of lighted charcoal

by the bird and waited to "hear him fall down from his perch." He lis-
tened for hours, but, hearing nothing, he crept into the room, lifted the
blanket, and stared at "the Eagle on his perch, with his bright
unflinching eye turned towards me, as lively and vigorous as ever."
Audubon resumed the experiment but after ten hours the bird still survived, "although the air of the closet was insupportable to my son and
myself." The next morning, Audubon added sulfur to the mix, but he
was "nearly driven from our home in a few hours by stifling vapours,
while the noble bird continued to stand erect." At last, Audubon
resorted "to a method always used as the last expedient." He took a
long pointed piece of steel and thrust it through the eagle's heart. "My
proud prisoner fell dead," he reported, "without even ruffling a
feather."[43]

In death, the eagle nearly cost Audubon his life. The artist stayed
awake all night outlining the bird; he worked incessantly for a fortnight
to complete the drawing. Suddenly, Audubon was "seized with a spasmodic affliction" that left him prostrated for days. He recovered, but
his family feared the worst. For over a year, a bilious disease had
plagued America, and residents of port cities seemed especially vulnerable. The boats journeying west from Europe brought more than
goods and travelers to American shores. They brought contagion as
well.

Throughout the year, Americans watched nervously as a cholera
epidemic spread west. The epidemic began in India in 1817 and
reached China by 1820. A few years later, it crossed the border into
Siberia; by 1830, it had reached Moscow. On June 26, 1831, residents
of St. Petersburg first exhibited symptoms of the disease. By September, it had swept across Europe and made its appearance in Liverpool.
One newspaper reported during the summer that Europe stood
"awestruck at the approach of this terrific disease, the most formidable which ever scourged the world." The *Boston Medical Journal* predicted confidently in July that the cholera was "destined to be arrested
in its progress only by the ocean which divides us from Europe," but
that was only wishful thinking. Although the Atlantic may once have

served as a divider, now more than ever it was a connector. By the fall, it became clear to all that "this disease will ravage the United States."[44]

It carried many names: Indian cholera, epidemic cholera, spasmodic cholera, malignant cholera, cholera morbus. Russian peasants called it the black illness. Physicians tried to categorize various forms of the disease, but whatever it was called, it attacked the body with the rapidity and fury of a tornado. One would be walking or working and suddenly feel cramps in the stomach. Severe vomiting and diarrhea would ensue. As dehydration set in, the skin turned cold and damp, its color darkening to a leaden purple or blue. The tongue whitened and flattened, like a piece of dead flesh, and the voice of the stricken diminished to an empty whisper. The eyes shrank in their sockets. In a matter of hours, the early symptoms of "violent vertigo, sick stomach, [and] nervous agitation," gave way to freezing-cold skin, faint pulse, and greenish-brown discharges. Insensibility and death usually followed. At the height of the epidemic, one citizen found it "appalling to the boldest heart" that he could "see individuals well in the morning & buried before night."[45]

Despite the evidence before them, as late as December, even with the news that the cholera had reached England, some Americans continued to believe that the United States would remain immune to the disease. Reports from Europe indicated that cholera mainly struck those who were filthy, hungry, and impoverished. No one at the time realized that the disease was transmitted through polluted water supplies and that the laboring poor in urban areas were therefore most susceptible to contamination. The wealthy, who drank spring water and fled the cities for the country, avoided sickness. Americans initially thought that they had nothing to fear. The epidemic was a foreign phenomenon, a judgment on the decrepitude of European societies. One writer reasoned, "Poverty is nearly unknown in the United States; and as nearly the whole population are well clothed and fed, cholera will be less likely to attack us." But the writer had it backward. Prosperity did not protect the nation—on the contrary, it made Americans vulnerable.

The country's love of trade and wealth and mobility led to unchecked growth and limitless interaction. Either Americans must be willing to "forego some of the benefits of commerce" by imposing quarantines and equalizing conditions or, one writer warned, "we must expect soon to find, *that the Cholera has commenced its ravages among us.*"[46]

The epidemic hit the United States with force in 1832. Thousands died in New York, Baltimore, New Orleans, and Cincinnati. All the port cities issued quarantines for both goods and passengers, but too late. Disease was upon the land. Some, like George Catlin, believed that the unsettled areas along the upper Missouri River, where "the atmosphere is so light and pure that nothing like fevers or epidemics has ever been known to prevail here," would provide a "delightful refuge . . . if the Cholera, should ever cross the Atlantic." But Catlin was mistaken. The troops traveling west to battle Black Hawk carried the disease with them to unspoiled land.[47]

Physicians debated methods of treatment, but most relied on the same regimen used during the yellow-fever epidemic of the 1790s: bloodletting. One physician exclaimed that he had drawn "blood enough to float the General Jackson steamboat." They also prescribed calomel, which contained mercury, and laudanum, which contained opium. Though the disease was months away from striking, one settler in Newport, Kentucky, copied a formula for treatment into his diary: "The moment any of the usual symptoms such as coolness and change of colour at the finger ends or sickness and sudden debility are perceived lose no time in resorting to the following receipt. From 20 to 30 drops of laudanum and the same quantity of aether to be taken in camphor, julep, or peppermint water." The treatments did nothing to help the afflicted, and in all likelihood further weakened those who might have recovered from the bacterium on their own. Recommendations offered by boards of health may have done more good: they advised citizens not to drink fetid water and to avoid raw fruits and vegetables.[48]

Pleas for Christian benevolence went forth. One writer prayed that among the unafflicted "the lovely charities of the human heart" would "expand and grow out into the fruits of sympathy for the sick and the dying." The ill, he hoped, would not be left to face their end in deso-

lation and terror. But those with financial resources ignored the call for
community action and abandoned the cities. Isaac Fidler, a missionary
traveling in the United States, thought that Americans shared no social
bond "sufficiently close to connect the different members of the politic,
so as to insure assistance from one another in seasons of general distress. 'Every man for himself,' is perhaps more fully and regularly
acted on in America than elsewhere." On July 3, 1832, the *New-York
Evening Post* described the roads as lined in all directions with "well-
filled stage coaches, livery coaches, private vehicles and equestrians,
all panic struck, fleeing from the city." On their way, they hurled blame
at the immigrants, the poor, the prostitutes, the free blacks, and the
intemperate for instigating the epidemic. Disdaining any celebration of
the United States as a "refuge for the poor of other countries," Philip
Hone declared simply that foreigners "have brought the cholera this
year and they will always bring wretchedness and want."[49]

Physicians concluded that "the sensual, the vicious, the intemperate" were most likely to be afflicted by the disease, but they disagreed
over how cholera was transmitted. It was unclear whether or not the illness was contagious upon contact. Some argued that cholera could not
be contracted merely by exposure to someone who had it, but others
insisted that the disease was both infectious and highly contagious. If
cholera was not spread by contact, then citizens might be encouraged
to bestow charitable care upon the sick. But, given evidence that was
inconclusive, most Americans acted on the assumption that exposure
meant contamination.

Some physicians offered an alternative explanation as to how it
spread. Noting that the disease erupted simultaneously at different
times and in different locations, they argued that the atmosphere rather
than contagion served as the mechanism of dissemination. James
Kennedy, who wrote one of the first histories of the epidemic, concluded that the disease was "propagated through the atmosphere. . . .
When cholera was most virulent, the weather was close and sultry, and
during the day the sun was obscured by whitish clouds." Isaac Fidler
offered this observation: "It was borne along on the wings of the wind."
One analyst concluded that cholera migrated "from place to place, in

consequence of a cause existing in the air, and derived from some exhalations from the surface of the earth, or some intemperies of the atmosphere." Another expressed it more simply: "All pestilence is essentially of the atmosphere."[50]

If that were the case, Americans knew they had much to fear. The year leading to the cholera epidemic had been filled with atmospheric phenomena: an eclipse, the aurora borealis, comets, meteors, severe blizzards, and raging thunderstorms. These had been seen as signs of coming evils, but now Americans learned that the atmosphere itself could turn poisonous. Everyone knew the disease was especially fatal to "the poor, the squalid, the ill-fed, and the intemperate," and Christian moralists used the epidemic as an occasion to attack those who consumed alcohol. The cholera, warned Francis Wayland, "is the curse of God going forth over all the earth, entering into every house, and unfolding the doom of every family, sparing neither age nor sex, rank nor station, parent nor child, but marking every intemperate man and woman for instant, agonizing, strange, and horrible death."

But the disease struck the redeemers as well as the unredeemed. No less a figure than Charles G. Finney contracted and survived the cholera. For all the reports compiled by physicians, ministers offered as compelling an explanation of the cholera epidemic as anyone: "All Christians must regard it in the light of a pestilence sent forth by the Lord of the whole earth as one of God's sore judgments inflicted upon idolatrous nations, upon an adulterous and apostate race of professed christians. We must regard it as a prelude to the woes which are fast coming upon all the earth."[51]

MOUNT AUBURN CEMETERY AND FRANCES TROLLOPE

As the cholera plague was bearing down on the United States, a new cemetery opened outside of Boston. Disturbed by overcrowding in the city, dismayed by the condition of urban burial grounds, and anxious over their own final resting place, leading citizens in Boston planned a rural cemetery and garden on seventy-two acres of land that adjoined the road from Cambridge to Watertown. A meeting held on June 8, 1831, was chaired by Justice Joseph Story, who appointed Daniel Webster and Edward Everett to the cemetery committee. Within weeks, these men managed to maneuver through the state legislature an act incorporating the Massachusetts Horticultural Society and authorizing the organization to establish a "rural cemetery." Three-hundred-square-foot lots were sold for sixty dollars each; within weeks, more than a hundred lots were assigned.[52]

Various addresses laid bare the feelings that led to the creation of this "garden of graves." Edward Everett spoke of the need for a place of burial that citizens "may contemplate without dread or disgust; one that is secure from the danger of being encroached upon, as in the graveyards of the city, secluded from every species of uncongenial intrusion; surrounded with everything that can fill the heart with tender and respectful emotion; beneath the shade of a venerable tree, on the slope of a verdant lawn, and within the seclusion of the forest; removed from all the discordant scenes of life." Jacob Bigelow, a physician who led the rural-cemetery movement, urged that burial must take place "amidst the quiet verdure of the field, under the road and cheerful light of heaven, where the harmonious and ever-changing face of nature reminds us, by its resuscitating influence, that to die is but to live again."

The terror of death had given way to romance. The fate of all humans was to be met not with dread but with quietude. Planted in nature and surrounded by the peaceful solitude of nature, the city of the dead became a city of eternal life. "We are glad," thought one mourner, "when we see a sunbeam on the green roof of their narrow mansion, as if we could light up the darkness below; and if we see a tree or a flower planted above them, we feel as if they must revive and rejoice in the pledge that their memory is still treasured by some who loved them." At the new cemetery, remarked one observer, "Nature throws an air of cheerfulness over the labors of Death."[53]

On Saturday, September 24, Mount Auburn Cemetery was consecrated. Two thousand people filled a "natural amphitheatre" formed within a slight valley surrounded by trees. The sky was cloudless and the atmosphere clear, cleansed by thunderstorms that had passed through during the night. The ceremonies began with instrumental music. A prayer offered by Henry Ware followed. Justice Joseph Story then stepped forth to deliver a dedication address. Story at first had difficulty containing his emotions and at times paused to wipe his eyes. Five months earlier, his youngest child, Louisa, had died at age ten of the scarlet fever. "Sunk in utter desolation and despair," Story had admitted that "life would be to me a burden, a grievous burden, if it were not for the belief in another and better state of existence." Still, thoughts of her returned him to a state of "settled and miserable gloom."

Story began by reminding his listeners of "the duty of the living to provide for the dead" and the universal concern with "the time and place and manner of our death." Religion might teach that we are all dust, but "dust as we are, the frail tenements, which enclose our spirits but for a season, are dear, are inexpressibly dear to us." Story spoke of the spiritual impulse to be buried in one's homeland with one's family and friends, and of the importance for mourners to be near the burial ground of the dead: "As we sit down by their graves, we seem to hear the tones of their affection, whispering in our ears. We listen to the voice of their wisdom, speaking in the depths of our souls. We shed our tears; but they are no longer the burning tears of agony. They relieve our drooping spirit, and come no longer over us with a deathly faintness. We return to the world, and we feel ourselves purer, and better, and wiser, from this communion with the dead."

Story went on to review the burial practices of ancient civilizations and reminded listeners that the word "cemetery" meant "place of sleep or repose." He denounced the tradition of depositing "the remains of our friends in loathsome vaults, or beneath the gloomy crypts and cells of our churches, where the human foot is never heard." He despaired over city burial grounds that were "crowded on all sides" and left neglected and vandalized. No wonder graveyards carried with them feelings of terror.

But, located in nature, surrounded by beauty, the rural cemetery allowed mourners to banish the belief that the grave "is to be the abode of gloom, which will haunt the imagination by its terrors, or chill the heart by its solitude." To stand at the grave was to stand "upon the borders of two worlds"; the gravesite served as boundary "beyond which the living cannot go nor the dead return." Yet, by placing us within nature and furnishing a location for meditation and solitude, cemeteries such as Mount Auburn, Story predicted, would "tranquilize human fears" and "cast a cheerful light over the darkness of the grave."[54]

Mount Auburn was dedicated at the beginning of the fall, a season associated with miasma. One English traveler, Frances Trollope, left America in July so as to avoid another bout with "the noxious influence of an American autumn." Weak and feverish through the fall and winter of 1830–31, Trollope "felt persuaded that I shall never recover" from "the sickliness of the American autumn." While recuperating in Alexandria, Virginia, Trollope continued writing an account of her travels in America. Published a year after her return to England, *Domestic Manners of the Americans* became a publishing sensation. One observer reported, "The commotion it created amongst the good citizens is truly inconceivable. The Tariff and Bank Bill were alike forgotten, and the tug of war was hard whether the 'Domestic Manners,' or the cholera, which burst upon them simultaneously, should be the more engrossing topic of conversation."

Trollope, at age forty-seven, had arrived in the United States in 1827, accompanied by a son, two daughters, a servant, a maid, and a French artist who appended himself to the entourage. Also on board was Frances Wright, the mercurial lecturer and utopian, whose talk at the moment was full of her dreams for Nashoba, an experimental community near Memphis, Tennessee, aimed at preparing slaves for freedom. Trollope was facing financial difficulty and family problems—her son had dropped out of school and was looking to improve his prospects in America. Wright's vision thus seemed quite appealing, and together they left England, their sights set on Nashoba. But what Trollope encountered—a few flimsy cabins set near a swamp—bore no relationship to what she had imagined. Overcome by feelings of desolation, within weeks she left Wright and Nashoba behind. In February 1828, she arrived in Cincinnati, a frontier city that in a matter of years had been transformed from a remote outpost to a burgeoning metropolis of twenty thousand residents. At Cincinnati, Trollope formed her impressions of America, and lost a fortune in a failed attempt to open a bazaar that offered entertainment and a variety of goods for sale. She remained in Ohio just over two years before traveling east to Virginia, Maryland, and New York, and then leaving the country behind forever.[55]

But the country did not leave her. The publishing success of *Domestic Manners of the Americans* provided Trollope with the financial security that had eluded her in Cincinnati; she went on to write four novels set in America. Unlike many other travelers, however, Trollope offered neither lavish praise nor grudging admiration. She did not peer deeply into the structures of government or habits of the people. She offered impressions of the nation, impressions of slavery and religion, politics and character, and she concluded, "I do not like America. . . . I speak of the population generally, as seen in town and country, among the rich and the poor, in the slave states and the free states. I do not like them. I do not like their principles, I do not like their manners, I do not like their opinions."

Trollope highlighted the contradiction of Americans boasting of their liberty while enslaving Africans and killing Indians. "You will see them," declared Trollope, "with one hand hoisting the cap of liberty, and with the other flogging their slaves. You will see them one hour lecturing their mob on the indefeasible rights of man, and the next driving from their homes the children of the soil, whom they have bound themselves to protect by the most solemn treaties." But she also denounced the delusion of equality, suggesting that the slave system was "less injurious to the manners and morals of the people than the fallacious idea of equality" which allowed those with money to command the services of those without. Contemplating both slavery and equality, she threw up her hands and concluded that by some strange "political alchymy" Americans had contrived "to extract all that was most noxious both in democracy and in slavery, and had poured the strange mixture through every vein of the moral organization of their country."

Much as the British aristocrat was irked by the pretension to equality, manifested by an " 'I'm as good as you' " attitude that "would make of mankind an unamalgamated mass of grating atoms," she reserved her most bitter comments for the slaveholders. It disturbed her that laws made it criminal to teach slaves how to read and shocked her that slave owners often shipped their slaves to plantations in the Deep South which "are the terror of American Negroes." Especially galling was the lack of human sympathy accorded the enslaved, whom their masters often treated as if invisible. While Trollope was in Virginia, she boarded with a family consisting of a widow, four daughters, and several slaves. One of the slaves, an eight-year-old girl, found some biscuits in the cupboard and ate them. Unknown to her, they had been sprinkled with arsenic and placed there to kill off rats that had infested the kitchen. Trollope prepared an emetic of mustard and water and then held the girl in her lap and comforted her. The white family members started giggling. " 'My! If Mrs. Trollope has not taken her in her lap, and wiped her nasty mouth,' " one exclaimed. For Trollope, here was the tragedy of slavery: "The idea of really sympathizing in the sufferings of a slave, appeared to them as absurd as weeping over a calf that had been slaughtered by the butcher." The institution of slavery "paralyzed . . . the greatest and best feelings of the human heart."[56]

The icy heart of the American needed to be thawed, but Trollope dismissed as little more than a humbug evangelical attempts to do so. The "endless variety of religious factions" astonished her, as did the "vehement expressions of insane or hypocritical zeal" offered by itinerant ministers. In Indiana, she attended a revivalist camp-meeting and witnessed "hysterical sobbings, convulsive groans, shrieks, and screams the most appalling." "I felt sick with horror," Trollope reported. She viewed the preachers as actors playing to a participating audience that consisted mainly of young women. Once she saw a girl, in a fit of ecstasy, fall twelve feet from a gallery above into the arms of the congregation below. She watched with disgust as preachers sidled up to attractive women and whispered in their ears, "Sister, dear Sister," and the ladies responded by blushing and murmuring their confessions. The feminization of American religion astonished Trollope, who "never saw, or read, of any country where religion had so strong a hold upon the women, or a slighter hold upon the men." She believed that the reason religion attracted women more than men was that the clergy devoted to them "that sort of attention which is so dearly valued by every female heart throughout the world." And she chastised the good husbands and fathers of America for abandoning their wives and daughters to the domestic, evangelical realm, where ministers bound them in the "iron chains of a most tyrannical fanaticism."[57]

For Trollope, religion offered but one example of the evils of the illusion of equality in America. She despised the incessant political talk that inundated conversation. "Election fever," she noted, was "constantly raging through the land." The "electioneering madness alone," she exclaimed, even if everything else in America was attractive, "would make me fly it in disgust. It engrosses every conversation, it irritates every temper, it substitutes party spirit for personal esteem; and, in fact, vitiates the whole system of society." She was nauseated by the behavior of politicians who smoked cigars, swilled whiskey, and spit repeatedly; the title of her book might have been "the total and universal want of manners" in America. Despite all the statements, expositions, and editorials, the resignation of Jackson's Cabinet remained an enigma to Trollope, though she admired Edward Clay's caricature of the fleeing rats. Listening to deliberations in Congress, she gleaned a puzzling truth about the American polity: every debate seemed to pivot on the issue of "the entire independence of each individual state, with regard to the federal government." "The jealousy on this point," she commented, "appeared to me to be the very strangest political feeling that ever got possession of the mind of man."[58]

On only one day out of the year did the nation seem to be united and the people magnanimous: July 4. On that day, "the hearts of the people seem to awaken from a three hundred and sixty-four days' sleep; they appear high-spirited, gay, animated, social, generous." The rest of the year, however, Americans seemed an uncouth, inarticulate people driven only by the pursuit of wealth. In Cincinnati, trash was left in the streets to be disposed of by roving pigs; no one read books, only newspapers; and the only topic of conversation was enterprise. Trollope agreed with an English friend who proclaimed that, regardless of the location—on the street, in the home, in the field, at the theater—"he had never overheard Americans conversing without the word DOL-LAR being pronounced between them." "Such unity of purpose, such sympathy of feeling," Trollope insisted, "can be found nowhere else, except, perhaps, in an ants' nest. The result is exactly what might be anticipated. This sordid object, for ever before their eyes, must inevitably produce a sordid tone of mind, and, worse still, it produces a seared and blunted conscience on all questions of probity." Thus Americans, Trollope thought, gave fewer alms than any other nation in the world and averted their eyes from the problems of the poor.

But where profit was to be made, there the American commitment was limitless. Even Trollope marveled at "the boldness and energy with which public works are undertaken and carried through. Nothing stops them if a profitable result can be fairly hoped for. It is this which has made cities spring up amidst the forests with such inconceivable rapidity; and could they once be thoroughly persuaded that any point of the ocean had a hoard of dollars beneath it, I have not the slightest doubt that in about eighteen months we should see a snug covered rail-road leading direct to the spot."

Such grandiose scheming matched the grandeur of the American landscape, which offered forests and storms and vistas unlike any-where else. "The clearness and brightness of the atmosphere" aston-ished Trollope with its radiance and purity. "Every thing seems colossal on this great continent," she observed. "If it rains, if it blows, if it thunders, it is all done *fortissimo*; but I often felt terror yield to wonder and delight, so grand, so glorious were the scenes a storm exhibited."[59]

Trollope was giving voice to the romantic ideal of the sublime, a fascination with the power of nature to overwhelm the imagination and overturn the creations of humankind. At the precise moment when she was writing about the terrors and wonders of nature, an American artist in Europe was painting such a scene. Trollope, as with everything else, disdained the quality of the arts in the United States. She believed that American artists, whatever their natural talents, had to make their way "through darkness and thick night."[60] To the extent that she was correct, artists groped along by leaving the United States for study in Europe. One such artist, Thomas Cole, was in his second year of travel in England and on the Continent when he painted his *Tornado in an American Forest*, a work he described as "the greatest picture, perhaps, I have painted."

A storm has enveloped a forest and it threatens devastation. The sky has turned black; only a patch of light remains. The wind pushes against the trees. A man seeks cover between two gnarled trunks, but he is as inconsequential as a fallen branch. What power hath nature. How insignificant the worldly pursuits of man. Those caught in the storm's fury might survive, but the experience would change them, and their society, forever.

Cole exhibited the painting in England and then traveled the continent before returning to New York. "Completely tired of voyaging," he escaped the civilization of Europe for the landscape of America. Upon his return, he began his famous cycle of five works on *The Course of Empire* (1833–36). The paintings depicted the inevitable decline and destruction of all great commercial empires. Try as it might, America could not escape the fate of previous republics, and the current low condition of society, suggested Cole, would only hasten the disappearance of the nation before it had survived a century.[61]

Trollope took the opposite journey from Cole. She fled America for England, but not before experiencing a terrible storm like the one depicted in *Tornado*. She stood with her children on a hill, mesmerized as the tempest approached and unleashed its fury. The air grew heavy. The sky turned blue-black. Birds dived to the ground seeking shelter.

19. Thomas Cole, *Tornado in an American Forest*, 1831, 1835, oil on canvas, 46³/₈ x 64⁵/₈ in. (117.7 x 164.1 cm) (Courtesy of the Corcoran Gallery of Art, Washington, D.C., Gallery Fund)

Slowly, but inescapably, the darkening heavens moved overhead until "the inky cloud burst asunder, and cataracts of light came pouring from behind it. . . . The heavens blazed and bellowed above and around us, till stupor took the place of terror, and we stood utterly confounded. . . . Torrents of water seemed to bruise the earth by their violence; eddies of thick dust rose up to meet them; the fierce fires of heaven only blazed the brighter for the falling flood. . . . The wind was left at last the lord of all, for after striking with wild force, now here, now there, and bringing worlds of clouds together in most hostile contact, it finished by clearing the wide heavens of all but a few soft straggling masses, whence sprung a glorious rainbow, and then retired, leaving the earth to raise her half-crushed forests."

Some weeks later, Trollope looked heavenward again and witnessed the solar eclipse. She described it as "nearer total than any I ever saw, or ever shall see." Though "the darkness was considerable," the snow lessened the effect by reflecting what light shone through. It was a freezing day in Alexandria, but Trollope spent the entire time outdoors, on a rise near the Potomac River. "In this position," she noted, "many beautiful effects were perceptible; the rapid approach and change of shadows, the dusky hue of the broad Potomac, that seemed to drink in the feeble light . . . the gradual change of every object from the colouring of bright sunshine to one sad universal tint of dingy purple, the melancholy lowing of the cattle, and the short, but remarkable suspension of all labour."[62] The day seemed mysterious, pregnant with meaning; its hues would linger for a long time to come.

NOTES

ECLIPSE

1. *Ash's Pocket Almanac*, quoted in the *Saturday Bulletin*, February 5, 1831; *Daily Chronicle*, February 11, 1831. See also *Boston Evening Transcript*, February 14, 1831.

2. *Diary of Sarah Connell Ayer* (Portland, 1910), p. 312; *Boston Evening Gazette*, February 12, 1831; *Richmond Enquirer*, February 15, 1831.

3. *Daily Chronicle*, February 11, 1831; *Hampden Gazette*, quoted in *Daily Chronicle*, February 9, 1831.

4. *Philadelphia Gazette*, February 18, 1831; *Germantown Telegraph*, February 16, 1831; N. L. Frothingham, *Signs in the Sun: A Sermon Delivered on the Day After the Eclipse of the 12th February, 1831* (Boston, 1831), p. 6.

5. *National Intelligencer*, February 14, 1831; *Connecticut Mirror*, February 19, 1831; *Daily Chronicle*, February 14, 1831; *Hazard's Register*, February 19, 1831; *Boston Daily Evening Transcript*, February 12, 1831.

6. *Independent Chronicle and Boston Patriot*, February 19, 1831; *United States Gazette*, February 17, 1831.

7. Edward Everett to Charlotte Everett, February 12, 1831, Everett Papers, Massachusetts Historical Society; *United States Gazette*, February 16, 1831; *Philadelphia Gazette*, February 17, 1831.

8. *Saturday Bulletin*, February 12, 1831.

SLAVERY AND ABOLITION

1. *The Confessions of Nat Turner* (Baltimore, 1831), p. 11; *Boston Evening Transcript*, August 18, 1831.

2. Many of the newspaper accounts of Turner's insurrection are compiled in Henry Irving Tragle, *The Southampton Slave Revolt of 1831* (New York, 1971). Parenthetical page references below are to this volume; all dates are 1831. *Constitutional Whig*, August 23 (p. 35); *Richmond Compiler*, August 24 (p. 37); *American Beacon*, August 26 (p. 40). Turner discusses Travis in his *Confessions*. See also Samuel Warner, *Authentic and Impartial Narrative of the Tragical Scene* (New York, 1831).

3. *Constitutional Whig*, August 29 (p. 51); *Richmond Compiler*, August 27 (p. 47); *Richmond Compiler*, August 24 (p. 37); *Edenton Gazette*, August 31 (p. 56); *Richmond Enquirer*, August 30 (p. 45); *American Beacon*, August 29 (p. 49).

4. *Constitutional Whig*, September 26 (p. 91); *Petersburg Intelligencer*, August 26 (pp. 38–39); *Constitutional Whig*, August 29 (pp. 50–52).

5. *Constitutional Whig*, September 3 (pp. 66–72); *Constitutional Whig*, August 29 (pp. 50–52); *Lynchburg Virginian*, September 8 (pp. 73–75).

6. *Richmond Enquirer*, August 30 (p. 45); *Constitutional Whig*, September 3 (p. 68); *Constitutional Whig*, September 26 (p. 95).

7. William Parker to Governor John Floyd, September 14, in Tragle, *Southampton Slave Revolt*, pp. 420–21; *Richmond Compiler*, August 27 (p. 49); *Richmond Compiler*, September 3 (p. 60); *Lynchburg Virginian*, September 15 (p. 80); *Richmond Enquirer*, August 30 (p. 44); *Constitutional Whig*, September 3 (p. 70).

8. Warner, *Authentic Narrative*, p. 34; *American Beacon*, September 9 (p. 75); *Richmond Enquirer*, October 4 (p. 117); *Niles' Weekly Register*, October 29 (p. 131).

9. *American Beacon*, November 8 (pp. 132–33); *Norfolk Herald*, November 4 (pp. 134–35); *Petersburg Intelligencer*, November 4 (pp. 135–36).

10. *Richmond Enquirer*, November 8 (pp. 136–37). For a full discussion of Gray, see Daniel S. Fabricant, "Thomas R. Gray and William Styron: Finally, a Critical Look at the 1831 Confessions of Nat Turner,"*American Journal of Legal History* 37 (July 1993): 332–61. See also Kenneth Greenberg, ed., *The Confessions of Nat Turner and Related Documents* (Boston, 1996), pp. 1–35.

11. *Confessions of Nat Turner*, pp. 20, 3–5, 8–11, 18–19.

12. *Richmond Enquirer*, November 25 (p. 143).

13. *Niles' Weekly Register*, September 10 (p. 77); *Alexandria Gazette*, September 1831 (p. 88).

14. *Constitutional Whig*, September 26 (p. 92); *Richmond Enquirer*, September 27 (p. 102).

15. On Garrison, see John L. Thomas, *The Liberator* (Boston, 1963); Henry Mayer, *All on Fire: William Lloyd Garrison and the Abolition of Slavery* (New York, 1998). Quotations are from *Selections from the Writings and Speeches of William Lloyd Garrison* (Boston, 1852), pp. 44–61.

16. Wendell Phillips Garrison, *William Lloyd Garrison: The Story of His Life Told by His Children* (Boston, 1885).

17. Walter M. Merrill, ed., *The Letters of William Lloyd Garrison* (Cambridge, Mass., 1971), Vol. I, pp. 94, 97–103, 105.

18. Ibid., pp. 102, 106.

19. William Lloyd Garrison, *An Address Delivered Before the Free People of Color in Philadelphia, New York, and Other Cities* (Philadelphia, 1831), pp. 3, 8, 10–13, 14–15; W. P. Garrison, *William Lloyd Garrison*, vol. I, p. 260; *New York Evangelist*, September 20, 1831.

20. *New-Haven Register*, n.d., as cited in *College for Colored Youth: An Account of the New-Haven City Meeting and Resolutions* (New York, 1831), pp. 22–23.

21. Samuel J. May, *Discourse on Slavery in the United States Delivered in Brooklyn, Connecticut, July 3, 1831* (Boston, 1832), pp. 4–5.

22. *Liberator*, January 29, 1831; January 22, 1831.

23. Ibid., January 8, 1831; May 14, 1831; May 28, 1831.

24. Merrill, ed., *Garrison Letters*, vol. I, p. 129; *Liberator*, September 3, 1831.

25. *Richmond Enquirer*, September 27 (p. 101); Merrill, ed., *Garrison Letters*, vol. I, p. 139; *Liberator*, September 10, 1831.

26. *Liberator*, October 8, 1831.

27. Merrill, ed., *Garrison Letters*, vol. I, p. 113; *Liberator*, December 17, 1831; October 1, 1831.

28. *Liberator*, September 10, 1831; October 1, 1831.

29. *Free Enquirer*, September 17, 1831, p. 380

30. [Thomas R. Dew,] "Abolition of Negro Slavery," *American Quarterly Review* 12 (September 1832): 245.

31. John Floyd, diary entry for September 27, 1831, reprinted in Tragle, *Southampton Slave Revolt*, pp. 255–56.

32. [James Boardman,] *America, and the Americans* (London, 1833), p. 7; Godfrey T. Vigne, *Six Months in America* (London, 1832), vol. II, pp. 32–41.

33. Henry Tudor, *Narrative of a Tour in North America* (London, 1834), vol. II, pp. 68–78.

34. [Thomas Hamilton,] *Men and Manners in America* (Philadelphia, 1833), pp. 279–80; 57–58, 317–22.

35. J. M. Peck, *Guide for Emigrants* (Boston, 1831), pp. 75–76.

36. *Philadelphia Gazette*, September 21, 1831; *New York Evening Post*, December 26, 1831; James Alexander, *Transatlantic Sketches* (Philadelphia, 1833), p. 227.

37. Johann August Roebling, *Diary of My Journey* (Trenton, 1931), pp. 117–18.

38. George Wilson Pierson, *Tocqueville and Beaumont in America* (New York, 1938; reprinted Baltimore, 1996), pp. 43–44.

39. J. P. Mayer, ed., *Alexis de Tocqueville: Journey to America* (New Haven, 1962), pp. 50, 225, 116, 61, 70.

40. Mayer, ed., *Journey*, pp. 224–25; Gustave de Beaumont, *Marie, or Slavery in the United States* (Stanford, Calif., 1958), p. 4; Pierson, *Tocqueville and Beaumont*, p. 515; Mayer, ed., *Journey*, pp. 157–59.

41. Alexis de Tocqueville, *Democracy in America*, trans. Phillips Bradley (New York, 1945), vol, I, pp. 370–97.

42. Mayer, ed., *Journey*, p. 264. A comparison of Tocqueville's diaries and letters from his journey with the chapter on race in *Democracy* shows how closely the former informed the latter.

43. Mayer, ed., *Journey*, p. 100; Alexis de Tocqueville to Louis de Kergoly, June 29, 1831, in Roger Boesche, ed., *Alexis de Tocqueville: Selected Letters on Politics and Society* (Berkeley, Calif., 1985), p. 46; Tocqueville, *Democracy in America*, vol. I, pp. 370–88.

44. Mayer, ed., *Journey*, p. 242.

45. Tocqueville, *Democracy in America*, vol. I, pp. 388–97.

46. Beaumont, *Marie*, pp. 36, 55, 74, 214–16.

47. *Niles' Weekly Register*, September 24 (p. 89); *African Repository* 6 (February 1831): 362.

48. Merrill, ed., *Garrison Letters*, vol. I, p. 124; William Lloyd Garrison, *Thoughts on African Colonization* (Boston, 1832), part II, p. 31.

49. *Liberator*, April 23, 1831; "After Nat Turner: A Letter from the North," *Journal of Negro History* 55 (April 1970): 147; Alison Goodyear Freehling, *Drift Toward Dissolution: The Virginia Slavery Debate of 1831–32* (Baton Rouge, La., 1982), pp. 170–71.

50. [Boardman,] *America, and the Americans*, p. 249.

51. Jane Randolph quoted in Freehling, *Drift Toward Dissolution*, p. 6; Floyd to James Hamilton, November 19, 1831, in Tragle, *Southampton Slave Revolt*, pp. 275–76; Floyd diary in Tragle, *Southampton Slave Revolt*, pp. 261–62.

52. *Richmond Enquirer*, December 17, 1831.

53. Ibid., January 19, 1832.

54. Ibid., January 21, 1832; January 24, 1832.

55. *Speech of John Thompson Brown* (Richmond, 1832), pp. 5, 15, 18, 21.

56. *Richmond Enquirer*, January 24, 1832; January 28, 1832.

57. "The Kentucky Resolutions," in Merrill Peterson, ed., *The Portable Thomas Jefferson* (New York, 1975), p. 281; *Notes on the State of Virginia*, ibid., p. 186.

58. Edward Coles to Thomas Jefferson, July 31, 1814, September 26, 1814, in *William and Mary Quarterly*, 2nd ser., 7 (1927): 97–100; Thomas Jefferson to

Edward Coles, August 25, 1814, in Peterson, *Portable Thomas Jefferson*, pp. 544–47.

59. Thomas Jefferson to John Holmes, April 22, 1820, in Peterson, *Portable Thomas Jefferson*, p. 567.

60. Edward Coles to Thomas Jefferson Randolph, December 29, 1831, in *William and Mary Quarterly*, 2nd ser., 7 (1927): 105–7.

61. *The Speech of Thomas J. Randolph in the House of Delegates of Virginia on the Abolition of Slavery* (Richmond, 1832); *Richmond Enquirer*, January 28, 1832. On September 2, 1829, Garrison proclaimed in the *Genius of Universal Emancipation*: "The question of expediency has nothing to do with that of right and it is not for those who tyrannize to say when they may safely break the chains of their subjects."

62. *Speech of Thomas J. Randolph*, pp. 8–9.

RELIGION AND POLITICS

1. The Niagara Falls parable was first recorded by Asa Rand, "Depravity and Regeneration," *Volunteer* 1 (December 1831): 138–39. The sermon in which it appeared, "Sinners Bound to Change Their Own Hearts," was published in Finney's *Sermons on Various Subjects* (New York, 1836), pp. 14–15; [Lyman Beecher,] "The Necessity of Revivals of Religion to the Perpetuity of our Civil and Religious Institutions," *Spirit of the Pilgrims* 4 (September 1831): 478.

2. Garth M. Rosell and Richard A. G. Dupuis, eds., *The Memoirs of Charles G. Finney: The Complete Restored Text* (Grand Rapids, Mich., 1989), p. 325; "The Recent Revivals of Religion," *Spirit of the Pilgrims* 4 (August 1831): 409; Rosell and Dupuis, eds., *Memoirs of Finney*, p. 307.

3. *Memoirs of Rev. Charles G. Finney* (New York, 1876), p. 24. On Finney, see Keith J. Hardman, *Charles Grandison Finney: Revivalist and Reformer* (Syracuse, New York, 1987); William McLoughlin, *Modern Revivalism: Charles Grandison Finney to Billy Graham* (New York, 1959).

4. James Boardman, *America and the Americans* (London, 1833), p. 131.

5. [Beecher,] "Necessity of Revivals," p. 467. On the Great Awakening in Rochester, see Paul Johnson, *A Shopkeeper's Millennium: Society and Revivals in Rochester, New York, 1815–1837* (New York, 1978).

6. Rosell and Dupuis, eds., *Memoirs of Finney*, pp. 299–302; account of Finney's preaching quoted in Hardman, *Finney*, pp. 201, 207.

7. Rosell and Dupuis, eds., *Memoirs of Finney*, pp. 330, 343–45.

8. "Sinners Bound to Change Their Own Hearts," in Finney, *Sermons on Various Subjects;* William McLoughlin, ed., *Lectures on Revivals of Religion* (Cambridge, Mass., 1960), pp. 209, 220.

9. Asa Rand, *The New Divinity Tried* (Boston, 1832). Benjamin Wisner responded to Rand's attack in *Review of "The New Divinity Tried"* (Boston, 1832). Rand then issued *A Vindication of "The New Divinity Tried"* (Boston, 1832), to which Wisner responded with *Reply to Rand's "Vindication"* (1832). See also *Spirit of the Pilgrims* 5 (March 1832): 161–69.

10. "Thoughts on Some of the Dangers of the Times," *Spirit of the Pilgrims* 4 (November 1831): 574; William Sprague, *Lectures on Revivals of Religion* (New York, 1836), p. 37; Rand, *New Divinity Tried*, p. 14.

11. Walter Balfour, *Tricks of Revivalists Exposed* (Boston, 1831), p. 13.

12. Bernard Whitman, *Letter to an Orthodox Minister* (Boston, 1831), p. 51.

13. Ralph Waldo Emerson to Mary Moody Emerson, February 8, 1831, in *The Letters of Ralph Waldo Emerson*, ed. Ralph L. Rusk (1939), vol. I, p. 318; *Journals and Miscellaneous Notebooks of Ralph Waldo Emerson*, ed. William H. Gilman and Alfred R. Ferguson (Cambridge, Mass., 1963), vol. III, pp. 238, 246, 257, 259.

14. Gilman and Ferguson, eds., *Emerson Journals*, vol. III, p. 259; vol V, p. 477.

15. John Claiborne, *Life and Correspondence of John A. Quitman* (New York, 1860), pp. 108–9.

16. Charles Hall to Absalom Peters, December 17, 1830, quoted in Whitney Cross, *The Burned-Over District* (New York, 1950), p. 177; Rosell and Dupuis, eds., *Memoirs of Finney*, pp. 305–6; McLoughlin, ed., *Lectures on Revivals of Religion*, p. 259; Rebeccah Lee, *An Address Delivered in Marlbourough, Connecticut, September 7, 1831*, quoted in Nancy F. Cott, *The Bonds of Womanhood* (New Haven, 1977), pp. 131–32.

17. Lydia Maria Child, *The Mother's Book*, 3rd ed. (Boston, 1832); review of "The Mother's Book," *American Monthly Magazine* 3 (July 1831): 238. For an exhaustive study of Child, see Carolyn L. Karcher, *The First Woman in the Republic* (Durham, N.C., 1994).

18. Henry Ware, Jr., *On the Formation of Christian Character*, in Henry Ware, Jr., *Sermons* (Boston, 1847), vol. II, pp. 287–391. See also William Sullivan, *The Moral Class Book* (Boston, 1831).

19. *Spirit of the Pilgrims* 5 (May 1832): 277–96; Edward Everett, "Advantage of Knowledge to Workingmen: An Address Delivered as the Introduction to the Franklin Lectures in Boston, November 14, 1831," in Edward Everett, *Orations and Speeches on Various Occasions* (Boston, 1865), vol. I, p. 327.

20. *Working Man's Advocate*, November 5, 1831. On reactions to Mormons, see *Working Man's Advocate*, May 28, 1831; *New Jersey Mirror*, August 26, 1831; September 11, 1831; *Connecticut Mirror*, April 16, 1831; *Philadelphia Gazette*, August 20, 1831.

21. *First Annual Report of the Executive Committee of the New-York Magdalen Society* (New York, 1831), pp. 5, 8, 9, 13; *Connecticut Mirror*, July 23, 1831;

*Orthodox Bubbles, or a Review of the First Annual Report of the Executive Com-
mittee of the New-York Magdalen Society* (Boston, 1831), p. 11; *Working Man's
Advocate,* July 20, 1831; *Confessions of a Magdalen* (New York, 1831), p. 30.

22. *Orthodox Bubbles,* pp. 9–10; *Confessions of a Magdalen,* pp. 3, 29; *First
Annual Report,* p. 11; *Magdalen Facts* (New York, 1831), p. 95.

23. *Confessions of a Magdalen,* p. 29; *Orthodox Bubbles,* p. 9; *Working Man's
Advocate,* July 25, 1831; *Remarks on the Report of the New-York Magdalen
Society* (New York, 1831), p. 11.

24. Samuel Whitcomb, Jr., *An Address Before the Working-Men's Society of Dedham* (Dedham, Mass., 1831), pp. 18–20.

25. Stephen Simpson, *The Working Man's Manual* (Philadelphia, 1831), p. 20.

26. "Imprisonment for Debt," *North American Review* 31 (April 1831): 491, 502;
Sixth Annual Report of the Board of Managers of the Prison Discipline Society
(Boston, 1831), p. 66; Simpson, *Working Man's Manual,* pp. 189–90.

27. "Report of the Select Committee on So Much of the Governor's Message As
Relates to Imprisonment for Debt," Assembly Doc. 190, *New York Assembly
Documents* (Albany, 1831), pp. 1–32; *An Act to Abolish Imprisonment for Debt
and to Punish Fraudulent Debtors* (New York, 1831); *Laws of the State of New-
York Passed at the Fifty-fourth Session of the Legislature* (Albany, 1831),
pp. 396–406.

28. Allan Nevins, ed., *The Diary of Philip Hone, 1828–1851* (New York, 1927),
vol. I, p. 35; Thomas Skidmore, *The Rights of Man to Property* (New York,
1829), quoted in Sean Wilentz, *Chants Democratic* (New York, 1984), p. 185;
Free Enquirer, December 24, 1831, p. 71.

29. Robert Dale Owen, *Moral Physiology; or, A Brief and Plain Treatise on the
Population Question* (New York, 1831), pp. 16, 42; *Free Enquirer,* March 26,
1831, p. 176.

30. Thomas Skidmore, *Moral Physiology Exposed and Refuted* (New York, 1831),
pp. 71, 75, 37, 9.

31. Evans quoted in Walter Hugins, *Jacksonian Democracy* (Stanford, Calif.,
1960), p. 86; *Free Enquirer,* November 5, 1831, p. 16.

32. *Free Enquirer,* December 24, 1831, p. 69; Thomas Hamilton, *Men and Manners in America* (Philadelphia, 1833), p. 156; J. P. Mayer, ed., *Alexis de
Tocqueville: Journey to America* (New Haven, 1962), pp. 170–71.

33. Edward Giddins, *An Account of the Savage Treatment of William Morgan in
Fort Niagara* (Boston, 1830); *An Impartial Statement of the Facts in the Case
of Rev. George Witherell* (Boston, 1831); *A Letter on Freemasonry by the Hon.
Richard Rush* (Boston, 1831).

34. *Memoirs of John Quincy Adams* (Philadelphia, 1876), vol VIII, pp. 378, 368;
John Q. Adams, *Letters and Opinions of the Masonic Institution* (Cincinnati,
1851), pp. 9–27.

35. Josiah Johnston to Henry Clay, September 26, 1831, in Robert Seager, ed., *The Papers of Henry Clay* (Lexington, Ky., 1984), vol. VIII, p. 406; *New York Register and Antimasonic Review*, January 1, 1831, p. 14; *Proceedings of the Antimasonic State Convention of Massachusetts* (Boston, 1831), p. 17.

36. William H. Seward, *An Autobiography* (New York, 1891), pp. 89–90, 208.

37. John P. Kennedy, *Memoir of the Life of William Wirt* (Philadelphia, 1851), vol. II, p. 298; *The Proceedings of the Second United States Anti-Masonic Convention* (Boston, 1832), pp. 63–67.

38. *New York Evening Post*, October 1, 1831; *Niles' Weekly Register*, January 21, 1832; Henry Clay to James F. Conover, October 9, 1831, in Seager, ed., *Clay Papers*, vol. VIII, p. 417; *New Jersey Journal of Commerce*, quoted in *Maine Working Men's Advocate*, October 20, 1831; Kennedy, *Memoir of the Life of William Wirt*, vol. II, p. 312.

39. Calvin Philleo, *Light on Masonry and Anti-Masonry* (Providence, 1831); James Thompson, *An Address Delivered Before the Fraternity at Leicester, Massachusetts* (Cambridge, Mass., 1831), p. 3; *Free Enquirer*, November 27, 1830, p. 39.

40. Seward, *Autobiography*, pp. 208–9.

41. Harriet Martineau, *Retrospect of Western Travel* (New York, 1838), vol. I, p. 173; Calvin Colton, ed., *The Private Correspondence of Henry Clay* (Boston, 1856), pp. 304, 308–9; *Journal of the National Republican Convention* (Washington, 1831), pp. 20, 24, 25. On the history of the Whigs in America, see Daniel Walker Howe, *The Political Culture of the American Whigs* (Chicago, 1979); Michael Holt, *The Rise and Fall of the American Whig Party* (New York, 1999). See also Harry Watson, *Liberty and Power: The Politics of Jacksonian America* (New York, 1990).

42. Clay wrote in August, "I fear the public mind is not yet ripe for gradual emancipation." The month before, he sought to buy "three or four young negro men." (Henry Clay to Thomas Speed, August 23, 1831, and Henry Clay to George Corbin Washington, July 24, 1831, in Seager, ed., *Clay Papers*, vol. VIII, pp. 390, 378. Quote in text is from Calvin Colton, ed., *Works of Henry Clay* (New York, 1897), vol. V, p. 439.

43. Martineau, *Retrospect of Western Travel*, vol. I, p. 172; Charles Wiltse, ed., *The Papers of Daniel Webster: Speeches and Formal Writings* (Hanover, N. H., 1986), vol. I, pp. 347–48.

44. Daniel Webster to Elisha Whittlesey, May 10, 1831, in Charles Wiltse, ed., *The Papers of Daniel Webster* (Hanover, N. H., 1977), vol. III, p. 112; Daniel Webster to Albert Haller Tracy, January 15, 1831, ibid., p. 97; Daniel Webster to Ambrose Spencer, November 16, 1831, ibid., p. 134.

45. Speech at public dinner in New York, March 24, 1831, in Wiltse, ed., *Papers of Daniel Webster*, vol. I, p. 458.

46. *Diary of Philip Hone*, vol. I, p. 39; Daniel Webster to Charles Miner, August 28, 1831, in Wiltse, ed., *Papers of Daniel Webster*, vol. III, p. 120; Robert Remini, *Daniel Webster: The Man and His Time* (New York, 1997), quote following p. 542, p. 29n; Hamilton, *Men and Manners in America*, p. 285; Daniel Webster to Ambrose Spencer, November 16, 1831, in Wiltse, ed., *Papers of Daniel Webster*, vol. III, p. 135.

47. Hamilton, *Men and Manners in America*, p. 154; Daniel Webster to Henry Clay, October 5, 1831, in Wiltse, ed., *Papers of Daniel Webster*, vol. III, p. 129; Henry Clay to Francis Brooke, May 1, 1831, in Seager, ed., *Clay Papers*, vol. VIII, p. 342; Josiah Johnston to Henry Clay, January 7, 1831, ibid., p. 318.

48. James Parton, *Life of Andrew Jackson* (New York, 1868), vol. I, p. 104; Hamilton, *Men and Manners in America*, pp. 276–77, 228–29; Gustave Beaumont, quoted in George Wilson Pierson, *Tocqueville and Beaumont in America* (New York, 1938; reprinted Baltimore, 1996), p. 664; Henry Tudor, *Narrative of a Tour in North America* (London, 1834), p. 470.

49. Hamilton, *Men and Manners in America*, p. 282; Clyde N. Wilson, ed., *The Papers of John C. Calhoun* (Columbia, S.C., 1978), vol. XI, pp. 173–91.

50. Wilson, ed., *Calhoun Papers*, vol. XI, p. 295.

51. Monroe to Madison, April 11, 1831, in Stanislaus Murray Hamilton, ed., *The Writings of James Monroe* (New York, 1898). See Lucius Wilmerding, Jr., *James Monroe: Public Claimant* (New Brunswick, N.J., 1960); Harry Ammon, *James Monroe: The Quest for National Identity* (New York, 1971).

52. Charles Francis Adams, ed., *Memoirs of John Quincy Adams* (Philadelphia, 1876), vol. VIII, p. 360, 401–2; John Quincy Adams, *Eulogy on the Life and Character of James Monroe* (Boston, 1831); Gilman and Ferguson, eds., *Emerson Journals*, vol. III, p. 282.

53. John Quincy Adams to John C. Calhoun, January 14, 1831, in Wilson, ed., *Calhoun Papers*, vol. XI, p. 296; Daniel Webster to Henry Clay, April 4, 1831, in Seager, ed., *Clay Papers*, vol. VIII, p. 331; Andrew Jackson to Charles J. Love, March 7, 1831, in John Spencer Bassett, ed., *Correspondence of Andrew Jackson* (Washington, D.C., 1929), vol. IV, p. 246.

54. John C. Calhoun to James H. Hammond, January 15, 1831, in Wilson, ed., *Calhoun Papers*, vol. XI, p. 299; Andrew Jackson to John C. McLemore, April 1829, in Bassett, ed., *Jackson Correspondence*, vol. IV, p. 21; Louis McLane, quoted in Robert V. Remini, *Andrew Jackson and the Course of American Freedom, 1822–1832* (New York, 1981), p. 162; Charles Ambler, ed., *The Life and Diary of John Floyd* (Richmond, 1918), pp. 148–49; Gaillard Hunt, ed., *The First Forty Years of Washington Society: The Letters of Margaret Bayard Smith* (New York, 1906), p. 318.

55. A full account of the Eaton affair is offered in John F. Marszalek, *The Petti-coat Affair: Manners, Mutiny, and Sex in Andrew Jackson's White House* (New York, 1997).

56. Andrew Jackson to Richard Call, July 5, 1829, in Bassett, ed., *Jackson Correspondence*, vol. IV, p. 52; Jackson to Stiles, March 23, 1829 in Parton, ed., *Life of Andrew Jackson*, vol. III, pp. 188–89.

57. Andrew Jackson to John C. McLemore, April 1829, in Bassett, ed., *Jackson Correspondence*, vol. IV, p. 20; Andrew Jackson to Samuel Swartwout, September 27, 1829, ibid., p. 78; Andrew Jackson to Andrew Donelson, March 24, 1831, ibid., p. 253; Andrew Jackson to John Coffee, May 13, 1831, ibid., p. 288.

58. *Philadelphia Sun*, April 28, 1831; *National Intelligencer*, May 4, 1831.

59. C. F. Adams, ed., *Memoirs of J. Q. Adams*, vol. VIII, pp. 359–60; *National Gazette*, April 28, 1831.

60. Marszalek, *Petticoat Affair*, p. 161; *United States Gazette*, April 29, 1831.

61. C. F. Adams, ed., *Memoirs of J. Q. Adams*, vol. VIII, p. 317; *Philadelphia National Gazette*, quoted in *Maine Working Men's Advocate*, May 4, 1831.

62. Boardman, *America and the Americans*, p. 76; Tocqueville, *Journey to America*, pp. 266, 239; Hamilton, *Men and Manners in America*, p. 245.

63. Henry Clay to Edward Everett, June 12, 1831, in Seager, ed., *Clay Papers*, vol. VIII, p. 360; Andrew Jackson to Martin Van Buren, September 21, 1831, in Bassett, ed., *Jackson Correspondence*, vol. IV, p. 351.

STATE AND NATION

1. Edward Everett to Charlotte Everett, February 22, 1831, in Everett Papers, Massachusetts Historical Society.

2. Wirt quoted in R. Kent Newmeyer, *Supreme Court Justice Joseph Story: Statesman of the Old Republic* (Chapel Hill, N.C., 1985), p. 425; Joseph Story to Sarah Story in William W. Story, ed., *Life and Letters of Joseph Story* (Boston, 1851), vol. II, p. 87; Charles Francis Adams, ed., *Memoirs of John Quincy Adams* (Philadelphia, 1876), vol. VIII, pp. 315–16; *Niles' Weekly Register*, March 26, 1831, p. 68.

3. See Francis P. Prucha, *American Indian Policy in the Formative Years* (Cambridge, Mass., 1962); Jackson quoted in Michael Paul Rogin, *Fathers and Children* (New York, 1975), p. 131.

4. *Cherokee Phoenix*, November 12, 1831, in Theda Perdue, ed., *Cherokee Editor: The Writings of Elias Boudinot* (Knoxville, Tenn., 1983), pp. 140–43.

5. Godfrey Vigne, *Six Months in America* (Boston, 1832), vol. I, pp. 216–17; Jackson's public pronouncements can be followed in James D. Richardson, *A*

Compilation of the Messages and Papers of the Presidents, 1789–1908 (Washington, D.C., 1908), vol. II, esp. pp. 456–59, 519–23, 554–55, 603–5.

6. *Register of Debates in Congress* (Washington, D.C., 1830), vol. VI, part 1, pp. 309–20, 343–57.

7. Ibid., part 2, pp. 1058–79.

8. *Register of Debates in Congress* (Washington, D.C., 1831), vol. VII, pp. 618–19, 682–84.

9. Ibid., pp. 685–717. Opponents of removal also published Everett's speech separately in pamphlet form.

10. Wirt to Ross, June 4, 1830, in Gary E. Moulton, ed., *The Papers of Chief John Ross* (Norman, Okla., 1985), vol. I, p. 190. Wirt's exchange with Gilmer was widely reprinted in the newspapers; see, for example, *Niles' Weekly Register*, September 18, 1830, pp. 69–71. Wirt's correspondence with Carr is in John P. Kennedy, *Memoirs of the Life of William Wirt* (Philadelphia, 1851), vol. II, pp. 253–58.

11. *Niles' Weekly Register*, January 8, 1831; Joseph Story to John Ashmun, January 30, 1831, in W. W. Story, ed., *Life and Letters of J. Story*, vol. II, pp. 47–48.

12. The oral arguments in the case are reported in Richard Peters, *The Case of the Cherokee Nation Against the State of Georgia* (Philadelphia, 1831). Peters, the court reporter, published the volume to promote public sentiment in favor of the Cherokee; he dedicated it to Joseph Story. See pp. 92, 95, 155–56, 158–59.

13. C. F. Adams, ed., *Memoirs of J. Q. Adams*, vol. VIII, p. 343.

14. Peters, *Cherokee Nation Against State of Georgia*, pp. 15–80; Joseph Story to Mrs. Joseph Story, January 13, 1832, in W. W. Story, ed., *Life and Letters of J. Story*, vol. II, p. 79.

15. *Richmond Enquirer*, March 24, 1831.

16. The account of the meeting was widely reprinted. See, for example, ibid., June 24, 1831.

17. *Vermont Telegraph*, quoted in John Ehle, *Trail of Tears: The Rise and Fall of the Cherokee Nation* (New York, 1988), p. 252; Joseph Story to Mrs. Joseph Story, February 26, 1832, in W. W. Story, ed., *Life and Letters of J. Story*, vol. II, pp. 83–84.

18. *Worcester v. State of Georgia*, 6 Peters 515 (1832), p. 243; Joseph Story to George Ticknor, March 8, 1832, in W. W. Story, ed., *Life and Letters of J. Story*, vol. II, p. 83.

19. Andrew Jackson quoted in Robert V. Remini, *Andrew Jackson and the Course of American Freedom, 1822–1832* (New York, 1981), p. 276; Evans Jones quoted in William G. McLoughlin, "The Reverend Evan Jones and the Cherokee Trail of Tears, 1838–1839," *Georgia Historical Quarterly* 73 (1989): 569.

20. Ellen Whitney, ed., *The Black Hawk War, 1831–32* (Springfield, Ill., 1973), vol. II, pp. 3, 13.

21. William Clark to Edmund Gaines, May 28, 1831, in Whitney, ed., *Black Hawk War*, p. 17; "Memorandum of Talks between Edmund P. Gaines and the Sauk, June 4, 5, 7, 1831," ibid., pp. 27–33. See also the account provided by Black Hawk first published in 1833, in Donald Jackson, ed., *Black Hawk: An Autobiography* (Carbondale, Ill., 1964).

22. Roger L. Nichols, *Black Hawk and the Warrior's Path* (Arlington Heights, Ill., 1992).

23. Jackson, ed., *Black Hawk Autobiography*, pp. 114, 139.

24. Brian Dippie, *Catlin and His Contemporaries: The Politics of Patronage* (Lincoln, Neb., 1990), p. 5. See also George Catlin, *Letters and Notes on the Manners, Customs, and Conditions of North American Indians* (London, 1844; New York, 1973).

25. Catlin recounts the story of Wi-jun-jon in *Letters and Notes*, vol. II, pp. 194–200. See also the discussion in Dippie, *Catlin*, pp. 61–63.

26. Tocqueville to his mother, December 25, 1831, in Roger Boesche, ed., *Alexis de Tocqueville: Selected Letters on Politics and Society* (Berkeley, Calif., 1985), pp. 70–73.

27. "First Annual Message," in Richardson, *Compilation*, vol. II, p. 458; James A. Hamilton to Andrew Jackson, January 4, 1830, in John Spencer Bassett, ed., *Jackson Correspondence* (Washington, D.C., 1929), vol. IV, pp. 111–14; "Second Annual Message," in Richardson, *Compilation*, vol. II, pp. 519–20.

28. Biddle to Jonathan Roberts, January 15, 1831, quoted in Robert V. Remini, *Andrew Jackson*, p. 304; [George Bancroft,] "Bank of the United States," *North American Review* 33 (January 1831): 22; A Merchant [David Henshaw,]; *Remarks upon the Bank of the United States* (Boston, 1831), pp. 14–15.

29. *Register of Debates in Congress*, vol. VII, pp. 46–78.

30. Stephen Simpson, *The Working Man's Manual* (Philadelphia, 1831), pp. 253, 263.

31. Jackson to John Randolph, December 22, 1831, in John Spencer Bassett, ed., *Jackson Correspondence* (Washington D.C., 1929), vol. IV, p. 387.

32. McLane quoted in John A. Munroe, *Louis McLane: Federalist and Jacksonian* (New Brunswick, N.J., 1973), p. 319.

33. C. F. Mercer to Nicholas Biddle, December 12, 1831, in Reginald McGrane, ed., *Correspondence of Nicholas Biddle Dealing with National Affairs, 1807–1844* (Boston, 1919), p. 141; Henry Clay to Nicholas Biddle, December 15, 1831, in Robert Seager, ed., *The Papers of Henry Clay* (Lexington, Ky., 1984), vol. VIII, p. 433; Daniel Webster to Nicholas Biddle, December 18, 1831, in Charles Wiltse, ed., *The Papers of Daniel Webster* (Hanover, N.H., 1977), vol. III, p. 139.

34. Thomas Cadwalader to Nicholas Biddle, December 21, 1831, in McGrane, ed., *Correspondence of Nicholas Biddle*, p. 148.

35. James Madison to Charles Ingersoll, June 25, 1831, in *Letters and Other Writings of James Madison* (Philadelphia, 1865), vol. IV, pp. 183–187; Andrew Jackson quoted in Robert V. Remini, *Andrew Jackson and the Bank War* (New York, 1967), pp. 15–16.

36. "Veto Message," in Richardson, *Compilation*, vol. II, pp. 576–91.

37. Nicholas Biddle to Henry Clay, August 1, 1832, in McGrane, ed., *Correspondence of Nicholas Biddle*, p. 196.

38. James Martin, Jr., to Willie P. Mangum, December 27, 1831, in *The Papers of Willie Person Mangum* (Raleigh, 1950), vol. I, p. 441; free-trade proponent quoted in William Freehling, *Prelude to Civil War: The Nullification Controversy in South Carolina, 1816–1836* (New York, 1965), p. 94.

39. Thomas Hamilton, *Men and Manners in America* (Philadelphia, 1833), p. 108; Mary E. Dewey, ed., *Life and Letters of Catherine Sedgwick* (New York, 1872), p. 215.

40. Vigne, *Six Months in America*, vol. I, pp. 211–12; James Hamilton, Jr., *Speech at Waterborough* (Charleston, 1828), in William Freehling, ed., *The Nullification Era* (New York, 1967), pp. 48–61.

41. South Carolina Exposition and Protest, in Clyde N. Wilson and W. Edwin Hemphill, eds., *The Papers of John C. Calhoun* (Columbia, S.C., 1977), vol. X, pp. 444–539; *Richmond Enquirer*, quoted in *Banner of the Constitution*, June 1, 1831.

42. Hamilton, *Men and Manners in America*, p. 169; James Madison to David Hoffman, June 13, 1832, in *Letters of Madison*, vol. IV, p. 223; James Madison to Reynolds Chapman, January 6, 1831, in *Letters of Madison*, vol. IV, pp. 143–50.

43. James Madison to Joseph G. Cabell, September 16, 1831, in *Letters of Madison*, vol. IV, p. 196; James Madison to Townsend, October 18, 1831, ibid., p. 200; James Madison to James Robertson, March 27, 1831; ibid., p. 167; James Madison to Henry Clay, October 9, 1830, ibid., p. 117; James Madison to Townsend, October 18, 1831, ibid., p. 199; James Madison to Nicholas Trist, December 1831, ibid., p. 204.

44. James Madison to Joseph C. Cabell, September 16, 1831, ibid., p. 196; James Madison to Mathew Carey, ibid., p. 192.

45. Jackson quoted in Remini, *Andrew Jackson*, p. 70; "Second Annual Message," in Richardson, *Compilation*, vol. II, pp. 511–18.

46. Andrew Jackson to Martin Van Buren, November 14, 1831, in Bassett, ed. *Jackson Correspondence*, vol. IV, p. 374; Jackson to Van Buren, July 23, 1831, ibid., p. 316; Jackson to Van Buren, September 18, 1831, ibid., p. 351; Jackson to Robert Y. Hayne, February 8, 1831, ibid., p. 242.

47. Hamilton, *Men and Manners in America*, pp. 168–69, 111; J. M. Peck, *Guide for Emigrants* (Boston, 1831), pp. 5–6.

48. J. P. Mayer, ed., *Alexis de Tocqueville: Journey to America* (New Haven, 1962), pp. 66, 182; Alexis de Tocqueville to Ernest de Chabrol, October 7, 1831, in Boesche, ed., *Tocqueville: Letters*, p. 59.

49. Alexis de Tocqueville, *Democracy in America*, trans. Phillips Bradley (New York, 1945), vol. I, p. 427; George Wilson Pierson, *Tocqueville and Beaumont in America* (New York, 1938; reprinted Baltimore, 1996), pp. 71, 131.

50. *New York Evening Post*, May 21, 1831; *The Journal of the Free Trade Convention, Held in Philadelphia* (Philadelphia, 1831), pp. 51, 62; "Address to the People of the United States," in *Journal of the Free Trade Convention*, pp. 31–41.

51. *Banner of the Constitution*, November 30, 1831.

52. *Journal of the Proceedings of the Friends of Domestic Industry* (Baltimore, 1831), p. 16.

53. *Saturday Bulletin*, July 2, 1831; *Speech of the Hon. George McDuffie, at a Public Dinner Given to Him by the Citizens of Charleston, (S.C.) May 19, 1831* (Charleston, 1831), pp. 4, 25, 28–29.

54. Quoted in Freehling, ed., *Nullification Era*, p. 104; Duff Green to John C. Calhoun, May 31, 1831, in Wilson and Hemphill, eds., *Calhoun Papers*, vol. XI, pp. 398–401; John C. Calhoun to Christopher Vandeventer, May 25, 1831, ibid., p. 396.

55. John C. Calhoun to James H. Hammond, May 16, 1831, in Wilson and Hemphill, eds., *Calhoun Papers*, vol. XI, p. 383; John C. Calhoun to Christopher Vandeventer, May 25, 1831, ibid., p. 394; John C. Calhoun to David Caldwell, May 1, 1831, ibid., pp. 375–76; John C. Calhoun to the *Pendleton Messenger*, July 26, 1831, ibid., pp. 413–40.

56. Hammond quoted in Freehling, *Prelude to Civil War*, p. 166; Richard E. Ellis, *The Union at Risk: Jacksonian Democracy, States' Rights and the Nullification Crisis* (New York, 1987), p. 127; *United States Gazette*, August 24, 1831; John Quincy Adams to Henry Clay, September 7, 1831, in Seager, ed., *Clay Papers*, vol. VIII, p. 397; Henry Clay to James Conover, August 26, 1831, ibid., p. 392; Andrew Jackson to Martin Van Buren, September 5, 1831, in Bassett, ed., *Jackson Correspondence*, vol. IV, p. 346.

57. *Proceedings of the Celebration of the Fourth of July at Charleston, South Carolina* (Charleston, 1831); Robert Hayne, *An Oration, Delivered in the Independent or Congregational Church, Charleston, Before the State Rights & Free Trade Party, the State Society of Cincinnati, the Revolution Society, the '76 Association, and Several Volunteer Companies of Militia; on the 4th of July, 1831, Being the 55th Anniversary of American Independence* (Charleston, S.C., 1831), pp. 10–11, 13, 20–21.

58. *Proceedings of the Celebration*, pp. 46, 64.

59. Francis T. Brooke to Henry Clay, September 4, 1831, in Seager, ed., *Clay Papers*, vol. VIII, p. 397; *Liberator*, January 8, 1831, p. 7; *United States Gazette*, September 24, 1831.

60. Citizen of Abbeville, *Signs of the Times* (Columbia, S.C., 1831), pp. 24–25, 30.

61. William Drayton, *An Oration Delivered in the First Presbyterian Church, Charleston, on Monday July 4, 1831* (Charleston, S.C., 1831), pp. 41, 21–23, 26–29.

62. *Memoirs of John Quincy Adams* (Philadelphia, 1876), vol. VIII, p. 377; John Quincy Adams, *An Oration Addressed to the Citizens of the Town of Quincy, on the Fourth of July, 1831, the Fifty-Fifth Anniversary of the Independence of the United States of America* (Boston, 1831), pp. 6, 26, 34–36.

63. Quoted in Merrill Petersen, *The Great Triumvirate* (New York, 1987), p. 214.

64. Freehling, ed., *The Nullification Era*, includes many of the relevant documents; *Richmond Enquirer*, quoted in *Banner of the Constitution*, June 1, 1831.

MACHINES AND NATURE

1. *Free Enquirer*, December 10, 1831.

2. *Philadelphia Gazette*, March 23, 1831; *Saturday Bulletin*, October 8, 1831; James Alexander, *Transatlantic Sketches* (Philadelphia, 1833), p. 290; *Philadelphia Gazette*, August 1, 1831; *Report of the Camden and Amboy Railroad and Transportation Company* (Camden, N.J., 1831), p. 17; Henry Booth, *An Account of the Liverpool and Manchester Railway* (London, 1831), p. 197; *Saturday Bulletin*, April 2, 1831.

3. William Seward, *An Autobiography* (New York, 1891), pp. 195–96; *Niles' Weekly Register*, April 23, 1831.

4. John H. White, Jr., *The John Bull: 150 Years a Locomotive* (Washington, D.C., 1981), p. 24. See also John H. White, Jr., *American Locomotives* (Baltimore, 1997); James Vance, Jr., *The North American Railroad* (Baltimore, 1995).

5. John K. Brown, *The Baldwin Locomotive Works, 1831–1915* (Baltimore, 1995); *Saturday Bulletin*, April 30, 1831.

6. *Railroad Journal*, January 14, 1832; *Annual Report of the South Carolina Canal and Rail-Road Company* (Charleston, S. C.: 1831), p. 16; Alexander, *Transatlantic Sketches*, p. 232; *New Orleans Advertiser*, in *Philadelphia Gazette*, May 10, 1831.

7. James Dilts, *The Great Road: The Building of the Baltimore and Ohio, the Nation's First Railroad, 1828–1853* (Baltimore, 1993), p. 11. See also John Stover, *History of the Baltimore and Ohio Railroad* (West Lafayette, Ind., 1987).

8. Donald Jackson, ed., *Black Hawk: An Autobiography* (Carbondale, Ill., 1964), p. 145.

9. Evans quoted in Edwin Burrows and Mike Wallace, *Gotham: A History of New York City to 1898* (New York, 1999), p. 564; Gilbert quoted in *Free Enquirer*, November 15, 1831.

10. Dilts, *Great Road*, p. 138; *Railroad Journal*, June 9, 1832.

11. Abraham Lincoln, "To the People of Sangamo County," March 9, 1832, in Andrew Delbanco, ed., *The Portable Abraham Lincoln* (New York, 1992), pp. 5–9.

12. Dilts, *Great Road*, pp. 109–21.

13. See Stanley I. Kutler, *Privilege and Creative Destruction: The Charles River Bridge Case* (Philadelphia, 1971); Morton J. Horwitz, *The Transformation of American Law, 1780–1860* (Cambridge, Mass., 1977).

14. R. Kent Newmeyer, *Supreme Court Justice Joseph Story: Statesman of the Old Republic* (Chapel Hill, N.C., 1985); Dilts, *Great Road*, p. 110; *Charles River Bridge* v. *Warren Bridge*, 11 Peters 420 (1837).

15. J. Leander Bishop, *A History of American Manufactures from 1608 to 1860* (Philadelphia, 1868), pp. 351–65.

16. Salem D. Pattison, *The McCormick Extension Case of 1848* (Chicago, 1900), n.p.; William T. Hutchinson, *Cyrus Hall McCormick* (New York, 1930), p. 83.

17. Gustave de Beaumont, *Marie, or Slavery in the United States* (Stanford, Calif., 1958), p. 200; *The Reaper: Argument of William H. Seward in the Circuit Court of the United States* (Auburn, N.Y., 1854), pp. 3, 9, 29.

18. "Letters from Ohio," *New England Magazine* 1 (December 1831): 490; Nicholas Wood, *A Practical Treatise on Railroads* (Philadelphia, 1832), p. 467; *Saturday Bulletin*, June 25, 1831.

19. Charles Knight, *The Results of Machinery* (Philadelphia, 1831), pp. 29, 26; "Effects of Machinery," *North American Review* 34 (January 1832): 225, 233, 237; Stephen Simpson, *The Working Man's Manual* (Philadelphia, 1831), p. 133.

20. W. L. Fisher, *Pauperism and Crime* (Philadelphia, 1831), p. 18.

21. Tocqueville to Beaumont, April 4, 1832, in Roger Boesche, ed., *Alexis de Tocqueville: Selected Letters on Politics and Society* (Berkeley, Calif., 1985), p. 77; Tocqueville to Ernest de Chabrol, October 7, 1831, ibid., p. 59.

22. Gustave Beaumont and Alexis de Tocqueville, *On the Penitentiary System in the United States and Its Application in France* (Philadelphia, 1833; reprinted Carbondale, Ill., 1964), p. 84; Tocqueville quoted in George Wilson Pierson, *Tocqueville and Beaumont in America* (New York, 1938; reprinted Baltimore, 1996), pp. 662, 473.

23. Beaumont and Tocqueville, *On the Penitentiary System*, p. 60; J. P. Mayer, ed., *Alexis de Tocqueville: Journey to America* (New Haven, 1962), p. 204.

NOTES TO PAGES 185–199

24. Tocqueville quoted in Pierson, *Tocqueville and Beaumont*, pp. 546–47; Mayer, ed., *Journey*, p. 205; Beaumont and Tocqueville quoted in Pierson, *Tocqueville and Beaumont*, pp. 47, 115; Tocqueville to Ernest de Chabrol, June 9, 1831, in Boesche, *Tocqueville Letters*, p. 40.

25. Beaumont quoted in Pierson, *Tocqueville and Beaumont*, pp. 190–93; Mayer, ed., *Journey*, pp. 183, 123.

26. Mayer, ed., *Journey*, pp. 129–33, 321–22.

27. Ibid., pp. 135, 198–99, 329–30.

28. Ibid., pp. 199–201, 364, 350, 348–49.

29. Ibid., pp. 353, 355, 361, 367.

30. Hall J. Kelley, *A General Circular to All Persons of Good Character Who Wish to Emigrate to the Oregon Territory* (Charlestown, Mass., 1831).

31. Mayer, ed., *Journey*, pp. 333, 340, 357, 372–74.

32. Ibid., p. 370; Tocqueville to his mother, December 25, 1831, in Boesche, ed., *Tocqueville Letters*, p. 69; Beaumont quoted in Pierson, *Tocqueville and Beaumont*, p. 171.

33. Thomas Hamilton, *Men and Manners in America* (Philadelphia, 1833); John James Audubon, *Ornithological Biography* (Philadelphia, 1831), vol. III, p. 486.

34. "Audubon's Ornithological Biography," *Blackwood's Edinburgh Magazine* 30 (July 1831): 2; Thomas Nuttall, *A Manual of the Ornithology of the United States and Canada* (Cambridge, Mass., 1832), p. 1.

35. Quoted in Brian Dippie, *Catlin and His Contemporaries: The Politics of Patronage* (Lincoln, Neb., 1990), pp. 30, 60.

36. Audubon, *Ornithological Biography*, vol. I, p. v; "Ornithological Biography," *American Quarterly Review* 20 (December 1831): 245–58; "Audubon's Ornithological Biography," *American Monthly Review* 1 (May 1832): 349–60.

37. "Remarks on Audubon's 'Birds of America' and 'Ornithological Biography,' " *Edinburgh New Philosophical Journal* 10 (January–March 1831), pp. 322, 327; "Audubon's Ornithological Biography," pp. 14–15.

38. "Ornithological Biography," p. 258; *United States Gazette*, July 13, 1831; "Remarks on Audubon's 'Birds of America' and 'Ornithological Biography,' " p. 326; "Audubon," *Monthly American Journal of Geology* 1 (April 1832): 465.

39. John James Audubon to Mrs. Audubon, November 23, 1831, in Howard Corning, ed., *Letters of John James Audubon* (Boston, 1930), vol. I, p. 154; "Letter from J. J. Audubon to the Editor, December 31, 1831," *Monthly American Journal of Geology* 1 (March 1832): 413; John James Audubon to Robert Havell, September 20, 1831, in Corning, ed., *Audubon Letters*, vol. I, 136.

40. Charles P. Ambler, *The Life and Diary of John Floyd* (Richmond, Va., 1918), p. 163; John James Audubon to Mrs. Audubon, October 9, 23, and 30, 1831, in Corning, ed., *Audubon Letters*, vol. I, pp. 140, 142–45; "Audubon," p. 468.

41. "The Long-Billed Curlew," in Audubon, *Ornithological Biography*, vol. III, pp. 240–45.

42. John James Audubon to Mrs. Audubon, October 23, 1831, in Corning, ed., *Audubon Letters*, vol. I, p. 144; John James Audubon to Mrs. Audubon, November 23, 1831, ibid., p. 154; "Letter from Audubon to the Editor, December 7, 1831," *Monthly American Journal of Geology* 1 (February 1832): 359; "Letter from J. J. Audubon to the Editor, December 31, 1831," *Monthly American Journal of Geology* 1 (March 1832): 408–9.

43. "Letter of J. J. Audubon to Editor, December 31, 1831," p. 408; "The Golden Eagle," in Audubon, *Ornithological Biography*, vol. I, pp. 464–69.

44. *Maine Working Men's Advocate*, June 20, 1831; *Boston Medical Journal* quoted in *Philadelphia Chronicle*, July 23, 1831; *Maine Working Men's Advocate*, September 22, 1831.

45. "Board of Health—Cholera," *Periscope*, October 1, 1831; "Cholera," *American Quarterly Review* 10 (December 1831): 334–55; diary entry quoted in Charles Rosenberg, *The Cholera Years* (Chicago, 1962), p. 3.

46. "Cholera," pp. 354–55; *Boston Daily Advertiser*, quoted in *Poulson's*, September 10, 1831.

47. George Catlin, July 15, 1832, quoted in Dippie, *Catlin and His Contemporaries*, p. 33.

48. Physician quoted in Rosenberg, *Cholera Years*, p. 66; diary of Johnson Mason, Jr., American Antiquarian Society. I am grateful to Ellen Dunlap for bringing this entry to my attention.

49. "Cholera," p. 355; Isaac Fidler, *Observations on Professions, Literature, Manners, and Emigration in the United States and Canada* (New York, 1833), p. 163; Allan Nevins, ed., *The Diary of Philip Hone* (New York, 1927), vol. I, p. 78.

50. Physician quoted in Rosenberg, *Cholera Years*, p. 96; James Kennedy, *The History of the Contagious Cholera* (London, 1832), p. 113; Fidler, *Observations*, p. 162; "Cholera," p. 345; *Precautions Necessary to Be Taken Against the Cholera* (New York, 1832), p. 6.

51. "Cholera," *American Monthly Review* 1 (May 1832): 386; Francis Wayland, *An Address Delivered Before the Providence Association for the Promotion of Temperance* (Providence, 1831), pp. 4–5; *Millennial Harbinger*, August 6, 1832.

52. On the history of Mount Auburn, see David Charles Sloane, *The Last Great Necessity: Cemeteries in American History* (Baltimore, 1991); Blanche Linden-Ward, *Silent City on a Hill: Landscapes of Memory and Boston's Mt. Auburn Cemetery* (Columbus, 1989); Stanley French, "The Cemetery as Cultural Institution: The Establishment of Mount Auburn and the 'Rural Cemetery' Movement," *American Quarterly* 26 (March 1974): 38–59.

53. Jacob Bigelow, *A History of the Cemetery of Mount Auburn* (Boston, 1840), pp. 133–43; "Mount Auburn Cemetery," *North American Review* 33 (October 1831): 399.

54. Joseph Story to Reverend John Brazer, May 25, 1831, in William W. Story, ed., *Life and Letters of Joseph Story* (Boston, 1851), vol. II, pp. 54–55; Joseph Story, *An Address Delivered on the Dedication of the Cemetery at Mount Auburn* (Boston, 1831).

55. Fanny Trollope, *Domestic Manners of the Americans* (London, 1832; New York, 1997), p. 239; observer quoted in Pamela Neville-Sington, "Introduction," p. vii; See Donald Smalley, "Introduction," *Domestic Manners of the Americans* (New York, 1949).

56. Trollope, *Domestic Manners*, pp. 314, 168, 140, 246, 190–91.

57. Ibid., pp. 130–31, 160, 60, 266.

58. Ibid., pp. 197, 257, 172.

59. Ibid., pp. 68, 234, 270, 81, 69.

60. Ibid, p. 268. Thomas Cole quoted in Louis Noble, *"The Course of Empire," "Voyage of Life," and Other Pictures of Thomas Cole* (New York, 1853), pp. 122–23, 127.

61. On Thomas Cole, see Matthew Baigell, *Thomas Cole* (New York, 1981); Ellwood Parry, *The Art of Thomas Cole: Ambition and Imagination* (Newark, 1988); William Truettner and Alan Wallach, eds., *Thomas Cole: Landscape into History* (New Haven, 1994).

62. Trollope, *Domestic Manners*, pp. 223–24, 229.

INDEX